Steven F. Dansky, CSW

C000075794

Now Dare Everything: Tales of HIV-Related Psychotherapy

Pre-publication
REVIEWS,
COMMENTARIES,
EVALUATIONS . . .

"**S** teven Dansky has given us AN INFORMATIVE, STEREOTYPE-SMASHING, AND DEEPLY MOVING BOOK. In the midst of the suffering that defines the age of HIV/AIDS, this book is an act of healing and an act of love."

Robin Morgan
Author, New York City

"**A** N ENCOMPASSING, WELL-WRITTEN, THOROUGHLY RESEARCHED WORK by Steven F. Dansky on the experiences and challenges of working with persons with the HIV diagnosis. Mr. Dansky provides a landscape for viewing and understanding the pandemic of HIV disease. This historic perspective will be of interest to cultural historians, anthropologists, sociologists, and anyone seeking a world view of a current crisis."

Muriel Gladstein, MSW, ACSW
Associate Professor,
Hunter College School of Social Work

More pre-publication
REVIEWS, COMMENTARIES, EVALUATIONS . . .

"In *Now Dare Everything*, Steven Dansky DISPLAYS A PROFOUND UNDERSTANDING OF THE POLITICIZATION OF AIDS AND THE DEEP ROOTS OF SOCIETY'S UNWILLINGNESS TO DEAL WITH IT. As a therapist in New York City serving the most underprivileged class of those with the disease, Dansky's understanding of the human pain and tragedy it causes is profound. Dansky's tale is at its most moving when he relates the stories of his clients–the poor, the female, the IV-drug user, and not-always-gay PWAs Dansky counsels and cares for–often unto death. For those willing to follow Dansky on this journey, an uncommon enlightenment is the reward. This is not just a book for therapeutic social workers, though it is their story as much as that of the PWAs Dansky counsels, but instead offers every read-er a rare insight into the humanity of these particular sufferers in this particular place with this particular disease. This is about the situation where the 'personal' and the 'political' meet head on."

John Knoebel
President,
The Advocate

"Steven Dansky has successfully integrated aspects of HIV disease, human sexuality, and psychology in his book. Not only does the book provide insight into the case presentations, but it concurrently integrates in each chapter numerous and valuable medical and psychologic references. This enables the reader to understand each case with a proper perspective. The topic has been professionally researched, and the author provides us with excellent documentation. Mr. Dansky completed a monumental task by successfully addressing issues with sensitivity and in-depth analysis.

Chapters six and seven deal with the silent epidemic of HIV in women and the book dramatically brings to light an important aspect of the epidemic that has until recently been neglected and misunderstood. THIS BOOK IS A QUILT ON THE HUMAN IMMUNE DEFICIENCY DISEASE."

Pascal J. de Caprariis, MD
Chief of AIDS Services,
Department of Medicine,
Division of Infectious Diseases,
Lutheran Medical Center,
Brooklyn, New York

Harrington Park Press
An Imprint of the Haworth Press, Inc.

Now Dare Everything
Tales of HIV-Related Psychotherapy

HAWORTH Social Work Practice
Carlton E. Munson, Senior Editor

New, Recent, and Forthcoming Titles:

Now Dare Everything
Tales of HIV-Related Psychotherapy

Steven F. Dansky, CSW

Harrington Park Press
An Imprint of The Haworth Press, Inc.
New York • London • Norwood (Australia)

Published by

Harrington Park Press, an imprint of The Haworth Press, Inc., 10 Alice Street, Binghamton, NY 13904-1580

The Haworth Press, Inc., 10 Alice Street, Binghamton, NY 13904-1580

Library of Congress Cataloging-in-Publication Data

Dansky, Steven.
    Now dare everything : tales of HIV-related psychotherapy / Steven Dansky.
      p.   cm.
    Includes bibliographical references and index.
    ISBN 1-56023-037-1 (alk. paper).
    1. AIDS (Disease)–Patients–Mental health. 2. HIV infections–Psychological aspects. 3. Psychotherapy. 4. HIV infections–Patients–Counseling of. I. Title.
    [DNLM: 1. HIV Infections–psychology. 2. Psychotherapy. WD 308 D191n 1993]
RC607.A26D37   1993
616.97′92′0019–dc20
DNLM/DLC
for Library of Congress   92-48376
                                                                      CIP

This book is dedicated to Chester Chappell
and to the memory of Glennon Chamberlain

ABOUT THE AUTHOR

Steven F. Dansky, CSW, is a long-time political activist and writer who has been involved in the AIDS epidemic for over a decade. His HIV experience comes from diverse settings, ranging from hospital-based and grass roots community-based organizations to a private psychotherapy practice. He has lectured on AIDS throughout the country and his work was presented at the Fifth International Conference on AIDS. Currently, Mr. Dansky serves as a consultant to HIV-related programs in addition to his private practice. He is preparing a book, *Children of Survival: Orphans of the HIV Epidemic,* also to be published by The Haworth Press. He received his Master of Social Work degree from Hunter College School of Social Work.

CONTENTS

Acknowledgements

The writing of this book was so much a result of interactions with other people, colleagues, and friends, that whatever merit it may have must be shared with them.

I am indebted to my friends and colleagues: Barbara Agatstein, Donna Bersch, Pascal de Caprariis, Maria Corbo, Gerald Friedland, Lynn Friedman, Lauren Gordon, Robert Klein, Joyce Kravets, Sally Levy, Inez Madera, Elaine Magalis, Susan Meadvin, Lynn Meehan, Renee Shanker, and Herb Tillman–all of whom offered steadfast support.

I would like to thank my mentors, from whom I have learned: Mera Eisen, Sandi Feinblum, Fred Nenner, Linda Lightstone, Laura McCarthy, Natalie Jacobson, Michelle Saracco, and Ellen Siegal. And especially to Wendy Walker.

I am grateful to Jeanne Swinton, the librarian at Planned Parenthood of New York City (PPNYC), for her invaluable assistance. I am also grateful to Glen Campbell, Ron Hufham, and Sarah Ramirez for their extraordinary commitment.

I praise the courage of the members of the Gay Men's Health Crisis' (GMHC) Monday evening PWA Support Group; the members of the PPNYC's Wednesday evening Women's HIV Support Group; and to all those struggling to live on during this epidemic.

The confidentiality of individuals presented in this book is protected. Names and circumstances have been changed. Some people and events are presented in the form of a composite.

Introduction

For my purpose of defense, reality can be distorted not only in memory but in the very act of taking place.*

–Primo Levi, *The Drowned and the Saved*

After a decade-long involvement with the human immunodeficiency virus (HIV) disease, it is almost inconceivable to remember life before this epidemic. The epidemic transformed my life–personally, politically, and professionally. Indeed, even the dominion of my unconscious dream life tolerates representations of suffering and losses through illness, separation, and death. During lunch at a Spanish-American restaurant in New York's South Bronx, a colleague once told me, "Most of my gay friends don't sleep well at night, awakening with the images of their friends. I took care of my best friend the last year of his life; I found him dead in his apartment one cold winter morning." I'm reminded of the penultimate wish-fulfillment dream, the closing scene of the film *Longtime Companion*, a film about the devastation of HIV disease in the gay community. The sequence is an enraptured, impressionistic homecoming between those alive and dead that takes place on a beach.

A couple of years into the epidemic, while serving as a volunteer for Gay Men's Health Crisis (GMHC)–the first and largest HIV disease service organization–I returned to school in a graduate social work program, driven by grievous necessity. Continuously, for more than eight years, I continued volunteering, offering my assistance for persons living with acquired immune deficiency syndrome (AIDS). I defected from a career as a literary agent–representing writers for book publishing, theater, film, and television–with never a regret, hardly a backward glance.

---

*Primo Levi (New York: Summit Books, 1986), p. 33.

The volunteer experience changed my life. After graduation, I co-led a persons living with AIDS (PLWA) therapy group at GMHC and also became an HIV social worker for a Brooklyn hospital in a high drug-using neighborhood. Over the years, I practiced social work in an AIDS treatment center at a major medical center in the Bronx. After that, I provided HIV-related psychotherapy treatment for a community-based organization (CBO) with sites in Manhattan and Brooklyn. I was also the administrative director of an HIV primary-care training program associated with a hospital center in the South Bronx, an epicenter of the epidemic with one of the highest incidences of HIV infection in the world. Currently, I have a private psychotherapy practice, specializing in HIV disease, sexual identity, and substance use.

I have worked with hundreds of PLWAs, their families, and significant relationships with the realization of the difference of HIV-related practice–and of the enormity of biopsychosocial issues that face clients. This perception of difference is resounding. It compels me to explore my professional roots and question whether a moral imperative propels and sustains me from sheer burnout. I must turn to the continuity of political commitment.

As my determination positioned me within the eye of the epidemic, I never imagined what lay ahead in the front lines. In a speech given on November 22, 1991, Larry Kramer, a founder of GMHC and the AIDS Coalition to Unleash Power (ACT-UP), said the following:

> *There's got to be a higher vision for your reason for being. You've got to want to end this!* Instead, I see layer upon layer of bureaucracy, hordes of employees, and thousands of volunteers spending hours and days at endless useless meetings, just like all the bureaucrats in Washington. Plus, all those useless board members, who have absolutely no sense of urgency, no sense of urgency, no sense of urgency, no sense of urgency that 40 million people are going to die in a few short years' time. [Author's emphasis][1]

Kramer's chant of "no sense of urgency" is compelling. The HIV activist movement is unparalleled as the synthesis of politics and health concerns, a movement distinguished by the emblematic statement "Silence = Death." Often, I reflect on the discrepancy between the cottage industry of HIV disease–with its attendant aura of power politics displayed by governmental bureaucracies, the pharmaceutical industry, and biomedical institutions–and the desperate reality of individuals infected with HIV disease, many of whom live in despairing poverty, trapped within the diseased cycle of drug dependency. I, too, have sat at endless meetings where the main topic of discussion is the mutually destructive political game pitting government funders against the fundees, with both groups tearing each other apart for a piece of the pie. I suspect those infected with the HIV virus would view these scenes with incredulity as they endure the adversity of living with HIV disease while managing family and societal systems that sustain an epistemology of domination–male, white, class, and heterosexual supremacy.

Madonna received the Award of Courage from the American Foundation for AIDS Research (AmFAR). Fair enough. She is a steadfast financial contributor to HIV organizations. President Bush praised the courage of Magic Johnson's disclosure of his HIV seropositive status. Bush (several months earlier, responding to an ACT-UP demonstration at his Kennebunkport, Maine, home, said with cynicism the cause of HIV was people's behavior and that no additional monies would forthcome.)

My roots are in activism, political writing, and poetry. To be quite up-front, my *higher vision* proceeds from an enduring, life-long commitment to struggle against all manifestations of oppression. In the early 1960s, I joined Students for a Democratic Society (SDS) and the peace movements against the war in Vietnam. I was a community organizer during the late 1960s on New York City's Lower East Side, a poor, multi-ethnic and racial community. I was the editor of a bilingual newsletter, *Basta!*, which my partner and I handed out on street corners. I was on the staff of *I-Kon*, a magazine that owned a bookstore on East 4th Street. The store was a clearing-house for radical books, magazines, and newspapers, and it was the setting for weekly poetry readings.

In 1969, I was a drug addiction counselor at a therapeutic community (TC), the Odyssey House, when I was confronted by administration and staff (including mental-health professionals) about my sexual identity. Point-blank, they told me to begin psychotherapeutic treatment–the sole reason being that I was a gay man. I declined and they terminated my employment. Within a month of leaving the TC, the Stonewall Rebellion occurred in New York's Greenwich Village. I became a founder of the Gay Liberation Movement and a member of the Gay Liberation Front (GLF). I was on the editorial collective of the first new-wave gay liberation newspaper, *Come Out!*, which initially published my theoretical article "Hey Man." The article was controversial because it "carried the struggle against sexism and its expression in maleness to the heart of gay liberation."[2] The article was reprinted widely in this country and worldwide, and it was the first to confront the male-dominated gay movement for its sexism toward women and lesbians, who were part of the early gay (male-dominated) movement.

During the early 1970s, I became an antisexist, most influenced by the work of feminists, principally Robin Morgan. I published *Faggotry*, a journal of poetry and articles with an antisexist partiality. Jill Johnston reviewed the journal and said its contributors were the "first men to confess the inappropriateness of their manhood and to withdraw from the classic male demand of support from the female."[3]

I then founded the Effeminist Movement, with Kenneth Pitchford and John Knoebel, to formulate pro-feminist politics by men. Kenneth, John, and I wrote the "Effeminist Manifesto," which appeared in our magazine *Double-F*. The manifesto appeared in several books and magazines, generating fierce debate within the gay movement. Some called it "a milestone in political thought."[4] Certain circles of the women's movement considered the manifesto to be the "most imaginative, profound, and persuasive analysis of gender developed by any men anywhere."[5] Martin Duberman reviewed *Double-F*, saying the magazine was "formulating basic questions on gender."[6]

During the summer of 1981, a couple of years past the tenth anniversary of the Stonewall Rebellion and the birth of the current gay liberation movement, *The New York Times* reported the story of several gay men who were presenting with a rare pneumonia and cancers. Doctors treating them began to speculate as to the cause of the underlying problem of immunodeficiency. The notion of an epidemic was an abstraction–for many gay men the use of antibiotics was widespread for treating sexually transmitted diseases (STDs)–so at first, the general reaction was denial. They assumed there would be an uncomplicated medical solution.

The resistance to behavioral change continued unabated, for the most part, into the mid-1980s despite the prevalence of this new disease in the gay community. The ideological stance of the gay movement was quite different during the first ten years than it is currently. There was a steadfast alignment with the male-dominated sexual politics of the counterculture and such institutions as *Playboy* and male liberation. Theoretically, sexual acts were equated with identity so that an attempt to examine behavior, no matter how self-destructive the behavior might be, was labeled homophobic. Sex, itself, was the primary medium for liberation: to question sex, therefore, contradicted and threatened the aspiration of the movement. Even for nonpolitically aligned gay men, the movement and the politics of sexual freedom changed the mores of the subculture. Compliance with safer sex by gay men has been a painful process and has taken years to implement. Currently, there has been slippage with private sex clubs emerging once again.

* * *

Now Dare Everything is a collection of tales of HIV-related psychotherapy involving those persons affected by the HIV retrovirus. Mental-health professionals (MHPs)–psychiatrists, psychologists, and social workers–have played a pivotal role during the HIV pandemic. Before the identification of HIV by medical science as the etiological agent that causes HIV disease, MHPs intervened with PLWAs, since those ill clients required services in many settings. It has been a decade-long global struggle to alleviate the impact of HIV disease on individuals and communities, and there are many pioneers in various disciplines. MHPs have been in the forefront of working with PLWAs and those affected by HIV disease. MHPs have worked in a variety of settings, from non-HIV specific CBOs, hospital settings, private practice, mental-health clinics, family planning agencies, HIV anonymous test sites to those HIV-specific organizations.

I got the idea for *Now Dare Everything* during a coffee break in a Manhattan hotel ballroom during an AIDS conference. I had just come from a workshop where panelists criticized didactic approaches, particularly in certain communities, when attempting to reach people at risk for HIV infection. At times, academic methodology favors a context of separation without discussion or communication. Curiously, the workshop panelists themselves used didacticism when addressing the audience. The panel members became the experts, the *them*. The *us* were the inactive listeners. This structural dichotomy, sanctioned by our culture, reflects most therapeutic relationships: the authoritarian expert/professional treating the patient/client.

This form of social interaction extends into entire communities. The central premise is that the community knows nothing and that the professional knows everything. Within HIV practice, as well, there must be a recognition of the people's intrinsic right to self-determination. This must be coupled with an understanding of the ways in which a culture perceives reality, and how it copes with adversity. This requires more than cultural sensitivity training. Within a political context, various communities may have differing agendas regarding health education, belief systems, and prevention.

I stayed behind in the gaudy ballroom, lingering over coffee, making mental notes, thinking about individuals with whom I worked. A fundamental challenge of HIV-related psychotherapy converges on the specificity of the disease medically, psychologically, and within a sociopolitical and historical continuum. When investigating the distinctiveness of the HIV pandemic, one is aware of the challenge it has presented various professionals and communities from the beginning. The implications reach beyond biomedical health into the institutional and cultural foundations of society. GMHC existed before governmental funding. The founders proclaimed that GMHC would have been unnecessary if there had been an appropriate governmental response. Remember, President Reagan didn't publicly mention AIDS until 1987, six years after the Centers for Disease Control [CDC] had identified HIV disease as an epidemic. It was the advocate, chairperson of AmFAR, and megastar Elizabeth Taylor who accomplished the coup, getting the President to utter the word "AIDS."

The professional relationship involving an examination of how working with PLWAs makes necessary the different therapeutic models, the examination of theory bases, and the challenge to restyle the technical procedures of therapeutic training. The relationship between therapist and client must signify a fundamental encounter, as one human being encounters another. The theory base cannot be restrictive; that is, it must incorporate what is intrapersonal, interpersonal, and intersystemic.

The therapist must develop a personal style to manage the difficulties of HIV practice and combine it with therapeutic technique. HIV practice has compelled the reevaluation of therapeutic boundaries and goals. The focus on the therapist's personal perspective is vital, because any accurate discourse about working with PLWAs demands conscious self-reflection. Continual movement back and forth from client to therapist, therapist to client, is axiomatic within the therapeutic relationship. With HIV disease, this interactivity is quintessential. The therapist's conscious use of self is elemental when working with PLWAs due to the nature of the disease and to the biopsychosocial issues it raises, such as confronting issues of mortality. The self-reflective process has been painful for therapists. It is difficult to unmask camouflages that have hidden assumptions about sexual orientation, gender, culture, and race and to confront stereotypes about drug users. Burnout occurs when professionals have been unable to face and make peace with these formidable issues.

Now Dare Everything, to my mind, is part of a genre of HIV art, such as the work of Keith Haring (See Figure 1) and literature. From the beginning of the HIV pandemic, moving personal works of literature, confessional in style, often journal accounts, detailed the anatomy of human suffering. This literature described the private universe of individuals transformed by pain. The memoirs have been self-transcendent in nature. These works are within a tradition in Western literature, such as novels in which the central character stricken with disease becomes metamorphosed. The hero/ine becomes symbolic of moral, social, or political ideals. The hero/ine, an individual, represents an epoch, and the character is analogous to the sickness of the State.[7]

Accounts by Holocaust survivors are another example of this form of literature. It is within the nature of human experience to deny and subsequently forget painful experiences. HIV-related literature preserves historical and personal reality against the cultural

FIGURE 1

and individual defense mechanisms of denial. These narratives also serve a political function to promote change by asserting the humanity of PLWAs (who often confront discrimination) and by promoting the dignity of personal relationships and community. These existential works inspire and celebrate human experience–despite the threat of death–by imparting meaning to suffering and by negating individual mortality.

The introduction follows with Chapter 1, "The Phenomenology of Contagion," which interprets the occurrence of fear from contamination throughout recorded history. Chapter 2, "The Metaphysics of a Pandemic," explores HIV disease and the connection to sexuality and gives an overview of the disease process. Chapter 3, "Beyond Good and Evil," focuses on issues of HIV antibody testing and disclosure. Chapter 4, "A Chronology of Exile," is an early account in the course of the epidemic with a case study exemplifying long-term hospitalization prior to services such as supportive housing or hospice care for advanced HIV patients. Chapter 5, "Hocus Pocus is Coming," examines the complexities of living with the chronicity of HIV disease. Chapter 6, "The Silent Epidemic," addresses the manner in which women have been challenged and underserviced during the epidemic. Chapter 7, "Another Voice," presents the group process, using a women's group as a prototype. Chapter 8, "Frankie," is a case study of a homeless person with HIV who became institutionalized in a skilled nursing facility (SNF). Chapter 9, "Jose," is a study in suicide. Chapter 10, "The Substance of Dandelions," is a case study exploring somatization.

Now Dare Everything attempts to integrate existential experience with clinical knowledge. The case studies serve as prototypes of HIV-related psychotherapy from the initial crisis of an HIV seropositive diagnosis through the emergence of other issues, such as substance use, disclosure of diagnosis, homelessness, poverty, sexual and emotional abuse, biophysical debilitation, access to treatment, and the impact of sexism, racism, and homophobia to individual functioning. Each case example in the book is part of a quilt. Each panel represents a profound professional relationship. The joined panels portray the landscape of my involvement during the HIV epidemic.

* * *

On Semantics

1. HIV disease replaces AIDS as the complex or syndrome that follows the diagnosis of specific diseases and qualifications.

The term AIDS is obsolete; HIV infection more correctly defines the problem. The medical, public health, political, and community leadership must focus on the full course of HIV infection rather than concentrating on the later stages of the disease (ARC and AIDS). Continual focus on the later stages of disease rather than the entire spectrum of HIV infection has left our nation unable to deal adequately with the epidemic.[8]

2. HIV seropositive (HIV+) is the presence of the HIV antibody, indicating retroviral infection conducted by reactive screening through serologic testing. Each of the Western blot and enzyme-linked immunosorbent assay (ELISA) blood tests determine the presence of the antibody to HIV. Approximately, 95% of individuals seroconvert within six months from infection. An HIV+ diagnosis can be asymptomatic (without any infections) or symptomatic (with infections associated with HIV disease).

3. In 1983, the Advisory Committee of People with AIDS rejected the "victim" label to characterize those living with HIV disease. They wrote that the word "victim" not only "implies defeat, and we are only occasionally 'patients' [but it also] implies passivity, helplessness and dependence on the care of others."[9] They instead chose "people with AIDS" (PWAs).

4. The phrase "risk groups" is a delusive epidemiological conceit. Sexual identity or behavior, gender, race, community of origin (Greenwich Village or Haiti), and illicit drug use are not intrinsic risks. Singular activities constitute risk when there is blood inoculation from an infected individual to another.

5. For linguistic precision and political clarity, the term "gay" implies male same-sex eroticism and lesbianism, as distinguished from "homosexuality," a classification within medical and psychiatric nomenclature. In this context, use of the expression "gay" is agnostic from an ontological perspective. The term does not imply etiology, either from variants of social structure or biologic and genetic conjecture, sidestepping the essentialist/constructivist controversy. Sedgwick expressed apprehension about current methodologies applied to investigate the origins and development of gay identity, be-

cause they are "structured by an implicit, trans-individual Western project or fantasy of eradicating that identity."[10]

6. Sexual identity refers to the intrapsychic core orientation, lifestyle, and preferences of convention, such as hair length (flattop or ponytail).

7. The term "affected by HIV" reflects the extensiveness of the specialty. It includes persons and communities throughout the spectrum of infection–HIV seropositive asymptomatic, symptomatic, and fully diagnosed HIV disease–together with family members, significant relationships, care partners, and the category of the worried well.

* * *

To resound Kramer's phase of urgency, I attest to the urgency to keep alive those who died and those who live.

REFERENCE NOTES

1. Larry Kramer, "129,001 and Counting," *The Village Voice*, December 10, 1991.

2. Jeffrey Weeks, *Coming Out* (London: Quartet Books, 1977), p. 70.

3. Jill Johnston, *The Village Voice*, 1972.

4. *The Gay Liberator*, Detroit, MI, 1972.

5. Susan Rennie and Kirstin Grimstad, *The New Woman's Survival Sourcebook* (New York: Alfred A. Knopf, 1975), p. 222.

6. Martin Duberman, *The New York Times Book Review*, 1972.

7. Jeffrey Meyers, *Disease and the Novel, 1880-1960* (New York: St. Martin's Press, 1985), p. 1.

8. Report of the Presidential Commission on the Human Immunodeficiency Virus Epidemic, Washington, DC, Presidential Commission on the Human Immunodeficiency Virus Epidemic, 1988, p. xvii.

9. *Surviving and Thriving With AIDS*, Michael Callen, editor, People with AIDS Coalition, 1987.

10. Eve Kosofsky Sedgwick, *Epistemology of the Closet* (Berkeley: University of California Press, 1990), p. 41.

Chapter 1

The Phenomenology of Contagion

All is not lost, they say, all is not lost,
but with the startling knowledge of the blind
their fingers flinch to feel such flimsy walls
against the siege of all that is not I!*

–Tennessee Williams, "The Siege"

THE VIOLENT AGAINST NATURE

Pandemics recurrent throughout the millennia have been portentous historical turning points, stimulating evolutionary change by transforming social, religious, and biomedical institutions. By definition, pandemic eruptions have widespread consequences, extending across whole countries and continents, with the decimation of entire populations. Until the middle of the nineteenth century, time itself was measured through occurrences of epidemic cataclysms.[1]

By 1983, when scientists first isolated the human immunodeficiency virus (HIV) in the laboratory and designated it as the sole etiological agent that causes acquired immune deficiency syndrome (AIDS), occurrences of HIV disease were worldwide. From 1979 through 1986, according to the United Nations World Health Organization (WHO) Collaborating Centre on AIDS, there were 6328 cases in Europe, 7 in the Southeast Asia Region, 454 in the West Pacific Region, 43,319 in the American Region (including the Caribbean and Latin American), and 4084 in Africa. (See Figure 2.) No doubt, the profound global

---

*Tennessee Williams, *In The Winter of Cities* (New York: New Directions, 1964).

FIGURE 2. The Global Future of AIDS

Estimates and Projections of Cumulative Cases in Thousands

	HIV+ Adults '92 (est.)	HIV+ Adults '95 (proj.)	Adults with AIDS '92 (est)	Adults with AIDS '95 (proj.)
North America	1167	1495	257.5	534.0
Western Europe	718	1186	99.0	279.5
Australia/Oceania	28	40	4.5	11.5
Latin America	995	1186	173.0	417.5
Sub-Saharan-Africa	7803	11449	1367.0	3277.5
Caribbean	310	474	43.0	121.0
Eastern Europe	27	44	2.5	9.5
Southeast Mediterranean	35	59	3.5	12.5
Northeast Asia	41	80	3.5	14.5
Southeast Asia	675	1220	65.0	240.5
TOTAL	11799	17454	2018.5	4918.0

consequence of the HIV pandemic on humanity during the last decades of the twentieth century will be significant to history.

One reaction to HIV disease is the fear of contagion. This dread of contagion has been a critical element during this current epidemic, as it has been historically with others. To an extent, this dread has informed the establishment, or lack, of public policy and societal reactions by the general population. The specter of HIV disease conjures up pervasive danger from contagion. Public debate still focuses on the misconception of casual transmission despite secure scientific knowledge that confirms the blood-borne constituent of the retrovirus–that is, to infect an individual, the retrovirus must enter the blood stream from an infected individual. HIV is neither self-generating within the human system nor is the retrovirus transmitted solely through certain sexual acts or drug-using behavior unless one person is HIV-infected.

During the exigency of an epidemic, as a result of profound individual and collective disequilibrium, secular and ecclesiastical institutions assume a restorative function. Society institutes counteractive measures to reestablish order, frequently discerning moral normalcy as concomitant to the resolution of specifically biomedical concerns, such as cure and prevention. Accordingly, the terror that a populace experiences during an epidemic transcends exclusively biomedical concerns. Disclosure by patients, and dental and medical providers of their HIV-positive serostatus has been debated for the past several years. Medical and dental providers, particularly when performing invasive procedures, regard risk from HIV-positive patients as hazardous. The Centers for Disease Control (CDC) unyieldingly maintains that the guidelines for universal precautions adequately safeguards professionals from infection. The HIV-positive individuals encounter intimidation and refusal of services when they disclose their serostatus so they are reluctant. These issues result in persistent conflicts–without adequate resolution–when formulating public-health policies and maintaining protection of individual civil liberties. The Kimberly Bergalis case captured media attention after she claimed that she contracted HIV during a dental procedure from an HIV-infected dentist. She brought her case to the U.S. Congress, seeking HIV antibody testing of all health professionals who perform invasive procedures. The prospective law would require such professionals to disclose their serostatus if HIV positive. The Bergalis Bill met with opposition from activists and experts in public-health administration. She attracted media attention, with steadfast reinforcement from conservative and fundamentalist factions, until her death from HIV disease in December 1991.

Fear combined with abhorrence–the manner by which certain people, vis-à-vis the construction of subcategories of people or so-called risk groups–characterizes the social response during an epidemic. In her influential monographs on illness (and recently on AIDS), Sontag argues that throughout history, the belief prevails that "illness reveals, and is a punishment for, moral laxity or turpitude."[2] A thorough understanding of disease must appreciate the intersection between illness and difference because the constituents of health, well-being, and sickness and disease incorporate both the physical and moral arenas. These dual concerns, the corporeal and spiritual, proceed reciprocally, each reflecting the prevailing belief system of a culture. The therapeutic institutions of society emerge conjoined, whether secular or religious, from a social process inextricably bound within, and influenced by, cultural factors. According to Foucault:

> In that experience, medical space can coincide with social space, or, rather, traverse it and wholly penetrate it. One began to conceive of a generalized presence of doctors whose intersecting gazes form a network and exercise at every point in space, and at every moment in time, a constant, mobile, differentiated supervision.[3]

Discernment of public health is only one dictate of organized society. There is a juxtaposition between biomedical interventions and public-health legislation and moral and religious sanctions when a society attempts to reestablish equilibrium and assign meaning to disease during a large-scale epidemic. Concepts of disease defined by science are not objective realities; instead, the dialectics of scientific methodology transpire within the social matrix of culture.

The problem of contagion, Foucault maintained, is inappreciable without analysis using a perceptual structure that considers the full characteristics of the epidemic phenomena. Indeed, the historical individuality of an epidemic transcends transmission by one individual to another; rather, epidemics occasion a collective experience within an historical continuum. Within the context of disease perception is a simultaneous social process that occurs beyond biomedicine, regardless of technology. The physiological and material manifestation of illness, affecting an individual or community, emerges as a metaphoric visitation, curse, or judgment:

> Any disease that is treated as a mystery and acutely enough feared will be felt to be morally, if not literally, contagious. Contact with someone afflicted with a disease regarded as a mysterious malevolency inevitably feels like a trespass; worse, like the violation of a taboo.[4]

A moral implication is a fundamental response to all diseases, regardless of transmission, but especially to HIV disease, which is contracted primarily through sexuality and drug use. As a result, the disease elicits indignation and blame, and, at times, blamelessness or innocence. Recipients of infected blood product, such as hemophiliacs, have been *innocents*. Children have not captured the imagination of the American public as *innocents*, because their mothers are often intravenous drug users (IVDUs)–something too remote from public experience. Ali Gertz touched many because she stated that she contracted the virus from a single occasion of sexual intercourse. Excessive reliance on the juncture of biomedical knowledge of disease itself–the scientific knowledge of an epidemic–fails to assess the significance of historic specificity. The nomenclature of disease reflects attitudes about disease perception, and what the disease process entails, because science and medicine are part of a social process.

The occurrence of HIV disease transpires within a distinctive historical continuum because of extensive social, legal, and institutional ramifications. The continuum in the late twentieth century includes the emergence of a religious fundamentalism, an ecclesiastical facism, opposed to the rights of women, lesbians, gay men, and–when incorporated within white supremacy–against people of color. When David Duke, supposedly disavowed Grand Master of the Klu Klux Klan, declared his presidential candidacy in December 1991, he proclaimed the United States a Christian nation that

should close its borders to immigrants, particularly those from
Third World countries.

The moralistic theme of punishment through disease has profoundly impacted the consciousness of our culture, with ideas that
propose the pathogens of disease as "divine retribution." Disease
pathology in the individual assumes greater meaning as the representation of the body politic itself. The Biblical theme of contamination of one group by another is an early historical example of the
communal reaction to disease. Leviticus is particularly rich in disease references, notably to leprosy; but some symptomatology described suggests the possibility of gonorrhea or syphilis. Throughout Leviticus, there is an association between sexuality and disease,
with many references to hygiene and cleanliness. For example, it is
written in Leviticus: "Every thing, whereon he sitteth, shall be
unclean" (15:4); "And he that sitteth on any thing whereon he sat
that hath issue" (15:6); and "And what saddle soever he rideth
upon that hath the issue shall be unclean" (15:9).

In Biblical text, "secret" or "private" are terms used to denote
an anatomical body part stricken with disease. The designation of
the anus as "secret" connotes something sinister, hidden, and private. The theme of privacy, the human attempt to hide from God, is
a component within the myth of the Fall, as related in the Book of
Genesis. The associations between feces and the various organizations with which it is correlated remain deeply repressed.[5] The
distinction between sexual taboo and the anal sex taboo is the
centrality of spirituality–Christianity strives toward eternal, but human flesh decays. Death is a disturbing prospect, and defecation
represents the bodily reenactment of death vis-à-vis physical functions:

> Excrement was always the clearest and most persistent re-
> minder of the fate of man. Humans usually defecate in secret,
> and in Western imagination the anal function became a symbol
> of evil, darkness, death, and rebellion against the moral order.[6]

Therefore, anal intercourse has particular intrapsychic significance,
and in the so-called sodomy trials, the imagery of animals and
bestiality–the other fear of sexuality–was always in evidence: "Thus
the morbid attempt to get away from the body can only result in a

morbid fascination (erotic cathexis) in the death of the body."[7] Another reference to plague appears in I Corinthians 10:8, when Paul admonishes the Israelites by equating idolatry with disease and warning that fornification causes death.

The Old Testament survives as an early written account of the communal reaction to disease visited as moral punishment. The Book of Samuel prophesied plague as punishment for moral disobedience to Yahweh. The following passage in the Old Testament, Book of Samuel, is an epidemic narrative. Within the religious context, mythologies encourage a prophetic and moral function:

> Then the Lord laid a heavy hand upon the people of Ashdod; he threw them into distress and plagued them with tumours, and their territory swarmed with rats. . . . There was death and destruction all through the city; for the hand of God lay heavy upon it.[8]

Punishment through disease has profoundly impacted the consciousness of our culture with ideas that propose the etiology of disease as divine intervention, a form of microorganismic retribution for the sin of sexuality. Plague is the metaphor. Plague functions to reestablish order when the community does not conform to a dominant religious, political, or moral code of ethics.

The manipulative application of Biblical interpretations promotes dubious political and social goals. A debatable modern interpretation of a recurrent theme is the classification of so-called pagan rites, as described in the Old Testament, to include homosexuality. Plague was Yahweh's punishment when the Philistines refused to liberate the Ark from their community, returning it to the Hebrews for transportation back to Israel. As French indicates, the destruction of Sodom and Gomorrah is an allegory about the esteemed value of community in Biblical times. The wickedness involved in the tale is noncompliance with traditional laws of hospitality, essential to any nomadic culture, and not about sexual promiscuity or homosexuality: "Abraham and Sarah receive their angelic guests properly and are rewarded; the men of Sodom do not, and they are punished (along with the women, children, and all inhabitants of Gomorrah as well)."[9] Later interpretations placed sexual connotations on the tale, but the story itself does not, and the idea of sex as sin probably emerged much later:

> Homosexuality lies within the domain of sin, of a foetidness that can pass from one being to another and which has a tendency to strike high: it affects the highly placed people more often than the humble.[10]

During the Middle Ages, Albert the Great defined the often ambiguous term of "sodomy" as a sin against nature, of a man with a man, or of a woman with a woman. There is no explanation of what is *natural*. Precise Biblical references are what led him to state that the malady is innate and reputedly contagious.

In literature throughout the centuries, as in the works of Boccacio, Chaucer, Wagner, and Camus, the sickness of the individual is "analogous to the sickness of the State," symptomatic of moral, social, or political pathology. Daniel Defoe was five years old when the Great Plague of London occurred. His fictionalized account of the epidemic, *A Journal of the Plague Year*, published over a half-century after the outbreak, functions as treatise and critique of society:

> It was not the least of our misfortunes, that with our infection, when it ceased, there did not cease the spirit of strife and contention, slander and reproach, which was really the great troubler of the nation's peace before.

The interpretation of illness in the individual has a dual function when it encompasses a social diagnosis.[11] The hero, simultaneously isolated and exposed, experiences an intense transformation with disease as the modus operandi for heroic conversion, which assumes the form of redemptive salvation or the loss into damnation. Illustrative of this proposition is Wagner's hero Parsifal, in which the hero's sickness is always indicative of his not being in a state of grace. Redemption is the question, not healing, so the hero becomes saved, not cured. When Dante reserves Circle Seven in *The Inferno* for "The Violent Against Nature," whom he describes as "all clerks and men of worth, great men of letters, scholars of renown; all by the one same crime defiled on earth." In fact, Dante's notion of contagion is more than catching something. It carried more the sense of contamination or defilement–not so much as sick, but unclean or inhuman.

The paradigmatic shift substituted religious with scientific institutions, reconstructing the collective organization of society and theories of intrapsychic life. The ascendancy of scientific institutions transposed Biblical iconography–the Garden and original sin–into the medical nosology of pathology. Human experience became divided into categories of normalcy and deviancy in later centuries, with the medicalization of sexuality and gender. This medical consciousness associated individual existence with the collective life of society:

> The definition of political status for medicine and the constitution, at state level, of a medical consciousness whose constant task would be to provide information, supervision, and constraint, all of which 'relate as much to the police as to the field of medicine proper'.[12]

Biblical interpretation must proceed from communal, social, and religious circumstances. The Bible is neither a uniform faith-response nor a single book. Rather, as Schussler-Fiorenza points out, it is a bookshelf, a collection of various literary texts, spanning a millennia of ancient history and culture:

> The political appeal to the moral authority of the Bible can be dangerous if it is sustained by the 'community of the forgiven' but not by the *ecclesia semper reformanda*. It can be dangerous, especially if the Christian community is shaped by the remembrance of 'the historical winners' while abandoning the subversive memory of innocent suffering and of solidarity with the victims of history.[13]

The systematization or unification of Biblical themes rests with the dogma of religious institutions, including the translator and interpreter.

The culture medicalizes and then forms categories to fit into medical models of disease and pathology. Homosexuality, as a designation within psychiatric and medical nomenclature, came into usage toward the end of the nineteenth century. Foucault observed that the expression "homosexuality" was less representative of same-sex relatedness or sexuality than of the characteristic of a distinctive sexual sensibility, a metaconstruction of gender:

> Homosexuality appeared as one of the forms of sexuality when it was transposed from the practice of sodomy onto a kind of interior androgyny, a hermaphrodism of the soul. The sodomite had been a temporary aberration; the homosexual was now a species.[14]

The homosexual became a third gender, with a distinct anatomy over and above lifestyle and sensibility. In the nineteenth-century mind, the etiology of homosexuality and the pathology of behavior derives from a singular nature, an active principle, rooted in each biological manifest destiny and childhood development.

THE THEMATICS OF BLOOD

Blood is primary to the institutions that sustain power–which are replete with metaphors about blood relation, bloodline, to have a certain blood, to be of the same blood, class distinction of blue blood, and the mixing of blood (i.e., miscegenation). As Allport explains, the symbolism of blood derives from an essential and instrumental function within the hierarchical social structure.

During World War II, the Red Cross separated blood donated by people of African descent from that of caucasian donors. As Allport says, "Science could not tell the blood apart, but social mythology could."[15] Scientifically, all blood types are in all races, so the exaltation of so-called pure blood is a misnomer, a simile for racial supremacy and class division. This symbolization communicates diverse meanings–as in the ability to shed blood; to risk one's blood; and to its being easily spilled, subject to drying up, too readily mixed, and capable of being quickly corrupted.[16] The image of blood conjures powerful associations, particularly when it is contaminated.

References throughout the Old Testament contain evidence that the Hebrews accepted the divinity and worshipped goddesses. Sev-

eral books of the Bible transcribe the critical transition from poly-
theistic, goddess-worshipping cultures to patriarchal, monotheistic
societies. Within ancient culture, as Patai indicates, Hebrews recognized and worshipped goddesses. In Judges 3:7, it says, "The Israelites did what was wrong in the eyes of the Lord; they forgot the
Lord their God and worshipped the Baalim and the Asheroth";
there are additional references to goddess worship in Judges, Kings,
and Chronicles. Continual attempts within Hebrew society to dis-
credit matriarchal divinities were simultaneous with repeated wars
fought against matriarchal countries neighboring Israel.

One justification for man's domination over woman derives from
the mythology of the Fall: Eve, functioning as the species of
woman, breaks God's commandment by reaching for divine power.
The apple is less a symbol of sexuality than it is the scepter of
divinity.[17] The Book of Genesis presents the female as synonymous
with the sin of sexuality and with sin itself.

Eve is the prototype of woman. She provoked banishment from
the Garden by defying God's commandment and over-reaching His
male authority. Eve's quest for the divine, represented by the apple,
is an example of women's supposed venality. The apple also symbolizes sexuality, the power of the erotic. The punishment for sexuality is annihilation. The Fall established the subcategory of "Other" by gender. Daly considers the destructive image of women
reflected in the myth of the Fall as elemental to the modern psyche:
"Silence about the destructiveness of the myth's specific content is
oppressive because it conveys the message–indeed becomes the
message–that sexual oppression is a nonproblem."[18]

Eve contaminated Adam. Therefore, women contaminate men.
The myth survives into Christianity, and the Fall became analogous
to the rejection of Christ's redemption. Genesis proscribes that the
moral relation to God be unequivocal and open. The projection of
moral meaning and spiritual relation to God into the physical and
sexual realm constitutes several of the most predominant and recurrent teachings in early human consciousness. Any transgression
will have grave physical consequence to the individual and to the
social order. Annihilation is the power of the erotic.

Until monotheism, procreation was fundamental to the perception of creation with the central matriarchal figure being the Great

Mother, the Goddess of All Things. The cosmogony of Genesis attributes Creation to God alone, omitting all pre-existing elements or beings considered divine.[19] Gould Davis characterizes patriarchal creation myths as perpetrations to controvert both the "tradition of the female creator" and the "original supremacy of the female sex."[20] Horney formulated that male bias toward women derives from two intersecting elements. First, is women's reproductive capacity, partly contradicted and partly denigrated. Second, is male anxiety toward women, which is deeply rooted in sexuality.[21]

During the Middle Ages, Albertus Magnus devoted one of his treatises on animals to delineating the impregnation of the eyes during menses. He theorized that because the eye is a passive organ, menstrual fluid can contaminate it: "Every object placed in form of a 'menstrual eye' will be infected. In the absence of the notion of contagion, it is the air which, being corrupted on contact with a harmful source, transmits the disease."[22] Further, there was the belief that a woman could cloud a mirror's surface blood red during her menstrual cycle.

Many fundamental primitive taboos relate to women and sexual intercourse:

> Tabus on the approach of men to women during and after parturition, and during menstruation, are the most strictly observed primitive tabus. All the world over, and not only among savages, the tabus attaching to menstrual women are similar.[23]

The predominant theme of contamination of one group by another is a *lief motif* within the Bible. The systematic division of power between men and women imposed punitive sanctions against women. The patriarchy transformed women into a social subset, a category. In Hebrew tradition, "the dangers of contact and contagion are so great that women are nearly always scheduled or forced to reside apart during their monthly periods."[24] When a woman is menstruating, she is forbidden to prepare meals, eat with, or use the same utensils as men. During her menstrual cycle, sexual contact is sinful and punishable by the death penalty. From antiquity to the present, menstrual blood has been, in effect, poisonous. The Roman naturalist Pliny the Elder believed having intercourse with a menstruating woman resulted in stillborn births or children sick with purulent blood serum.[25] Jerome, a Church founder, wrote that children conceived during menstruation will be leprous and hydrocephalic and that corrupted blood causes plague-ridden bodies.[26]

The belief that menstrual and vaginal fluids are naturally hazardous contaminants caused male-dominated societies to exercise authority over contact between men and women: "Blood also plays a decisive part in feminine taboos, which from the earliest times until far into the patriarchal cultures and religions have caused men to turn away from all feminine matters as though from something numinous. The blood of menstruation, defloration, and birth proves to men that women have a natural connection with this sphere. But in the background there is a dim knowledge of the Great Mother who, as chthonic mistress of life and death demands blood and appears to be dependent upon the shedding of blood."[27]

Rich submits the plausibility that menstrual taboos originated from woman's self-perception that menstruation and reproductive capacity were sacred mysteries:

> Whether or not woman was actually the originator of taboo, the mere existence of a menstrual taboo signifies, for better or worse, *powers only half-understood; the fear of women and the mystery of her motherhood.* [Author's emphasis.][28]

Further, Rich suggests women separated themselves into communal living "to control and socialize the male" and that the menstrual taboo extended the power of woman by investing "them with the charisma of ritual." Paglia argues it is not menstrual blood itself that disturbs the imagination, "but rather the albumen in the blood, the uterine shreds, placental jellyfish of the female sea." She calls the chthonian matrix, the "evolutionary revulsion from slime," the site of biologic origins.[29]

Until the Middle Ages, the Church disapproved of menstruating women receiving Holy Communion. During the third century, the Patriarch of Alexandria suggested that "devout women would never even think of touching the sacred table or the Body and Blood of the Lord."[30] The theological dominion over sexual intercourse included interdictions on intercourse during menses after having a baby. Ranke-Heinemann writes that lochia, blood from childbirth, was regarded as more virulent than menstrual blood and so required women to undergo special purification, termed "churching," after childbirth. The practice of churching, which persists in contemporary society, requires a woman after childbirth to kneel or stand outside the church until she is purified with holy water and a priest's prayer. Only then may she enter the church.[31]

In Pliny's *Natural History,* a menstruating woman has supernatural power for moral or evil intentions:

> Her touch can blast vines, fade purple cloth, blacken linen in the wash-tub, tarnish copper, make bees desert their hives, and cause abortions in mares, but she can also rid a field of pests by walking around naked before sunrise, calm a storm at sea by exposing her genitals, and cure boils, erysipelas, hydrophobia, and barrenness. In the Talmud it is said that if a menstruating woman passes between two men, one of them dies.[32]

In Zambia, Stoller writes that villages subdivided by gender are configurations of specific networks and tabooed spaces, with traffic signs designated either "male" or "female." Segregation, by gender, safeguards the male from female contaminants, such as bodily fluids and scents. Zambians believe female scrutiny–including a woman's glance–detracts from male authority. The female body is considered lethal: female pollutants carry the power to osmose into food, water, or possessions, and they can inhabit a man's soul, corrupting his masculinity. All of these beliefs necessitate restrictions to keep females under surveillance. Male awe of the female converges on her reproductive capacity:

> When a woman goes into labor, she retires to the menstrual hut. There she is attended only by women; men are excluded. Mother and infant are thought to be infectious because of the mass of pollutants released there, so men fiercely avoid the area.[33]

Gender-driven taboos developed from the female biological capacity to menstruate and to bear children. Menstruation was considered defiling and dangerous, not an abstract principle. Taboos, as Briffault writes, originate from the dreaded effects of contact with females in these conditions. The Dene, an African tribe, believe contact with menstrual blood transmutates a male into a female. Similarly, the Orang Belenda, another African people, believe contact with a menstruating female deprives a male of masculinity. Some indigenous peoples believe touching a female during menses makes his bones soft and incapable of masculine pursuits.[34]

Campbell writes of male mutilation through a subincision wound that surgically equivocates a penis womb or vagina. This male-female, considered the "vaginal father," replaces a newborn's biological mother. Blood drawn from subincision wounds correspond in the male imagination to menstrual blood. Males appropriate the potent magical authority of menstrual blood, chanting the following:

> "We are not afraid of the bleeding vagina," they can now say;
> "we have it ourselves. It does not threaten the penis; it is the
> penis." And finally: "we are not separated from the mother;
> for 'we two are one.'"[35]

Foucault writes that the preoccupation with blood and the law relates to the political supervision of sexuality that began during the classical age. The *symbolics of blood*–which until the nineteenth century was held sovereign by laws prohibiting intermarriage, etc.– became an *analytics of sexuality*. Racism, in its modern biologizing form, became codified in the second half of the nineteenth century with a political system that was a statist formulation of colonization and settlement, family, marriage, education, social hierarchization, and property. The sexualization of white supremacy, to use Foucault's phrase, is a eugenic ordering of society, an extended state authority with biological rationalizations. The exaltation of "superior blood" became racially motivated to protect blood purity with laws governing the body, conduct, health, and everyday life:

> A eugenic ordering of society, with all that implied in the way
> of extension and intensification of micro-powers, in the guise
> of an unrestricted state control (etatisation), was accompanied
> by the oneiric exaltation of a superior blood; the later implied
> both the systematic genocide of others and the risk of exposing
> oneself to total sacrifice. It is an irony of history that the
> Hitlerite politics of sex remained an insignificant practice

while the blood myth was transformed into the greatest blood bath in recent memory.[36]

THE UNIVERSAL DISASTER

The aftershock of the bubonic plague that struck Europe during the fourteenth century (from 1347 through 1350) sent shock waves into the decades that followed. The epidemic was a universal disaster, decimating, at various estimates, from one-third to one-half of the population of Europe. Many historians concur that the bubonic plague, or Black Death, was a disaster with few parallels in recorded history. Throughout history, eruptions of infectious-disease epidemics had extreme consequences. Disease pathogens reached beyond geographic boundaries, allowing for new infections to cross-pollute populations that lacked any acquired immunity to fight off the disease. The plague pandemic has few parallels in history and was a consequential factor in the social, economic, religious, and cultural development of medieval Europe and in the beginning of the modern world.[37] Unfortunately, during the 100 years that followed the Black Plague, the Inquisition was established, which predominantly put to trial and executed women, but there were major episodic events of genocide toward lesbians and gay men.

Several historians contend that the bubonic plague was portentous by signaling the end of the Middle Ages and the beginning of the modern world. It changed the course of political and military events, promoted profound social change, fermenting intense class struggles between the bourgeoisie and the nobility and clergy. The bubonic plague also marked the appearance of an intense class struggle between the peasantry and the nobility. The plague precipitated the social reconstitution of medieval European society, its economics, religious life, and cultural development.[38]

Because of widespread misery in a restless population, the bubonic plague incited fanatical and superstitious religious beliefs that were motivated by contrition and repentance. The Brotherhood of the Cross resurfaced after suppression by the Catholic Church during the thirteenth century. The Order became a movement of self-flagellants who roamed through various countries organizing pilgrimages. The Order quoted self-serving Biblical passages to prove the claim that only penitence could deliver the population from the ravages of the plague. The self-flagellants believed they were divinely inspired redeemers of humanity. Religious fundamentalism provided the foundation for a mystical political movement that promoted fear in a population profoundly devastated by the plague. The etiology of the disease was unknown, so people resorted to moral indignation, prejudice, and religious explanations for the decimating effect of the plague.

The Order propagandized against the Jews by originating the mythic charge that Jews had poisoned public wells, thereby introducing the plague.[39] The self-flagellants fomented a genocidal attack on the Jewish community. They capitalized on the population's collective mental shock and mobilized themselves into a so-called preventative movement of mortification. The self-flagellants advanced through many medieval cities, presenting pageants in town squares and using the constant theme of death. They sentenced Jews before sanguinary tribunals and massacred them within their ghettoes:

> In Basle on January 9, 1349, the whole community of several hundred Jews was burned in a wooden house especially constructed for the purpose on an island in the Rhine, and a decree was passed that no Jew should be allowed to settle in Basle for 200 years.[40]

The Jews fought back, however. Already socially ostracized for centuries, Jews had suffered severe sanctions in European society, particularly at the hands of cruel and avaricious monarchs. They became a convenient scapegoat.

The plague was a central factor that contributed to the social choices of the era, and the Inquisition was a manifestation of an "extremist outbreak of hysteria."[41] (See Figure 3.) Scapegoats serve a purpose during an epidemic by stimulating the collective consciousnesses of a whole people to reinforce already existing prejudices: "Increasingly in the later Middle Ages both heretics and witches served as scapegoats, and the dangers of contamination from them become one of the favorite sermon topics."[42] Fear of

FIGURE 3. Burning of Plague Spreaders, Sebastian Munster, Cosmographia Universalis, Bettman Archive

contamination from women through the sexual act became a principal theme.

The Inquisition was the "purification of society," and it was "legitimated as a cleansing not only of the 'body politic,' [but also] to cleanse the whole organism from deviant and defiant individuals."[43]

The exploitation of the theme that originated in the thirteenth century was to be so successful that it gave birth to what might be called the great fear of women, intimately linked to all those sadistic elements that were unleashed at the time of the rise and subsequent repression of witchcraft.[44]

One calculation suggests that over the course of several hundred years, nine million people, mostly women, were tortured and burned at the stake.

The Catholic Church was in decline before the bubonic plague. Ironically, the plague helped reestablish the Church's supremacy with the rebirth of religious fervor during the plague and for a century thereafter. It is significant that the Inquisition established itself during the century that followed the bubonic plague, especially with the Church's ascendancy as a politically dominant institution.

The legislation enacted during the Black Plague was a form of so-called moral sanitation. It was not conjecture that the disease was sexually transmitted but, rather, that certain activities were morally offensive. As a result, moral legislation became the link to sanitary legislation during the epidemic years. Legislation ordered prostitutes and sodomites out of the city.[45] During the fifteenth and sixteenth centuries, health officials were anxious to fight the recurrent epidemics of plague. Cipolla notes that the etiology of plague disease–either pathogen or vectors–was unidentified. It was unknown at that time how disease spread and became epidemic:

> People were groping blindly in then as we are now in our search for ways to stop the spread of neoplasms. And working in the dark leads to errors, wasted resources, and the accusation of innocents.[46]

Historians agree that the Black Plague had a profound influence, but further research requires the specific connection between it and the later genocide and gynecide–the annihilation of women–of millions of people.

In 1496, the Parliament of Paris decreed that all persons infected with the disease should leave the city within 24 hours. In 1497, in Aberdeen, Scotland, the town council ordered "for protection from the disease which had come out of France and strange parts, all light women desist from their vice and sin of venery and work for their support, on pain, else, of being branded with a hot iron on their cheek and banished from the town."[47] An edict passed by the council ordered all inhabitants of Edinburgh that were afflicted with syphilis into banishment to the Island of Inchkeith.

The spread of syphilis during the fifteenth and sixteenth centuries was accompanied by xenophobic fervor in Italy, Spain, and France. The Spanish, who first recognized the disease, called it the disease of Espanolo, which meant the disease of Haiti. As Brandt writes, controversy continued into the early twentieth century regarding the origin of the disease, affecting immigration policies in the United States. But despite warnings that immigrants were bringing syphilis and other venereal diseases into the country, medical examinations at ports-of-entry showed low incidences of disease. Nativists called for a restriction of immigration, however.

> Theories of casual transmission of syphilis reflected deep cultural fears about disease and sexuality in the early 20th century. Syphilis was viewed as a threat to the entire late Victorian social and sexual system, which placed great value on discipline, restraint, and homogeneity. The sexual code of this era held that only sex in marriage could receive social sanction.[48]

During the syphilis epidemic, distinctions were made between innocent victims, depending on how the infection was contracted. Implicit in the notion of *innocent* infection was the suggestion of culpability for the epidemic.[49] The following moralistic statement refers to the syphilis epidemic in the United States during the 1930s:

> In general, the selective action of the disease is favorable to the perpetuation of strains endowed with altruism, self-control, idealism, and intelligence. It tends to eliminate some of the mentally deficient and mentally diseased, and also those lacking in self-control.[50]

In 1918, during World War I, the United States Congress established a "civilian quarantine and isolation fund" and quarantined more than 20,000 women. Barbed wire and guards secured many of the institutions.

Musto suggests that so-called drug experts in the early twentieth century considered quarantine to be a protection against contagion from substance users:

During the years just after World War I, for example, addicts in New York City were brought to North Brother Island in the East River. In the 1930s a federal narcotics hospital was built in the form of a prison in Lexington, Kentucky.[51]

The opinion that addiction is contagious (known as addictiphobia) drove public-health officials and governmental agencies to imprison individuals without Constitutional due process.

SELF-POLLUTION AND TOUCHING PHOBIA

The medical and psychiatric censure of masturbation, an almost universal practice, is a recapitulation of prohibitions within the ethics of Judeo-Christianity. The religious writings on masturbation, associated with sin and guilt, emerged diagnostically to have fatal physiological effects on mind and body. In 1835, an article entitled "Remarks on Masturbation" listed typical symptoms as feebleness and lack of vigor.[52] In a later article in the same journal, the author claimed masturbation led to insanity: "The victim of this practice passes from one degree of imbecility to another, till all the powers of the system, mental, physical and moral, are blotted out forever."[53]

St. Thomas Aquinas considered any nonprocreative ejaculation—and onanism in particular–a sin. For centuries, the sin of self-pollution and the sin against nature became medicalized with resultant bodily weakness, impotence, and ultimately suicide. For women, the surgical procedure of clitoridectomy became a medical intervention in England, introduced in 1858. Dr. Isaac Baker-Brown, president of the London Medical Society, considered the clitoridectomy imperative. He believed masturbation caused hysteria, epilepsy, and varicose veins. He performed the procedure on both children and adults and established a special home for women in London.[54]

According to Morgan, as of 1984, from 65 to 75 million women endure some form of genital mutilation. She notes the male supremacist prohibition against a woman's right to control her body extends beyond genital to "psychic clitoridectomy," citing Freud's declaration that "the elimination of clitoral sexuality is a necessary precondition for the development of femininity." It is crucial not to regard genital mutilation in racial, religious, or culture-specific terms because vaginal reconstruction was practiced in this country as recently as the 1970s.[55]

When anthropologists investigate the supernatural in other cultures, they often discover a school of "contagious magic." In contagious magic, the physical is integrated into the spiritual:

> A curious application of the doctrine of contagious magic is the relation commonly believed to exist between a wounded and the agent of the wound, so that whatever is subsequently done by or to the agent must correspondingly affect the patient either for good or evil.[56]

The capacity to combine distant objects and to convey an impression from one object to another accounts for the impact of contagious magic to evoke fear and fascination intrapsychically.

Freud attempted to synthesize the various disciplines of anthropology, social psychology, and psychoanalysis by proposing a relationship between recurring cultural themes. He turned to the very origin of taboo, which he considered a riddle, to provide a clue to "throw a light upon the obscure origin of our own 'cultural imperative'." He believed that the imposition of taboo serves the interests of a privileged caste or class, and it functions from a source of fear that is supernatural. The neurosis, "touching phobia," extends from the prohibition of physical contact to mere thoughts of the forbidden object:

> Anyone who has violated a taboo becomes taboo himself because he has possessed the dangerous quality of tempting others to follow his example. . . . Thus he is truly contagious in that every example encourages imitation, and for that reason he himself must be shunned.[57]

The central principle of taboo is the avoidance of physical and psychical contact with the object or person. The violation of taboo results in contagion.

In *Totem in Taboo*, Freud attempted to synthesize the various disciplines of anthropology, social psychology, and psychoanalysis to advance an interrelationship among recurrent cultural themes found within the neuroses common to Western civilization.

The truth of taboos is the key to our human attitude. We must know, we can know that prohibitions are not imposed from without. . . . If we observe the taboo, if we submit to it, we are no longer conscious of it. But in the act of violating it we feel the anguish of mind without which the taboo would not exist: that is the experience of sin.[58]

Freud felt that the imposition of taboo lay deeper than serving the interest of a privileged class: the source of fear must have a supernatural basis. However, this denial negates historical reality because the imposition of taboo promotes the division of classes. These categories are intrinsic to the social infrastructure of dominance. One group exercises power over another based upon the perception of the Other, which is believed to be a threat. Inherent to the foundation of power, dominance is a definition of Self and the objectification of the Other.

Phobia is a neurosis characterized by anxiety and fear of an object or anything outside of the individual. Within the neurosis designated as "touching phobia," the principal prohibition of physical contact extends from the physical to thoughts of the forbidden object. The identical prohibition is the basis of taboo. The central principal of taboo is the avoidance of physical and psychical contact with the designated object or person, the violation of which results in contagion:

The object is endowed with evil intentions and with all the attributes of a malefic power. In the phobic, affect has a priority that defies all rational thinking. . . . Contact alone is enough to evoke anxiety. For contact is at the same time the basic schematic type of initiating sexual action (touching, caresses–sexuality).[59]

The prohibition of contact with the object or person considered taboo has considerable consequences for an individual within the social order, as well as intrapsychically:

The humanity of the colonized, rejected by the colonizer, becomes opaque. It is useless, he asserts, to try to forecast the colonized actions. It seems to him that strange and disturbing impulsiveness controls the colonized. The colonized must indeed be very strange, if he remains so mysterious after years of living with colonizer.[60]

Illness and difference in our culture are reciprocal. Apprehensions about difference further prescribe the manner by which an authoritarian and dominant social group imposes sanctions and ostracizes the disenfranchised group. The construction of subcategories of people is fundamental to any social infrastructure whose organization is power dominance:

> Shame, rather than guilt, appears to arise when a person finds himself condemned to an identity as the complement of another he wishes to repudiate, but cannot. It is difficult to establish a consistent identity for oneself–that is, to see oneself consistently in the same way–if definitions of oneself by others are inconsistent or mutually exclusive. . . . To 'fit in with' them all or to repudiate them all may be impossible. Hence mystification, confusion, and conflict.[61]

The philosophy of male supremacy, buttressed by religious doctrine, legal sanctions, medicalization of behavior, and economic constraints, maintains our patriarchal social structure with its quintessential caste division based on gender.

In contemporary society, there has been a process of divestment by the criminal justice system, rarely prosecuting gays or lesbians: "Under the new system, society is said to be acting in a parental role (*parens patriae*)–seeking not to punish but to change or socialize the nonconformist through treatment and therapy."[62] The emphasis of the therapeutic state has been the growth of new controls in the arenas of mental health, where gays and lesbians are castrated, lobotomized, shock-treated, and experimented upon with aversion-style therapies. The authority of psychiatric diagnosis augments religious doctrine: "What had been 'unnatural acts' or 'acts against nature' in the religious perspective, became, in psychiatric terminology, 'perverted' acts or 'perverse' inclinations."[63] Institutions other than biomedical conjoin by promoting homophobic philosophies and legal constraints. The mass psychology of homosexual panic, the mere unconscious fantasy of same-sex relatedness, affects our entire prohibitive culture. The pervasive fear of homosexual contamination, a component of homophobia, requires the institutions of legal restraints.

During the Third Reich, Heinrich Himmler wrote in a Gestapo memorandum:

> Contamination is especially frequent when it comes to homosexuality, which, as we know, 'is the result of seduction.'. . . They must be evicted and transported to an area where their activities present no danger to Germandom.[64]

Plant calls the persecution of gays in Hitler's Germany the ultimate culmination of legal injustice. In 1986 a United States Supreme Court decision upheld state's rights to criminalize same-sex relatedness by stating the following:

> Sodomy was a criminal offense at common law and was forbidden by the laws of the original thirteen states when they ratified the Bill of Rights . . . in this Nation's history and tradition or 'implicit in the concept of ordered liberty' is, at best, facetious.[65]

Ecclesiastic natural law (unnatural and acts against nature), the doctrine of sin, when transformed into medical and psychiatric canonical law became diagnosable as a perverse psychosexual disorder. Justice White delivered the decision outlawing sodomy. Twenty-four states and the District of Columbia criminally penalize same-sex relatedness in private and between consenting adults. Justice Burger concurred that "proscriptions against sodomy have very "ancient roots":

> Decisions of individuals relating to homosexual conduct have been subject to state intervention throughout the history of Western Civilization. Condemnation of those practices is firmly rooted in Judaeo-Christian moral and ethical standards. . . . To hold that the act of homosexual sodomy is somehow protected as a fundamental right would be to cast aside millennia of moral teaching.[66]

Same-sex relatedness, characterized as degeneracy, was viewed less from revulsion than from the fear that it was somehow contagious.

THE EPISTEMOLOGY OF STIGMA

The essence of stigma is the complementary, dual symbolization of moral and physical chaos embodied in a reciprocal interrelationship, a personality type. Sontag offers the modern inclination to psychologize disease causality, the presumption of unhealthy mindedness, as the etiology of certain illnesses replacing moral retribution or a theological interpretation:

> A large part of the popularity and persuasiveness of psychology comes from its being a sublimated spiritualism: a secular, ostensibly scientific way of affirming the primacy of "spirit" over matter.[67]

The stigmatized are deviates, branded (as in Kaposi's sarcoma), and corrupted. Some are identifiable; others are clandestine. Each has a "spoiled identity." The shame of HIV, to use Sontag's analysis, is an accusation of wrongdoing, an imputation of guilt because "the illness flushes out an identity that might have remained hidden from neighbors, jobmates, family, friends."[68] The diagnostic procedure of HIV antibody testing requires the obligatory self-disclosure of bad conscience-inducing behavior. Sexuality and acts of sex are discussed with a counselor in a truncated session.

> Shame becomes a central possibility, arising from the individual's perception of his own attributes as being a defiling thing to possess, and one he can readily see himself as not possessing.[69]

Scientific theories of disease that are signified as entirely biological phenomenon have cultural meanings within society.

The development of modern medicine, even as an auxiliary to biology, was an intensified fascination with human sexuality. The medicalization of sexuality, the locus of pathology, constructed a binary system of licit and illicit. For a century, medicine, including psychiatry, formulated an iconography that placed homosexuality into clinical nomenclature as pathology. Sexual identity became medicalized with the addition of "homosexuality" into the lexicon at the end of the nineteenth century–a period marked by the ascendancy of biomedical and psychiatric institutions. The first reference to the term "homosexuality" in the Oxford English Dictionary is 1897, with a comment by Havelock Ellis, who called the word "barbarously hybrid."[70] During the mid-nineteenth century, the political and sexual models of degeneracy were most evident in the arena of public health. Theories of degeneracy were fundamental to the medicalization of homosexuality. The invert, as Other, was a third gender, a different species that required medical identification:

> Homosexuality appeared as one of the forms of sexuality when it was transposed from the practice of sodomy onto a kind of interior androgyny, hermaphrodism of the soul. The sodomite had been a temporary aberration; the homosexual was now a species.[71]

Freud viewed sexual instinct as two halves, male and female, attempting to reunite; he defined the third category as inverts. There are three types of inversion: the *absolutely inverted*, the *psychosexually hermaphroditic*, and the *occasionally inverted*.

The medicalization of homosexuality, legitimized as scientific, was understood in both theological and teleological terms:

> Thus disease-entities were invented which defined a clearly limited subset of human beings as the group solely at risk. For such diseases were labeled as inherited to one degree or another. The inherited diseases, whether masturbation, hysteria, neurasthenia, congenital syphilis, or even incest, all had this in common.[72]

Illich sees the capability of modern society and its institutions to scientifically define so-called deficiencies. Science conducts research that confirms prior opinion and then diagnoses individuals, subjecting "entire population groups to compulsory testing; to impose therapy on those found to be in need of correction, cure, or upgrading."[73]

> In this process, the imagery and vocabulary of morality were replaced by biological fantasy and psychiatric metaphor. Temptation–resisted or indulged–has been supplanted by drives, instincts, and impulses–satisfied or frustrated. Virtue and vice have been transformed into health and illness.[74]

Spiritual regeneration, "to be born again," the cultural imperative for salvation, in contemporary society became the cure through medical salvation, "to be healthy again."

Institutions of medicine exercise power in industrialized societies by medicalizing behavior different from culturally established standards:

> Only doctors now "know" what constitutes sickness, who is sick, what shall be done to the sick and those they consider *at a special risk*. [author's emphasis][75]

Historically, those judged "at risk" are inherently different and require isolation through segregation and quarantine, or are confined by institutionalization and imprisonment from the community. "Fear of seizure of power by the Other is inherent in all images of Otherness."[76] The stigmatized provoke fear because of their contagion–that they have the potential to transmute and consequently seize power.

Foucault proposed that purely biological events, such as the appearance of microorganisms, as interpreted by historians, is intrinsic to social organization. Within a context of pathology, the body was a target for disease:

> The political investment of the body is bound up, in accordance with complex reciprocal relations, with its economic use; it is largely as a force of production that the body is invested with relations of power and domination.[77]

Homophobia coextending to erotophobia insists that same-sex related sexual acts are distinct from heterosexual acts. The assumption that kissing, body contact, and anal or oral intercourse are dissimilar when engaged in by members of different genders than the same gender is fallacious.

The quest for social order criminalizes certain behavior, assesses individual blame, and proscribes therapeutic control. Gays and lesbians, not protected by the U.S. Constitution, are sexual outlaws who must endure the criminal aspect of same-sex related behavior:

> American homosexuals were condemned to death by choking, burning, and drowning; they were executed, jailed, pilloried, fined, court-martialed, prostituted, fired, framed, blackmailed, disinherited, declared insane, driven to insanity, to suicide, murder, pitied, castigated, and despised.[78]

Any attempt to understand the relation of lesbians and gay men within Western civilization is extremely complex and controversial because of the sociopolitical and religious sanctions against same-sex relatedness. For instance, within English law, same-sex orientation was the *crime not fit to be named*. Therefore, an aura of prohibition has cloaked open discussion. This exacerbates the difficulty, since legal documents are often destroyed in order to preserve reputations and avoid scandal. This necessitated intensive and painstaking historical research by primarily lesbian and gay historians. The Stonewall Rebellion in Greenwich Village occurred during the summer of 1969, and it marked the beginning of gay liberation as a major political movement.

Medically diagnosed subgroups subsume the individual into a category with the loss of autonomy and the capability to self-define. HIV disease is illustrative of the stigmatization process. Within the conceit of "risk groups" (i.e., gay men, IVDUs, and Haitians during the early years of the epidemic) is the interpretation that there is a *general population* and the Other, further branding already disenfranchised peoples. Thinly disguised phases, such as *special-interest groups* and *family values*, have come into popular usage. These phrases connote commonly held beliefs about moral principles, in contrast to deviant ones, and serve to further separate people from one another and to isolate experience. Laing describes alienation in terms of the creation of a Them and a They, each compelling the repudiation of true self-identity and the recognition of the humanity of others:

When we have installed Them in our hearts, we are only a plurality of solitudes in which what each person has in common is his allocation to the other of the necessity for his own action. Each person, however, as other to the other, is the other's necessity.[79]

Unfortunately, the HIV disease "risk group" categories established a fallacious health assumption–being a member of a group causes HIV infection.

The fear of contagion is one manner a dominant social group apprehends the difference of the less powerful subgroup and its subsequent ostracism. HIV infection has been designated as a sexually transmitted disease (STD), bringing to mind all cultural prohibitions against sexuality, and homosexuality in particular. Actually, the disease transmission occurs through blood-to-blood or through those bodily fluids with blood content, such as semen: HIV is transmitted by any practice that results in direct bloodstream contact with an infected partner's blood or semen. Those infected with HIV, or individuals who are HIV-antibody-positive, carry the severe stigmatization associated with sexuality and sexual differences and are, within stigma-theory, "subhuman":

We construct a stigma-theory, an ideology to explain his inferiority and account for the danger he represents, sometimes rationalizing an animosity based on other differences. . . . We tend to impute wide range of imperfections on the basis of the original one, and at the same time to impute some desirable but undesired attributes, often of a supernatural cast.[80]

In a classic work on prejudice, Allport examined all aspects of discrimination to illuminate the root causes of prejudice, with its devastating effect on civilization. For instance, he analyzed the fear of contact by the out-group as an expression of prejudice, suggesting that institutional sanctions against segregation provided the means to refute discrimination. However, he qualified any notion about prejudice to include complications caused by inner conflict within the individual. The collective character structure can obstruct positive results imposed by institutional and legal sanctions, such as desegregation:

Sometimes the source of the fear is not known, or has been forgotten or repressed. The fear may be merely a mounting residue of inner feelings of weakness in dealing with the hazards of the outer world. . . . There may, of course, be elements of realistic fear mingled with displaced fear.[81]

The cultural theme of contamination has taken many historical forms. Allport felt that the fear of contact with the out-group was one manifestation of discrimination. His analysis is inclusive of the intrapsychic constituent of prejudice that encompasses the social realm where it characterizes both collective behavior and the institutions of control.

The majority of those infected with HIV disease–gay men, IV-DUs, and people of color–are socially ostracized. Within a phenomenological context, reactions to HIV are far beyond purely biomedical issues (i.e., knowledge of the routes of transmission or etiology). The perception of an epidemic is a combination of those infected and how they contracted HIV. The fear of contagion has been a critical element during the HIV pandemic, as it has been historically with other epidemics. However, fear of contagion has greater meaning than *catching* something. It carries more the sense of contamination or defilement, not so much of becoming sick, but being unclean or inhuman. The fear of contagion has a fundamental intrapsychic component that is integral to human character structure; the fear is archetypal, part of the collective unconscious.

The unconscious fear of contagion is inherent to power dominance. Power dominance perceives the Other through the process of mystification and objectification. Feminist philosopher Simone de Beauvoir suggested that the expression of duality, Self versus Other, is primordial and that it informs the nature and structure of human consciousness. She maintained the duality that became a hostile division based on gender was a historical development.[82] To preserve the collective Self, dominion over the Other is institutionalized, with authority exercised through misguided stereotypes that stigmatize. Stigma is the belief that the Other is subhuman: "On this assumption we exercise varieties of discrimination, through which we effectively, if often unthinkably, reduce his life chances."[83]

There has been vigilant attention paid to the HIV pandemic by those concerned with both social justice and the biomedical community. The epidemic exacerbates many preexisting global conflicts; the complexity of issues that encompass HIV disease are interwoven and reverberate into other struggles that have characterized this century. HIV disease has provoked further investigation into our ideas about gender, class, racial, sexuality, sexual orientation, and substance use within a framework of HIV disease–a life-threatening disease that has infected millions of people.

It signifies the wide split in our social structure. For instance, even before the appearance of HIV disease, "approximately 500 million people suffer[ed] from hunger and malnutrition; the most seriously affected [were] children under the age of five and women. Twenty million persons die annually of hunger-related causes and one billion endure chronic undernourishment and other poverty deprivations; the majority are women and children."[84] The viability of our planetary ecosystem depends on a holistic interpretation of health, not solely the absence of disease, but survival itself and the quality of life of our population.

The conduct of social and historical inquiry, alongside biomedical questions, has been a formidable challenge to professionals and activists, including those individuals with HIV infection. Historical investigation serves a purpose: the defense mechanism of denial pervades our culture, so painful historical periods and events are recast almost as quickly as they occur. The mass media is reductionist in its approach. It projects images that represent an event–the emotion, anguish, joy, or pleasure of the phenomena–yet it stands uniquely by itself, without the richness of language or the connotations of interpretation. Humankind as well suffers the loss of identity without historical process.

In September 1987, 500 people encircled a grade school in Arcadia, Florida. It was a rally organized by a community organization called Citizens Against AIDS. They were protesting a court order obtained by Clifford Ray that allowed his three hemophiliac sons, who tested HIV-seropositive to enroll in school. Almost 50% of the students boycotted the first day of classes. The school received bomb threats. After the first week of classes, a fire bomb completely gutted the Ray home, causing them to lose all their possessions. The family fled to another part of the state.[85]

In 1988, neighborhood opposition in the Richmond Hill section of Queens, New York, forced the closing of a counseling center that was to service people with HIV infection. When the center first opened, "telephone callers threatened to firebomb it and vandals threw rocks against its window."[86]

When the Berlin Wall came down in 1989, the AIDS wall went up. East German Premier Hans Modrow, a leading reformer in Communist ranks, said that the Berlin Wall should stay open but remain standing to keep out AIDS, drugs, and crime from the West: "In our country there is little criminal activity. Cases of AIDS and drugs are virtually unknown. Our people are asking themselves why they shouldn't just leave that as it is."[87]

The phobia of contamination has manifested itself politically through institutionalized segregation, quarantine, ghettoization, and its most extreme expressions, gynecide and genocide. Themes of contamination have been the subject of anthropology in many cultures. This phobia has severe political ramifications when acted upon in any social system, and it has been an important component of human prejudice.

REFERENCE NOTES

1. Geoffrey Marks and William K. Beatty, *Epidemics* (New York: Charles Scribner's Sons, 1976), p. 278.

2. Susan Sontag, *AIDS and Its Metaphors* (New York: Farrar, Straus and Giroux, 1989), p. 57.

3. Michel Foucault, *The Birth of the Clinic* (New York: Vintage Books, 1973), p. 31.

4. Susan Sontag, *Illness as Metaphor* (New York: Vintage Books, 1977)

5. Joel Kovel, *White Racism: A Psychohistory* (New York: Columbia University Press, 1984), p. 87.

6. Arthur N. Gilbert, "Conception of Homosexuality and Sodomy in Western History," in *The Gay Past*, edited by Salvatore J. Licata and Robert P. Peterson (New York: Harrington Park Press, 1985), p. 65.

7. Norman O. Brown, *Life Against Death* (Middleton, CT: Wesleyan University Press, 1969), p. 75.

8. *The New English Bible* (New York: Cambridge University Press, 1971), I Samuel, 5-6.

9. Marilyn French, *Beyond Power: On Women, Men, And Morals* (New York: Summit Books, 1985), p. 269.

10. Danielle Jacquart and Claude Thomasset, *Sexuality and Medicine in the Middle Ages* (Princeton: Princeton University Press, 1988), p. 161.

11. Jeffrey Meyers, *Disease and the Novel: 1890-1969* (New York: St. Martin's Press, 1985), p. 1.

12. Foucault, *Birth of the Clinic*, p. 31.

13. Elisabeth Schussler-Fiorenza, "Discipleship and Patriarchy" in *Women's Consciousness, Women's Conscience*, edited by Barbara Hilkert Andolsen, Christine E. Gudorf, and Mary D. Pellauer (New York: A Seabury Book, 1985), pp. 145-146.

14. Michel Foucault, *The History of Sexuality* (New York: Pantheon Books, 1978), pp. 42-43.

15. Gordon W. Allport, *The Nature of Prejudice* (Reading, MA: Addison-Wesley Publishing Company, 1987), p. 55.

16. Ibid., p. 147.

17. Marielouise Janssen-Jurreit, *Sexism: The Male Monopoly on History and Thought* (New York: Farrar, Straus and Giroux, 1982), p. 97.

18. Mary Daly, *Beyond God The Father* (Boston: Beacon Press, 1973), p. 45.

19. Robert Graves and Raphael Patai, *Hebrew Myths: The Book of Genesis* (New York: McGraw-Hill Paperbacks, 1964), p. 27.

20. Elizabeth Gould Davis, *The First Sex* (New York: G. P. Putnam's Sons, 1971), p. 144.

21. Karen Horney, MD, *Feminine Psychology* (New York: W.W. Norton & Company, 1967), p. 112.

22. Jacquart and Thomasset, *Sexuality and Medicine*, p. 129.

23. Robert Briffault, *The Mothers: The Matriarchal Theory of Social Origins* (New York: Grosset & Dunlap, 1963), p. 126.

24. H. R. Hays, *The Dangerous Sex* (New York: G. P. Putnam's Sons, 1964), p. 40.

25. Uta Ranke-Heinemann, *Eunuchs for the Kingdom of Heaven* (New York: Doubleday, 1990), p. 21.

26. "Commentary on Ezekiel," 18:6. quoted in *Eunuchs for the Kingdom of Heaven*, by Uta Ranke-Heinemann (New York: Doubleday, 1990).

27. Erich Neumann, *The Origins and History of Consciousness* (Princeton: Princeton University Press, 1973), p. 57.

28. Adrienne Rich, *Of Woman Born: Motherhood as Experience and Institution* (New York: W. W. Norton & Company, 1976), p. 105.

29. Camille Paglia, *Sexual Personae*, (New York: Vintage Books, 1991), p. 11.

30. Ranke-Heinemann, *Eunuchs*, p. 24.

31. Ibid., p. 26.

32. Robert Graves, *The White Goddess* (New York: Farrar, Straus and Giroux, 1972), p. 166.

33. Robert J. Stoller, MD, *Presentations of Gender* (New Haven: Yale University Press, 1985), p. 187.

34. Robert Briffault, *The Mothers* (New York: Grosset & Dunlap, 1963), p. 241.

35. Joseph Campbell, *The Masks of God: Primitive Mythology* (New York: The Viking Press, 1973), p. 103.

36. Michel Foucault, *The History of Sexuality: An Introduction, Volume 1,* (New York: Vintage Books, 1990), p. 150.

37. Ibid., p. 9.

38. Nancy Siraisi in *The Black Death: The Impact of the Fourteenth Century Plague* (Binghamton, NY: Center for Medieval Early Renaissance Studies, 1982), p. 9.

39. Yves Renouard, "The Black Death as a Major Event in World History," in *The Black Death,* edited by William M. Bowsky (New York: Holt, Rinehart and Winston, 1971), p. 35.

40. Barbara Tuchman, *A Distant Mirror: The Calamitous Fourteenth Century* (New York: Alfred A. Knopf, 1978), p. 94.

41. Pennethorne Hughes, *Witchcraft* (New York: A Pelican Book, 1965), p. 173.

42. Vern L. Bullough, "Heresy, Witchcraft, and Sexuality," *Journal of Homosexuality,* Volume 1(2), 1974, p. 183.

43. Mary Daly, *Gynecology: The Metaethics of Radical Feminism* (Boston: Beacon Press, 1978), p. 185.

44. Jacquart and Thomasset, *Sexuality and Medicine,* p. 129.

45. Ann G. Carmichael, *Plague and the Poor in Renaissance Florence* (New York: Cambridge University Press, 1986), p. 99.

46. Carlo M. Cipolla, *Faith, Reason, and the Plague in Seventeenth-Century Tuscany* (New York: W. W. Norton & Company, 1979), p. 11.

47. Wm. Allen Pusey, *The History and Epidemiology of Syphilis* (Baltimore: Charles C. Thomas, 1933), p. 7.

48. Allan M. Brandt, "The Syphilis Epidemic and Its Relation to AIDS," *Science,* January 22, 1988.

49. Ibid.

50. Paul Popenoe, *Applied Eugenics* (New York: The Macmillan Company, 1933), p. 94.

51. David F. Musto, "Quarantine and the Problem of AIDS," in *AIDS: The Burdens of History,* edited by Elizabeth Fee and Daniel M. Fox (Berkeley: University of California Press, 1988), p. 80.

52. John Duffy, "Sex, Society, Medicine: An Historical Comment," in *Sexuality and Medicine, Volume II,* edited by Earl E. Shelp (Boston: D. Reidel Publishing Company, 1987), p. 75.

53. "Insanity Produced by Masturbation," *Boston Medical and Surgical Journal,* XII, 1835.

54. Ranke-Heinemann, *Eunuchs,* p. 317.

55. Robin Morgan, *Sisterhood Is Global* (New York: Anchor Books, 1984), p. 763.

56. James Frazer, *The Golden Bough* (New York: The Macmillan Company, 1941), p. 41.

57. Sigmund Freud, *Totem and Taboo* (New York: W. W. Norton & Company, 1963), p. 32.

58. Georges Bataille, *Death and Sensuality* (New York: Walker and Company, 1962), p. 37.

59. Frantz Fanon, *Black Skin, White Masks* (New York: Grove Press, 1967), p. 157.

60. Albert Memmi, *The Colonizer and the Colonized* (Boston: Beacon Press, 1972), p. 85.

61. R. D. Laing, *Self and Others* (New York: Penguin Books, 1987), p. 87.

62. Nicholas N. Kittrie, *The Right To Be Different*, (Baltimore: The Johns Hopkins Press, 1971), p. 11.

63. Thomas Szasz, *Ceremonial Chemistry* (New York: Anchor Press, 1974), p. 160.

64. Richard Plant, *The Pink Triangle: The Nazi War Against Homosexuals* (New York: A New Republic Book, 1986), p. 119.

65. Bowers v. Hardwick, 106 S.Ct. 2841 (1986).

66. Ibid.

67. Sontag, *Illness as Metaphor*, p. 54.

68. Sontag, *AIDS and Its Metaphors*, pp. 24-25.

69. Erving Goffman, *Stigma: Notes on the Management of Spoiled Identity* (New York: A Touchstone Book, 1986), p. 7.

70. *The Compact Edition of the Oxford English Dictionary* (New York: Oxford University Press, 1971).

71. Foucault, *The History of Sexuality*, p. 43.

72. Sander L. Gilman, *Difference and Pathology: Stereotypes of Sexuality, Race, and Madness* (Ithaca, NY: Cornell University Press, 1985), p. 213.

73. Ivan Illich, *Gender* (New York: Pantheon, 1982).

74. Thomas Szasz, *Ceremonial Chemistry* (New York: Anchor Press, 1974), pp. 159-160.

75. Ivan Illich, *Medical Nemesis* (New York: Pantheon, 1976), p. 47.

76. Gilman, *Difference and Pathology*, p. 213.

77. Michel Foucault, *The Foucault Reader* (New York: Pantheon, 1984), p. 173.

78. Jonathan Katz, *Gay American History* (New York: Thomas Y. Crowell Company, 1976), p. 11.

79. R. D. Laing, *The Politics of Experience* (New York: Ballantine Books, 1967), p. 84.

80. Goffman, *Stigma*, p. 5.

81. Gordon W. Allport, *The Nature of Prejudice* (New York: Addison-Wesley Publishing Company, 1987), p. 367.

82. Simone de Beauvoir, *The Second Sex* (New York: Vintage Books, 1975), p. 31.

83. Goffman, *Stigma*, p. 5.

84. Robin Morgan, *Sisterhood is Global* (New York: Anchor/Doubleday, 1984), p. 2.

85. *Newsweek*, September 7, 1989.

86. *The New York Times*, March 13, 1988.

87. *Daily News*, March 15, 1989.

Chapter 2

The Metaphysics
of a Pandemic

He had pieced the tale together, was accompanied by
complicated diagrams, with all the arrows and circles
centered on one person–the now famous Patient Zero.*

–Randy Shilts, *And the Band Played On*

THE NEXUS OF SEXUAL LIFESTYLE

In 1981, a foreboding of the outbreak of an epidemic alerted the
federal Centers for Disease Control (CDC) when the agency received several physician inquiries from Los Angeles and New York
for pentamidine. Pentamidine is a drug used to treat the rare form of
pneumonia known as *Pneumocystis carinii* pneumonia (PCP). Before the early 1980s, PCP was a rarely occurring, atypical form of
pneumonia, so the CDC stored the nation's entire supply of pentamidine due to infrequent demands for this medicine.[1] On June 5,
1981, the federal CDC reported five cases of atypical PCP cases in
its publication the *Morbidity and Mortality Weekly Report*
(*MMWR*).[2]

PCP was not a new infection, but until these citations it only
presented in individuals with immunosuppression. The CDC considered these cases atypical because the infection was present in
otherwise healthy individuals. The etiology of PCP is a protozoan
microbe found commonly in the lungs of most healthy people; the

---

*Randy Shilts (New York: St. Martin's Press, 1987), p. 438.

microbe is innocuous unless there is immunosuppression. The body's immune system in healthy individuals safeguards against disease-causing organisms. The immune system immediately responds through a community of cells that prevent infection. These cells, found throughout the body, are principally within the bone marrow, spleen, and lymphatic system. Early infection of PCP is insidious and undetectable, progressing slowly without symptoms. Eventually, the individual experiences fatigue, fever, chills, sweats, and exertional dyspnea (discomfort to the chest that is sometimes accompanied by nausea and vomiting).

At this time, PCP is the most common opportunistic infection (OI) associated with HIV disease in the CDC nomenclature for the diagnosis of AIDS. OIs are diseases caused by microorganisms present in the human body and environment, with illness developing when the immune system is weak or damaged. At the end of 1981, the CDC calculated more than 100 cases. By 1982, with a doubling of cases, the agency developed surveillance definitions for the syndrome.

Retrospective searches to determine the genesis of HIV indicated that the retrovirus existed decades before 1981. Undoubtedly, for many years there were many undiagnosed deaths. The CDC recognizes nine cases diagnosed as early as 1978–and 49 cases in 1980. In 1991, Dr. George Williams, a University of Manchester pathologist, detected the HIV retrovirus on tissue stored for 32 years. He used a new laboratory technique on the tissue of a 25-year-old sailor who died in 1959. Currently, this is the earliest documented case of HIV infection. In Zaire, a study conducted by African researchers on preserved blood samplings dating back to 1959 were tested for HIV. The results determined the presence of the retrovirus, verifying that HIV had existed for at least three decades.[3] Retroviruses with tumor-causing potential were known as early as 1909, but laboratory isolation of the HIV retrovirus did not take place until 1983 (by Dr. Luc Montagnier of the Pasteur Institute in Paris). The HIV retrovirus, then, existed for decades before its identification through scientific technology.

Epidemiologists at the CDC seized on the confluence of sexual identity, because in each of the five cases presenting the rare pneumonia the individuals were gay. The introductory report from the

CDC about the momentous epidemic published in the MMWR stated:

> The fact that these patients were all homosexuals suggests an association between some aspect of homosexual life-style or disease acquired through sexual contact and Pneumocystis pneumonia in this population.[4]

The CDC instantaneously correlated the cases of PCP with "some aspect of homosexual life-style" and speculated that it was "acquired through sexual contact." Epidemiologists advanced an exclusive hypothesis that assigned a complex process within a determinate social matrix. Epidemiologists speculated the probability of immune dysfunction causality based on sexual identity observed from an insufficient sampling of five gay men. The biomedical nexus of lifestyle, rather than microbe pathogenesis, was astonishing. The human organism, some aspect of sexuality, became the object itself:

> Whatever else it may be, however, AIDS in the United States came to be a story of gay men and a construction of a hypothetical male homosexual body. Obsession [is] the repeated feature of the AIDS story.[5]

The religious prototype of "unnatural" and the psychology of pathology transform the body into the consummate host. The transformation of both sexuality and the dimensions of human experience into pathology are divisions of normalcy/deviancy:

> Human sexuality, given its strong biological basis, not unnaturally is often perceived as out of the control of the self. Since fantasy is an innate part of human sexuality, it is not only the biological but also the psychological which can be understood as out of control. For a secure definition of self, sexuality and the loss of control associated with it must be projected onto the Other.[6]

The view that gay men were excessive and out-of-control touched all bases: gay men were generally thought to be selfish, with a lot of leisure time to have promiscuous sex, irresponsible, and *dirty*-a euphemism for a medical and psychically diseased condition. Sex with multiple partners defined as promiscuity formulates a value-laden "overload theory" of infection. An overload theory dismisses the pathonogenicity of microorganisms through evidence analogous to prescientific theories of disease causality. Patton characterized her overload theory as a myth that explains HIV disease through distinctions of class, so "people who share certain common characteristics are vulnerable to particular types of disease, in this case sexual practice":

> Hell-bent on destruction, they don't take the body's signs of minor infection as a hint that perhaps they are overdoing it. Instead, they get shots to conquer VD and caustic carcinogenic potions to wipe out amoebas.[7]

A study conducted by physicians associated anal intercourse with risk factors for anal cancer: "We found that in men, a history of receptive anal intercourse (related to homosexual behavior) was strongly associated with the occurrence of anal cancer."[8] The study, conducted after the outbreak of the HIV disease epidemic, scrutinizes same-gender sexuality under the guise of medical research. The institution of procreative intercourse is *natural*, without the risk of political or legal condemnation. HIV infection has predominantly stricken gay men (more than two-thirds of known cases), an oppressed group in Western society.

The cause-and-effect analysis of infectious disease necessitates medical knowledge and methodology, which despite all the advances of the last century are not adequately understood:

> Simple cause-and-effect analysis is inadequate for such systems. Since many variables are simultaneously at work, interacting constantly and altering their magnitudes at irregular rates, it is usually misleading to concentrate attention on a single "cause" and try to attribute a particular "effect" to it.[9]

Analyses of the juncture of host and agent on every level of organization–molecular, cellular, organismic, and social–are misrepresentative of biologic and social evolutionary patterns.

Epidemiology proceeds from a social dimension that can promote cultural biases, incorporating human relations, behavioral patterns, and experiences into an explanation of disease processes.[10] Science is the systematic study of phenomena when juxtaposed against social context, and it assigns biomedical significance or disease predisposition to entire groups of people organized by gender, class, ethnic, racial, or sexual identity.

Epidemiology is a multifactorial process that entails the systemic observation of certain infectious diseases. Epidemiologists implement a tripartite schemata that includes knowledge of the agent (the pathogen of a disease), the environment (the social connection), and the host (the infected individual). Epidemiologists examine predisposing constituents when advancing disease etiology, or causation.

This is not new biopower play within the medical establishment. With sexual orientation bound to HIV, biomedicine introduced additional medical stratagem that proposed a link between identity and illness. The pattern of professional dominion exercised by physicians as a class defines the therapeutic role as authoritarian over patients. This occurs beyond clinical boundaries into "arenas of moral and political action for which medical judgment is only partially relevant and often incompletely equipped."[11]

Shilts' popular book *And the Band Played On* is a saga that synthesizes journalism, medical gumshoe, and soap opera. The battlefields are a juxtaposition of various backroom scenes–including the excesses of gay sexuality and the infighting of the CDC. The gay protagonists are murderous, degenerate, or indifferent men subsumed in the excesses of out-of-control sexuality; some characters are activist prophets of doom. The gay airline steward, Gaetan Dugas, known as Patient Zero, is a "Typhoid Mary" fall-guy prototype who advances a major subtheme of the book: Anyone who called for decisive action early is a hero.

When *And the Band Played On* was published in 1987, 38% of people with HIV disease were people of color, more than 16% were intravenous drug users (IVDUs), and 7% were women. Among the most glaring deficiencies is the negligible attention Shilts gives to the tragic experience of HIV disease among minorities, intravenous drug users, and women.

"It never made any sense that AIDS would become a heterosexual disease," Shilts told one journalist. He further stated:

> It's not the biology that argues against it. It's the sociology. Gay activists don't want to admit that no heterosexual man could hold a candle to a moderately active gay man. Heterosexuals have never had institutions like bathhouses to amplify the contagion. Single bars are very different. There was a social milieu in which this disease spread, and to ignore those factors is foolish.[12]

Within predominant heterosexist culture, same-sexuality is as synonymous with promiscuity as same-sex relatedness is with perversity. From a cultural predisposition, epidemiologists seized on the exegesis of "life-style" as critical to a disease model that includes microbes.

Reaction to HIV disease has been complex due its definition as a sexually transmitted disease (STD):

> All along AIDS has been thought of as a sexually transmitted or venereal disease that is generally fatal. All of these claims, which have contributed greatly to fear of the disease, are false or misleading.[13]

Altman submitted that when HIV disease became inseparable from sexuality (although this is not the only way it can be transmitted), the politicization of the disease was intractable.[14] Divisions became framed by the widespread judgments of the condemned, individuals whose behavior wittingly brought the disease upon themselves: gay men, IVDUs, or sexual partners of IVDUs, and the innocent (those in the path of the infected). Ironically, even the so-called innocents could not elude public perception, as Ryan White reported when appearing before the President's Commission on AIDS. He acknowledged the homophobia of fellow students who knew he had HIV disease and scrawled "faggot" on his gym locker.

Within a month of the initial PCP citations, the MMWR reported 26 instances of Kaposi's sarcoma (KS). Again, KS was rare, limited to three populations: elderly men, especially of Mediterranean descent; African nationals; and adolescent males. Immunosuppression occurs when individuals receive medications for organ transplantation or other chemotherapies. KS is a tumorous cancer of the blood and lymphatic vessel wall tissues. These cases were also among gay men. In 1981, *The New York Times* reported that 41 gay men had been diagnosed with KS in New York and San Francisco. The *Times* news story stated that they had severe defects in their immune system and that "researchers did not know whether the immunological defects were the underlying problem or had developed secondarily to the infections of drug use."[15]

The medical vernacular expanded from such entries as Gay Bowel Syndrome or Bath House Syndrome to include PCP into the lexicon as the Gay Pneumonia. The introduction of KS as the Gay Cancer and Gay Lymph Node Syndrome to describe lymphadenopathy provided the underpinning for the homophobic designation of Gay-Related Immunodeficiency (GRID). Often, disease names reflect perceptions, not mere descriptions of appearance or subjective sensation. Some names probe a bit deeper but are still descriptive of pathologic anatomy, often defined by gross or microscopic appearance. On the other hand, the disease name may focus on some real or supposed causative factor.[16]

Disease names are important tools for thought and communication, since they are evocative of what a disease signifies. They mask differences among patients, and they have a way of influencing and narrowing our thinking. Disease names characterize the person transmogrified into the object itself. The homophobic specification of GRID associated etiology to sexual identity rather than to the pathogenesis of a retroviral agent. Causality of disease, when linked to human identity, is conceivable only when the process of medicalization differentiates between socially acceptable and unacceptable behavior.

During 1981, several New York City hospitals diagnosed PCP among the intravenous drug-using population, but the link to sexual identity remained unreconstructed. The New York City Department of Health (NYC DOH) estimated that 400,000 New Yorkers were HIV-seropositive. In its announcement, the NYC DOH admitted the discovery of 2,500 so-called lost cases, most of whom were heterosexual drug users and their sex partners:

This revelation meant that gays had never been the primary
risk group and that the potential for the eruption of AIDS in
the general community was greater than anyone had imagined.[17]

These cases went officially unregistered.

In 1982, the reluctant CDC replaced the acronym GRID with
acquired immunodeficiency syndrome (AIDS). Throughout the
biomedical community, there was an undeniable link between the
many heterosexual cases involving blood-to-blood contact either
through intravenous drug use, transfusions, or hemophiliacs who
received blood products. The appellation "acquired," which previously insinuated the nexus of sexual identity for transmission,
was expanded to include the practice of drug use.

Throughout 1982, heterosexuals in this country presented symptomatology consistent with GRID, including OIs such as PCP:
"word of other complications and of the transmission of the new
disease to other groups was arriving virtually month by month at the
CDC."[18] However, the CDC presented insubstantial information
and neglected publication of new case findings. The negligible
statistics of HIV infection among heterosexuals perpetuated false
security and promoted misleading information. The media fostered
this to a large extent. As late as 1985, *The New York Times* insisted
that HIV was a "slim threat to heterosexuals."[19] During 1985, the
NYC DOH identified 447 cases of women diagnosed with HIV
disease in New York City alone.[20] The statistic reported accounted
for women who conformed to the CDC classification of "full-
blown AIDS," which was differentiated from HIV infection. *The
New York Times'* editorial policy contradicted its news reporting, at
times within the same edition. Other statistical skew-ups by the
CDC included the calculation of gay men who used drugs intravenously into the epidemiological tabulation of "gay." This tilted the
demography, with a flawed recording of HIV infection contracted
through needle-sharing behavior.

Medical journals are replete with articles on each biomedical
aspect of HIV disease. By 1986, the medical literature included
more than 10,000 research papers on HIV disease, and was growing
at a rate of 600 citations per month. Many scientific studies pro-

ceeded from homophobic assumptions, attempting to establish the distinctiveness of gay sexuality as a cofactor in the development of HIV disease.[21]

A large portion of medical literature on HIV disease focused on the life-styles and sexual practices of gay men in order to interpret disease transmission. For instance, the "variables most strongly associated with Kaposi's sarcoma or pneumocystis pneumonia were those related to number of male sex partners and to meeting such partners in bathhouses."[22] As mentioned before, one recent medical study concluded that "homosexual behavior in men is a risk factor for anal cancer."[23] However, the findings of the study were scientifically disputable because of inadequate control-group selection. Further, the authors were criticized for "pervasive cultural bias that factors associated with homosexual behavior are necessarily of an unhealthy nature."[24]

> Sodomy, then, elicited the combined fears of sexuality, animality and anality. This triumvirate came to personify evil to the Western sexual imagination. Sexual acts involving the anal passage were regarded as the ultimate form of evil, a pact with the devil, a violation of the upwardly striving Christian attempt to find salvation. Fear of anal sex was certainly as powerful a force in the Western imagination as fear of homosexual relations.[25]

In a recent Kinsey Institute survey, a questionnaire posed, "a person can get AIDS by having anal (rectal) intercourse even if neither partner is infected with the AIDS virus?" Half of the respondents answered this question incorrectly, and the Institute received many letters from heterosexual, often sexually exclusive, couples "who have anal intercourse but now fear developing AIDS as a result."

> The false idea that AIDS can spontaneously develop as a result of a particular behavior in the absence of infection may be rooted in the taboo about anal sex, bias against homosexuality, and the belief that sexually transmitted diseases (STDs) are the inevitable consequence of engaging in "bad" behavior.[26]

From January 1, 1979, to July 2, 1987, the Associated Press (AP) published 2,794 accounts referring to HIV disease. A research study analyzed the effect of HIV-related news stories on public perception. The study focused on themes that require investigation for future HIV disease education and prevention programs. The texts of 987 stories, selected randomly, were computer-retrieved to determine the characteristics of the reporting. The study revealed that 81% had at least one paragraph predicting that HIV disease would be restricted to subgroups.[27]

Nonetheless, there appears to have been a modification of the public perception about the risk of HIV transmission during the late 1980s. The public is aware of certain basics of HIV transmission. It knows transmission occurs through bodily fluids, but not which fluids. Saliva cannot transmit the HIV retrovirus, yet this fact remains obscure to the public and constitutes much of the irrational fear about transmission. Additionally, the public is least aware of perinatal transmission.

THE FEMINIZATION OF THE EPIDEMIC

Women categorized as "sexual partners" of IVDUs confirms the sexual hierarchy in which women are seen only as recipients of HIV disease. Further, when providing risk education, the term "heterosexual transmission" disregards the efficacy of transmission from female to male. The risk of female-to-male transmission in the context of sexual behavior in this country is theoretical terrain.

From the onset, HIV-infected women remained unrecognized and underreported. The New York City Women and AIDS Resource Network (WARN), a community-based organization, referred to women with HIV as the "the silent epidemic." A review of current data on women with HIV infection revealed that reporting methods conveyed the false impression that women were unaffected by the epidemic. The CDC does not include data on mortality by gender in its routine reporting on HIV disease. Assurances were given, despite alarming figures:

> Please remember, the great majority of your potential sexual partners are not infected or infectious! At this point in time we

are not in the position of having to choose between giving up sex or merely reducing the risk with condoms. To date, the only real significant danger for us is in having sex with males who belong to one of the two relatively small high-risk groups: bisexuals or I.V. drug addicts.[28]

Women are the fastest-growing HIV-infected group in this country. According to a study from Hahnemann Hospital in Philadelphia, their numbers increased 45% between 1991 and 1992. According to the CDC, of the number of female HIV-disease cases, 52% became infected through intravenous drug use, 31% through heterosexual contact, 10% through blood transfusions, and 7% through an unknown mechanism. Women of color account for 73% of female HIV-disease cases in the U.S.

An important factor underlying the dismal statistics of women with HIV disease is that many of the women infected with HIV are poor. Over half of the women of color who are heads of households in the U.S. live below the poverty level. Many of these women have received inadequate and fragmented health care throughout their lives, and their access to benefit programs is limited. Although other causes of death among women 15 to 44 years of age have remained stable during the last decade, the death rate due to HIV infection quadrupled between 1985 and 1988. HIV disease has emerged as an important cause of mortality in U.S. women of reproductive age, especially in the Northeast and among black women.

The CDC definition ignores the anatomical differences between men and women. A woman's first HIV-related symptoms are often gynecological. The CDC definition focuses on the manifestations of HIV disease in gay men. Many related illnesses occur in women and IVDUs who are excluded or denied access to treatments, services, benefits, and from clinical trials of new drugs.

One simple, glaring example of the inadequacy of the CDC definition is candidiasis (thrush)–a yeast infection that affects both men and women. Oral candidiasis occurs in the esophagus, trachea, bronchi, or lungs, and it is considered one of the first-indicator infections of HIV disease. The CDC includes oral thrush as an opportunistic infection, while vaginal candidiasis, which of course occurs only in women, is not. This classification remains in spite of mounting evidence that chronic, intractable vaginal thrush can be an indication of HIV infection.

The CDC has already indicated that it will not consider collecting data on vaginal candidiasis because many women get it. But vaginal thrush that is chronic, unresponsive to treatment, and so severe that women develop lesions and other complications is different from that typically found in women without immunocompromised systems. The CDC definition includes the herpes simplex virus infection that causes a mucocutaneous ulcer that persists longer than one month; it does not simply list the herpes simplex virus, because many people get herpes. The listings above indicate that the same could be done for other opportunistic infections, yet many infected women are denied access to medical services and experimental protocols. HIV education has been misleading or vague.

As mentioned, by 1985 almost 500 women were diagnosed with full-blown AIDS in New York City alone, which should have constituted an alarming epidemic if no one else were stricken. This figure does not account for women infected with HIV who may have been asymptomatic or symptomatic with infections not recognized by the CDC as HIV-related due to the gay male classifications of the disease. This figure represents conformity to a narrow and arbitrary nomenclature that excluded the ways in which women present with HIV infection, such as vaginal candidiasis, chronic pelvic inflammatory disease (PID), and cervical cancer. During the early course of the epidemic, almost the entire first decade, little attention was paid to the issue of women and HIV disease except from outspoken advocates of women. Five hundred individuals in one region stricken with a disease should have been alarming; however, the official position, supported by the mass media, maintained that HIV infection remained a slim threat outside of certain "risk groups."

Women have been the primary caregivers to persons with HIV disease, whether as mothers, spouses, and other family members, or as professionals such as nurses, social workers, and therapists. Due to the sexism of our culture, women are overlooked in a myriad of ways–from the total male classification of the clinical presentation of HIV (with the resultant misdiagnosis of symptomatology) to their exclusion from clinical drug trials to their underservice by support agencies. Besides those women infected with HIV or those

HIV-disease-diagnosed, women were superfluous to the epidemic. Women were viewed simply as the mothers, sisters, sex partners, family members, teachers, home-care workers, nurses, social workers, volunteers, or friends.

The metaphors of HIV disease are replete with gender bias, as evidenced during the 1987 Third International Conference on AIDS. At this conference, some presentations identified women solely by their reproductive capacity as "vessels of infection and vectors of perinatal transmission."[29] Reproductive rights present a formidable challenge within the family-planning movement. What's more, women may not receive the most pertinent, unbiased, and up-to-date information about the risk of perinatal transmission. Further, women may be unable to obtain supportive perinatal, pediatric, and abortion services. Those concerned with HIV transmission give little attention to lesbian risk. A lesbian is at risk of HIV infection, as is any woman, to the extent of her risky behavior. Her identity is neither protective nor condemning. It is essential to discuss specific practices rather than sexual identity.

The metaphors of HIV disease are conspicuous. Women are categorized as "sexual partners" of IVDUs rather than as separate individuals. Reproductive rights take on new meaning when applied to the issues of HIV infection. Applied to HIV infection, it is the right of an infected or at-risk woman to obtain unbiased, factual, up-to-date information about birth control, safer-sex techniques, pregnancy, pregnancy outcome for herself and her child, and fully supportive perinatal, pediatric, and abortion services.

The objective reality of life-threatening illness is that it encourages powerlessness. In our patriarchal culture, women struggle from a subordinate status. HIV-infected women–the status of double jeopardy–confront complex situations in addition to the considerable biopsychosocial ramifications of HIV disease. Epidemiologically, the incidence of underreporting of women infected with HIV creates a misrepresentation of the epidemic and the risk of infection to females. In 1987, *Newsday* reported that HIV disease is the leading cause of death in New York City for women aged 25 to 34.[30] African-American women compose 52% of women with HIV disease.

Biomedically, male-defined CDC HIV-disease case definitions

do not adequately recognize the contrast of disease manifestation for females:

> Women have been forgotten in every aspect of AIDS medicine. Fundamental questions about the progression of this disease in women have not been asked or answered.[31]

Women who are HIV-seropositive often present treatment-resistant vaginal yeast infections, chronic pelvic inflammatory disease (PID), abnormal Papanicolaou (Pap) smear, or cervical cancer. Gynecological problems may indicate HIV infection and thus require medical diagnoses and assessment regarding social risk factors.

INTRAVENOUS DRUG USE

IVDUs are also illicit. IVDUs rarely escape the sanctions of the criminal justice system. In addition to using illegal substances, most IVDUs have to support their addiction by turning to crime. Currently, IVDUs compose the greater number of those individuals who are infected with HIV, are asymptomatic, and are without any clinical indications of the disease. Estimates of the incidence of HIV seropositivity among IVDUs in cities such as New York suggest more than 50% seroprevalence. HIV outreach strategies to IVDUs require an understanding of the correlation between high-risk behavior for the drug-using population and their environment. This estimate is based on drug-use patterns from studies of individuals in drug-treatment programs. Characteristics of the addict may vary with the type of drug used, geographic area, social class, and the local drug culture. The addicted person may be a teenager, athlete, or business person—in short, nearly anyone.

The sharing of needles by IVDUs is part of a subculture within the drug-use community, and it has certain psychosocial and sexual connotations. There is a sexual politic to drug use, with differences arising according to gender. Research indicated the following:

> A greater propensity for females, in contrast to males who are intravenous drug abusers, to affiliate sexually within the IV-drug abusing circle, because female drug users are initiated

into drug use by males. . . . [F]emales also receive monetary and emotional reinforcement for continued drug dependency from male partners.[32]

The influences on the IVDU are mainly through peer pressure, including claims made by friends that the needles are clean; economic pressures, since they often have limited funds to purchase equipment; and fatalistic attitudes.[33]

The IVDU community lacks political-organizing capability, so the challenge has fallen on those who work with IVDUs. This includes mental-health professionals (MHPs), counselors, and recovering addicts. In New York City, ADAPT, an organization directed by Yolanda Serrano, took its message about HIV disease into the community, actually going into so-called shooting galleries, in an attempt to alter needle-sharing behavior among injection users.

The IVDU suffers from numerous health-related problems associated with poor nutrition; lack of sanitary practices; repeated incidence of infection and life-threatening illness, such as hepatitis and endocarditis; high stress; and the absence of basic life satisfactions. IVDUs have a high prevalence of homelessness; many other IVDUs live in inadequate municipal shelters or have other precarious housing arrangements:

> In addition to the complexities of AIDS patient care, most of these patients must be found a drug treatment 'slot.' In New York City, the drug treatment system is currently operating at 110% of capacity and no new methadone program has been opened in over a decade.[34]

In New York City, estimates suggest there are more than 200,000 individuals who are substance users, of which 35,000 are enrolled in drug-treatment programs. This is due to the severe shortage of detoxification units.

PREVENTION STRATEGIES

HIV-related interventions extend into the community, with the integration of safer-sex guidelines into the therapeutic terrain. For example, preventive and educational strategies demand supportive individual psychotherapy and group modalities to explore and maintain behavioral modification as a prophylaxis to contracting HIV infection. The complexity of behavioral change requires more than condom distribution. Adaptation to safer-sex practices requires community support to remodel accepted cultural norms. The success of safer sex in the gay community depended on a shift regarding normative behavior, and the perception of risk, in a cultural framework. For instance, well-attended conferences conducted over the years in the gay community explored a range of subjects, such as safer sex, dating, and intimacy.

A MHP must promote prevention strategies through the skillful clinical assessment of an individual's particular life situation, their communication abilities, and the presence of opportunity with a partner. The assessment factors are gender, culture, race, ethnicity, class, sexual orientation, and religious beliefs. Due to the incidence of domestic violence in our male-dominated culture, women, in particular, are vulnerable to repercussions when negotiating condom usage by a partner. The MHP must be conscious that a woman advocating safer sex can suffer consequences if her male partner is physically or emotionally abusive. Women also fear abandonment and the loss of economic security when they attempt to exercise sexual control. For instance, before the threat of HIV, women usually had full responsibility for contraception. Often, they will not tell their partner that they are using birth control pills. Thus, condom promotion often targets women–the path of least resistance–rather than men.

Organizations, compelled to expand their stated mission to encompass HIV disease-related services, have had to change admission criteria for services and other policies. Many community-based organizations (CBOs) were confronted from within by HIV disease advocates; from without, they were pressed by the needs of the community–a virtual battleground on which to challenge prejudice toward gay men and IVDUs. It required extensive in-service training and education to address these issues while trying to assuage the community's fears about HIV transmission. These conflicts persist on many levels.

The role of the Roman Catholic Church has been striking during the HIV pandemic. The policy statement on AIDS issued by the United States Catholic Conference stated that "safer sex" compromises human sexuality: "That is why we call upon all people to live in accord with the authentic meaning of love and sexuality. Human sexuality, as we understand this gift from God, is to be genuinely expressed only in a monogamous, heterosexual relationship of lasting fidelity in marriage."[35] In the instance of two married, mutually monogamous individuals where one partner is HIV-seropositive, it would be considered immoral by the Church for that couple to use condoms to prevent infection. According to Church doctrine, sexual intercourse must be procreative and genital. New York's Cardinal O'Connor has been adamantly opposed to prevention efforts that promote condom usage or the bleach-cleaning of needles. He stated the following:

> Sometimes I believe the greatest damage done to persons with AIDS is done by the dishonesty of those health professionals who refuse to confront the moral dimensions of sexual aberrations or drug use. Good morality is good medicine.[36]

Health educators confront formidable obstacles when guiding people through the implementation of safer-sex guidelines. Often, the most conservative and unrealistic choices are presented to avoid the unresolved controversies of HIV transmission. Many propose that wet kissing is *possibly* safe, when there is no scientific evidence, anecdotal reporting, or a documented case of viral transmission through saliva. Safer options include massage, hugging, body rubbing, dry kissing, masturbation, hand-to-hand genital touching, mutual masturbation, and erotic movies and books. Additionally, safer-sex advocates circumvent the realm of sexual politics: having women dress in lingerie from a Fredericks of Hollywood catalog or the use of pornography is contemplated as erotic, but it objectifies and degrades women. While the introduction of latex condoms and dental dams are a priority along with imaginative skill-building and empowerment, the reinforcement of rigid gender roles should *not* be.

Risk-assessment questionnaires are another tool recommended by family planners. These such questions as, "have you ever had sex with a homosexual or bisexual man, a prostitute (male or female), a person born in central, eastern, or southern Africa, or some

Caribbean countries?" The assessment does not question the nature of sexual activity or the use of protection. The notion that an individual willingly discloses stigmatized behavior in such a counseling session is counterintuitive. The very structure of the risk assessment promotes several prejudicial attitudes. The critical issue to prevention strategies is education and the identification of HIV-related medical symptomatology:

> Use risk assessment results as a basis for deciding whether an HIV-oriented systems review might be warranted, looking for extrainguinal lymphadenopathy, unexplained fatigue, unexplained weight loss, or other signs of immune system impairment.[37]

A complete physical examination of women in terms of HIV-related symptomatology must include gynecological manifestations of the disease. The above quote is taken from a book on contraceptive technology dated 1991 through 1992, ten years into the epidemic, so the male-oriented model of HIV disease persists even in a publication targeted to the providers of care for women.

Family-planning clinics have an unequivocal responsibility to women's reproductive health. To a large extent, this was not the case as late as 1991, even when a study suggested that 19% of cervical cancer patients were HIV-infected. Women with HIV have a higher rate of cervical dysplasia:

> The consequences of cervical disease and HIV could have a significant impact on the health care of women. Gynecologists who take care of women in their reproductive age and internists who care for HIV-positive women should counsel their patients accordingly.[38]

Even women who know their HIV status and self-disclose may not receive appropriate gynecological care. Anecdotal reports suggest the misdiagnosis of women. A gynecologist recommended to an HIV-positive woman, who self-disclosed her status, that she douche when she had a vaginal discharge. Her vaginal candidiasis remained untreated for months. Within one family-planning clinic in New York City, a policy was set in 1991 that recommended that women whose HIV status was known from abnormal Pap smears should have a colposcopy. The policy change did not institute procedures for abnormal Pap smear results when the HIV status was unknown.

The authentic roots of the epidemic go deeper into our social structures and further back in history. We can only speculate about what measures might have prevented the rapid spread of HIV infection with current total U.S. AIDS cases exceeding 11,694. (See Figure 4.)[39] Due to the designation of the epidemic as primarily affecting gay men and intravenous substance users, other communities have been inadequately prepared. When the epidemic reached beyond the narrow and fallacious definitions of who were at risk it was already almost a decade into the epidemic. The collective denial of even those communities with high incidence of HIV disease is remarkable:

> AIDS is an area that was not addressed by the Secretary's Task Force on Black and Minority Health. However, it is clearly one of the most crucial health problems affecting the black community today.[40]

Currently, the most disenfranchised and underserviced are being affected by the epidemic–the homeless. The homeless and HIV-infected population often have a multiplicity of health problems, including active tuberculosis (TB) with new treatment-resistant strains. In New York City, programs are being implemented to provide supportive, scatter-site housing for these individuals with monitoring of medical compliancy, particularly TB medications.

THE BIOMEDICS OF HIV DISEASE

An HIV-infected individual's physical condition, including neuropsychiatric complications, is essential to both an assessment and formulation of treatment goals. The obstacles to activities, daily functioning, and psychosocial well-being caused by HIV disease are formidable. A psychotherapist cannot be effective without a thorough medical foundation about the disease. Expertise is required of physical functioning and of the client's attitude toward his/her health. Assisting the client to recognize, accept, and cope

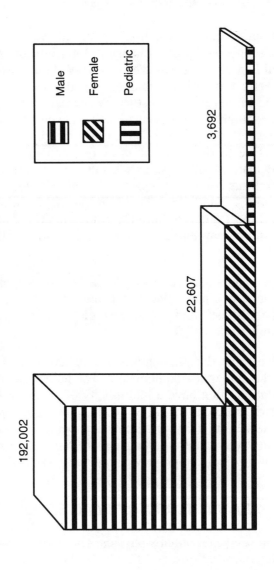

FIGURE 4. Total U.S. AIDS Cases

In thousands reported through March 1992

Male
Female
Pediatric

192,002

22,607

3,692

Total cases = 218,301

with medical chronicity and the reactions of their support system is fundamental to psychotherapeutic treatment of individuals with HIV disease. Individualizing should not exclude considering common factors of the disease entity. Although not primary, treatment goals must recognize obvious physical and neurologic deficits and knowledge of the manifestation of the disease, particularly if clients either deny or fail to recognize them.[41]

The HIV antibody test consists of an initial screening, called an enzyme-linked immunosorbent assay (ELISA) test, and a more specific confirmation test called the Western blot. Since the test, done with blood and tissue, is for HIV antibodies and does not directly measure the virus itself, it can label a small percentage of those tested as falsely positive, falsely negative, or indeterminate:

> In a study screening for HIV antibodies in 190 units of blood from 290,110 donors, a false-positive rate of no more than 0.0006 percent and a specificity of at least 99.9994 percent were obtained by sequential ELISA and Western blot testing.[42]

With most antibody tests, a positive result implies some immunity to the disease. This is apparently not the case with HIV antibody tests. The HIV antibody test does not diagnose HIV disease, and no single test will confirm, without clinical correlation, a diagnosis of HIV disease. However, certain laboratory tests, combined with clinical findings, may confirm a diagnosis.

The ELISA is the most widely used screening method for HIV antibody testing. Evaluation of a sample begins with the ELISA test. If the reactivity of the sample falls below a predetermined cutoff value, the result is negative. No further testing is undertaken. If the ELISA is reactive or borderline, the immunoblot, or Western blot, is routinely done. If the immunoblot pattern is ambiguous, for instance, if the observed bands are only faintly perceptible; the immunofluorescence assay procedure is more definitive.

Once infected, an individual probably remains infected. An infected individual may not be producing enough virus to be able to transmit it to others. Since there is no way to know when one is highly infectious and when one is not, consistent use of risk-reduction techniques is essential for people who are HIV-positive and for anyone else exposed but who does not know his or her antibody status.[43]

The sensitivity of current-generation ELISAs is close to 100% when the antibody is present in peripheral blood. However, these assays do not detect HIV antibody in the earliest stages of infection. The interval between HIV infection and the appearance of antibody in the blood is variable. In most patients, the period is less than six months after infection, although there are reports of longer periods of seronegativity–up to 34 months. Occasionally, there are patients who are initially HIV-seropositive who revert to a seronegative status. There is also a period late in HIV infection when the antibody may be undetectable because it has become complexed with excess antigen.

HIV TRANSMISSION AND INFECTION

Infection results from inoculation directly into the bloodstream of the HIV virus. This occurs through the following modes of transmission: (1) needle-sharing with intravenous drug use; (2) receipt of contaminated blood product; (3) through mucous membranes during vaginal or anal intercourse; and (4) perinatal transmission.

After inoculation, the virus replicates in one or more types of susceptible cells. The virus most commonly affects circulating CD4 lymphocytes and macrophages. Epithelial cells within the gastrointestinal tract, uterine cervical cells, and glial cells of the central nervous system may also be targets.

In the majority of individuals, the virus replicates sufficiently to produce detectable levels of viral antigens and elicit host antibody production within a few weeks to months. Theoretically, a latent stage develops, with little viral replication and with no antibody response. During the period of infection, an individual experiences a few days of symptoms similar to a viral illness or a mononucleosis-like syndrome.

As the host system mounts the initial antibody response to HIV, viral antigen neutralizes, disappears, or is detectable only at low levels. The patient usually becomes asymptomatic and remains so for a period that may range from weeks to many years. HIV antibodies are detectable in blood serum, and viral nucleic acid is detectable in infected cells.

As viral replication proceeds, the HIV virus and cell fusion destroy CD4 lymphocytes and monocyte-macrophages become dysfunctional. Damage to these key cells probably leads to abnormal activation of other immune mechanisms and also accounts for the observed dysfunction of B-cell and cytotoxic T-cell response. As the immune system deteriorates and HIV viral replication progresses, the host becomes vulnerable to opportunistic infections (OIs) and malignancies. Antibodies to HIV p24 antigen decrease in titer and may become undetectable, while viral core antigens reappear.

Antibodies are serum proteins that bind to specific antigens and begin the process that induces lysis. Lysis is the destruction of cells or the rupture of plasm membrane by the antigen, a substance that enters the blood. The antigen elicits an immune response and the formation of an antibody. The major cellular components of the immune system are lymphocyte groups of B and T cells and the macrophage. Functionally, the B cells are the precursors of antibody-producing plasma cells and the T cells promote or suppress the immune response.

The T-cell counts assist the diagnosis of immunodeficiency. An abnormal T-cell count infers, without confirming, specific diseases. A T-cell count within the typical range does not ensure a competent immune system. T-cell subgroups include the regulatory helper and suppressor T cells, which respectively enhance or suppress the development of immune responses, particularly antibody production.

CLINICAL SPECTRUM OF HIV DISEASE

During the post-inoculation period, some individuals develop a mononucleosis-like illness at the time of their initial infection with HIV. This process is known as HIV seroconversion. Development of antibodies to HIV occur anywhere from 19 to 56 days after the onset of illness. Not all patients appear to develop a clinically significant illness at the time of their initial infection: "Much is still unknown about the events occurring in the period immediately after inoculation of the host with HIV."[44] Seroconversion may or may not manifest with a discernable illness. The HIV antibody test most often, even in asymptomatic individuals, indicates antibodies. Clinically, a latent stage ranges from months to years before individuals manifest symptomatology or become infected with various illnesses.

Several factors pose risks for more accelerated progression of HIV infection. Older individuals, past fifty, appear to progress more rapidly, and this has been reported in several studies. Exposure to antigenic stimuli capable of activating the cellular immune system, such as sexually transmitted diseases (STDs), may increase risk for progression:

> There is no evidence that substance use advances immunosuppression or adversely influences prognosis. Whether malnutrition is an independent risk for progression is unclear. Presumably, malnutrition predisposes the progression of infectious diseases.[45]

Some studies suggest a relation between STDs and progression of infection.

HIV infection, either as a primary disease manifestation or as a secondary process, can affect virtually every organ system in the body, including the joints, heart, muscles, kidneys, and endocrine systems. HIV disease can cause a wide spectrum of clinical disease, ranging from acute infection to an asymptomatic state to severe immunodeficiency with chronic infections and wasting. HIV disease describes the more severe manifestations, particularly OIs and unusual tumors associated with immunodeficiency. An HIV-infected individual may be asymptomatic for several years–up to ten or more.

Most Frequent Opportunistic Infections (OIs) (See Figure 5)

Fungal

Pneumocystis carinii pneumonia (PCP) is a fungal lung infection rarely observed in immunologically healthy persons. It is the most commonly diagnosed OI in HIV disease. The symptoms, often mild, last for weeks or months, before diagnosis. The symptoms

FIGURE 5. Most Frequent Opportunistic Infections (OIs)*

	CLINICAL MANIFESTATIONS
FUNGAL	
Pneumoscystis Carinii Pneumonia (PCP)	Pneumonia
Candida Species	Stomatitis (inflamation of mucus membrane of the mouth); Esophagitis (inflammation of the esophagus); Systemic Infection
Cryptococcus Neoformans	Meningitis (inflammation in brain or spinal cord); Systemic Infection
VIRAL	
Cytomegalovirus (CMV)	Chorioretinitis (inflammation of the retina); Systemic Infection; Lymphadenopathy (disease affecting lymph nodes); Kaposi's Sarcoma
Herpes Simplex	Mucocutaneous Lesions
Herpes Zoster	Skin Lesions; Systemic Infection
Epstein-Barr Virus	Lymphadenopathy; CNS (involving central nervous sytem); Lymphoma (cancer of lymph tissue)
BACTERIAL	
Mycobacterium Avium Intracelluare (MAI)	Systemic Infection
Mycobacterium Avium Complex (MAC)	Pneumonia and Systemic Infection
PROTOZOAN	
Toxoplasma Gondii	Encephalitis (infection of the brain); Systemic Infection (relating to the entire body)
Cryptosporidium	Enterocolitis (inflammation of the colon)
METASTIC	
Kaposi's Sarcoma (KS)	Cancerous Lesions of Skin, Mucous Membranes, and Internal Organs
OTHER	
Idiopathic Thrombocytopenia Purpura (ITP)	Easy Bruising, Bleeding

*Adapted from Medical Answers About AIDS, prepared by Lawrence Mass, MD, New York: Gay Men's Health Crisis, 1989.

include coughing, fevers, and shortness of breath. PCP responds to treatment with trimethoprim sulfamethoxazole (Bactrim) and pentamidine isethionate. Both drugs may cause an allergic reaction and other side effects, and neither drug treats underlying HIV infection or immunodeficiency. An aerosolized form of pentamidine, with minimal or no side effects, is a prophylaxis treatment to prevent the onset of PCP. The protocol for prophylaxis is for persons with prior instance of PCP or when total lymphocyte and T-cell counts are below 200. Bactrim and dapsone are also preventive medications.

Cutaneous and oral infections with protozoal or bacterial organisms are also more common in patients with HIV infection. Oral candidiasis is a fungal disease most frequently caused by the species *Candida albicans*. Several factors can predispose patients to develop the disease: infancy, old age, antibiotic therapy, steroid and other immunosuppressive drugs, xerostomia, anemia, or endocrine disorders. Symptoms include complaints of a burning mouth, problems eating spicy food, and changes in taste. There are several classifications of candidiasis that exist, such as pseudomembranous candidiasis, known as thrush, which is characterized by a creamy white plaque on the oral mucosa. Other classifications of candidiasis may appear as a white or red lesion on the palate, tongue, or corners of the mouth.

Cryptococcus neoformans is a fungal infection that localizes in the pulmonary system, then spreads to other organ systems. Patients present with a mild headache, low-grade fever, nausea and vomiting, and other signs of meningitis.

Viral

Cytomegalovirus (CMV) is a virus that can infect many different organs, including the parotid gland, salivary gland, kidney, liver, lung parenchyma, and brain tissue; to a lesser degree, it can also infect the ovaries, bones, pancreas, and skin. Gastrointestinal involvement may result in diarrhea (colitis) and weight loss. Symptoms of dementia, confusion, and headaches indicate central nervous system (CNS) involvement. Fever, anemia, atypical lymphocytes, thrombocytopenia, and leukopenia are often present.[46]

Cytomegalovirus retinitis is a common and devastating complication of HIV disease, usually occurring with individuals quite immunocompromised. The symptomatic individual may present persistent generalized lymphadenopathy (PGL), which usually indicates an otherwise healthy patient who has swollen lymph nodes for three or more months. A high percentage of patients with HIV infection have PGL. A question posed by many clinicians is the efficacy of lymph node biopsies to determine HIV infection, since the pathologic findings in PGL are nonspecific and undetectable with antibody screening.

The most frequent occurring symptoms with individuals who are HIV-symptomatic are PGL, fatigue, skin rashes, fevers, diarrhea, muscle pain, night sweats, and weight loss. Some patients manage these disease manifestations; others become incapacitated. Symptomatic patients present with a spectrum of immunologic abnormalities–from minimal alterations in the immune system to severe cellular immunodeficiency comparable to persons with full-blown HIV disease.

The signs of the herpes simplex virus (HSV) include fever blisters or cold sores around the mucosal orifices of the face and genital areas, but these may also spread and infect the esophagus and laryngeal mucosa. The symptoms include fever, malaise, and pain due to herpetic infections.

Herpes zoster produces two different clinical syndromes: shingles and chicken pox. The dermatological indicators, localized to the infected dermatome, include mild itching or tingling to severe pain. It forms a lesion that ruptures and crusts. Crust formation may take a week to form and may persist for two to three weeks.

Epstein-Barr virus (EBV) is a member of the herpes virus family. Nearly 100% of gay men with HIV disease have reactivated antibodies to reactivated EBV. These patients may develop lymphomas for which EBV may be partially attributable.[47]

Bacterial

Typically, people with HIV-disease wasting syndrome experience considerable weight loss with the accompanying OIs. In advanced HIV disease there may be a diagnosis of Mycobacterium avium complex (MAC), formerly known as *Mycobacterium avium interacellulare* (MAI). MAC is an atypical tuberculosis that refers to organisms belonging to a particular group of mycobacteria. It is a disseminated or systemic infection, not limited to the lungs or any other organ, and is a common cause of bacterial infections in patients with HIV disease.

A person with MAC has had one or more bouts with PCP. As the prevention and treatment of PCP has advanced, other opportunistic diseases have become more prominent. The diagnosis of MAC may not be the cause of symptoms, since many patients have MAC infection without symptoms, such as weeks or months of weight loss, fevers, chills, night sweats, diarrhea, abnormal liver function tests, and rapidly progressive pancytopenia. There is a simultaneous decrease of red blood cells (anemia), white cells (neutropenia), and platelets (thrombocytopenia). Sputum and blood cultures, bone marrow biopsy, and tissue body specimens establish a diagnosis. The treatment of MAC, which is presently experimental and variable, is a combination therapy with drugs such as amikacin, clofazimine, ethambutol, rifampin, isoniazid, and ciproflaxacin 6.

Protozoan

Toxoplasmosis is the most frequent CNS infection occurring with HIV disease. Patients present with headache, fever, and focal neurologic defects such as seizures and cognitive disorders.

Cryptosporidium is an enteric protozoan infection characterized by general flu-like symptoms, including watery diarrhea with cramping, fever, malaise, and nausea. Another symptom of the infection is vomiting. The organism is seldom seen outside the bowel; however, it is sometimes seen in the gall bladder and biliary system, as well as in the sputum and the tracheobronchial tree.

Metastatic

Kaposi's sarcoma (KS) is a skin cancer that starts as one or more small, raised red or purple patches, often on the foot or ankle. It progresses slowly until the lesions grow and coalesce, eventually covering the surface of the lower legs. The lesions may spread to other areas of the body or the mouth lining. The lesions may ulcerate and become infected. Obstruction of blood vessels may prevent the return of fluid to the rest of the body, leading to swelling of the legs and new infections of the lesions and surrounding tissues. If the disease lasts long enough, it eventually spreads to the lining of the gastrointestinal tract and the lymph nodes. In late stages of HIV disease, KS affects the lungs and their lining membrane.[48]

The neurologic complications of HIV infection are common and varied. Neurologic involvement can occur within days to several weeks of the seroconversion and may take the form of encephalitis, meningitis, ataxia, or myelopathy. In the later stages of HIV infection, AIDS dementia complex (ADC) may develop, which is characterized by cognitive, motor, and behavioral dysfunction. Characteristically, this disorder manifests after patients develop major opportunistic infections or neoplasms.

Clinical Evaluation of Early HIV Dementia

- Memory deficits
- Inattentive and distractible
- Difficulty articulating (dysarthria)
- Lower voice volume (hypophonia)
- Decreased intellectual capacity
- Difficulty with abstract and sequential reasoning
- Deficit in visuospatial skills
- Motor abnormalities
- Personality changes

Adapted from Stephen L. Buckingham and Wilfred G. Van Gorp, "Essential Knowledge about AIDS Dementia," *Social Work*, Volume 33, Number 2.

Certain gynecologic conditions, in the setting of HIV disease, occur with increasing frequency and may behave more aggressively than those in seronegative women. STDs correlate to HIV infection. Genital ulcerative disease secondary to a variety of STDs may increase the risk for HIV transmission. Pelvic inflammatory disease (PID) occurs more often and is nonresponsive or more refractory to treatment. Herpes simplex virus (HSV) may be recurrent or chronic, when seen with vaginal candidiasis. Cervical dysplasia secondary to human papilloma virus (HPV) is more frequent, and it is possible that it may progress more rapidly to cervical intraepithelial neoplasia (CIN).

BIOPOLITICS

The CDC does not delineate or explain specific sexual and social activities that may put a person at risk of HIV transmission. The risk of sexual transmission relates to the exchange of specific bodily fluids and specific sexual activities. It has less to do with whether the person engaging in these activities self-identifies as gay, IVDU, lesbian, heterosexual, or a native of a Pattern II country. For example, persons who engage in cunnilingus are at risk of becoming infected through ingestion of vaginal secretions or blood.

The CDC has never considered cunnilingus as a potential transmission route for HIV. There is little known about lesbian transmission of the virus between infected women. There is no equivalent group for females compared to male homosexual/bisexual categories. The CDC does not consider lesbians as a risk group because there are only three documented cases of woman-to-woman transmission. From 1981-1984, there were 101 cases of HIV disease in self-identified lesbians or bisexuals. A woman outside a "risk group" who engages in anal intercourse is not likely to find articles, studies, or advice about her actual risk. Numerous people criticize the government for its negligent response before and after the formal CDC acknowledgement of the epidemic. They insist that the problem had been festering throughout the decade of the 1970s.

When someone fits the CDC definition, the health provider reports the case to the CDC or to their local surveillance unit. The CDC keeps statistics by case number (although the person's name exists). Other data they collect include age, race, sex, geographic location (by zip code), the "life-threatening" OI at the time of diagnosis, and the mode of transmission. The CDC collects no other information about the case until the person dies. This has constituted the data base of surveillance reports for the past ten years. No data is collected on what the person actually dies from (people do not die from HIV disease; they die from an HIV disease-related cause.) Many people become part of the CDC data only after death, when an autopsy reveals HIV.

The only information the CDC collects about HIV-related infections are "life-threatening conditions" at the time of an HIV disease diagnosis. They do not document the cause of death. There is no tracking of the complex of illnesses, their progression, interrelationship, co-factors, or regional differences. The current definition of the disease comes from a very select sample of people–predominantly gay white men. The diseases added in 1987 came about because the gay men tracked by the CDC were living longer due to the use of medications and prophylaxis. As some opportunistic infections became less prevalent (e.g., KS), others began to appear at a more advanced state of illness (e.g., HIV wasting syndrome). These gay men were not diagnosed with HIV disease until they had a more serious condition, usually one that occurs late in illness. Incidents of KS are declining, possibly because of links to other co-factors. The CDC has provided inadequate information about whether specific OIs have a relationship to the modes of transmission.

The CDC HIV disease definition also plays a key role in how funds for HIV disease-related services are allocated. Funding allocations for cities or regions relate directly to the number of HIV cases reported according to the CDC-defined classifications. Areas hit hard by non-CDC-defined HIV disease receive lower funding levels. The CDC's revised HIV case definition is not clear about the inclusion of additional HIV-related conditions, who they affect, or the standards of health care needed to deal with these conditions. Standards of health care, the national minimal guidelines for treatment, are set by the Public Health Service (PHS) and published in the CDC's MMWR, which is a directive resource by practitioners and policy-makers. One example is the CDC-published standard to administer certain drugs (AZT, bactrim, aerosolized pentamidine) to persons whose T-cell lymphocyte count has fallen below 200. Patients are treated with these drugs based on a T-cell count, yet this is not the diagnostic marker used by CDC for their HIV disease definition.

SELF-HEALING IN THE NEW AGE

In 1986, the United States spent $425 billion on health care. This amount is larger than the national defense budget; obviously, health care is a major industry. However, "health care, the most personal of subjects, is in our public discourse shunt aside as a vast, unapproachable enigma."[49] During the 1960s, public-policy changes took place regarding the accessibility of medical services, and that era marked the establishment of the federal government as insurer (vis-à-vis Medicaid and Medicare):

> The consumer as an active partner in the patient-therapist relationship is a comparatively new idea in medical care. This type of relationship has, however, had some expression in social work in the last decade.[50]

At a time when issues of consumerism began to surface in most major industries, planning and policy in American health care remain undefined.

Two philosophies have been critical of medical practice in our culture. They developed simultaneously and at times converge; but they can be mutually exclusive. One has to do with the over-medicalization of society that suggests that *iatragenesis* (i.e., physician-causing ills) promotes pain, sickness, and death rather than healing. The medical system reinforces industrial ill health, as well, at a social level. Medicine, as practiced in our technological society, alienates the individual from self-healing behavior. Also in the 1960s, psychosomatic replaced *somatization* as the "process by which the body (the soma) is used for psychological purposes for personal gain."[51] The so-called sick role is the label applied to those who attempt secondary gain from illness. Ford suggests that almost one-third of patients in several clinics are treated for organic disease complicated by psychiatric symptoms.

The second criticism of the health-care delivery system has to do with economics and the high cost of treatment. A victim-blaming ideology has emerged "alongside the 'limits of medicine' argument. Based in the irrefutable and increasingly obvious fact that medicine has been oversold, the new ideology argues that individuals may prevent most disease if they adopt life-styles which avoid unhealthy behavior."[52] There seems to be a delicate balance between blaming the victim and giving people the tools by which to live a healthy life.

In one research study, 100% of respondents (n = 47) felt a sense of personal responsibility for their health. This responsibility is congruent with implementation of a healthy lifestyle. For instance, only 26 respondents have been capable of making significant health changes when troubled by a hazardous pattern. The difficulty of making change is underscored by 65% of respondents having sought professional help to cope with a lifestyle-related health problem.[53]

While respondents rejected a moralistic approach when viewing ill people, more than two-thirds felt that an inability to express anger (or even misdirected anger) could cause illness. The expression of anger is often construed as crucial to health; the reinterpretation of anger is not. Anger in its various manifestations is not distinguished, so anger toward social injustice that might be appropriate is considered similar to anger toward another individual.

Fifty-five percent of respondents saw no correlation between illness and politics. Self-healing proposes that the human system is capable of "self-limiting," that the body is able to prescribe for itself. Immunologists investigate the purely physiological. Yet healing must consider an individual's state of mind; therefore, they choose to ignore psychosocial issues. Any "enlightened healer must have the courage to renounce what is practically medical dogma; that the body's immune system is totally self-contained and outside the influence of any other system in the body. By declaring that the mind can influence the way the body protects itself, one rejects 20 years of findings that indicate that the body's immunity operates without help of interference from any other physiological system."[54]

As considered, ideas about disease are absolute when medical diagnosis is imbued with moral authority. Moreover, in contemporary society there is a predilection for psychologizing about disease: "A large part of the popularity and persuasiveness of psychology comes from its being a sublimated spiritualism: a secular, ostensibly scientific way of affirming the primacy of 'spirit' over matter."[55]

> The systematic cultivation of healthy-mindedness as a religious attitude is therefore consonant with important currents in human nature, and is anything but absurd.[56]

On self-healing, Bernie Siegel suggests that "there are no incurable diseases only incurable people. The doctor works in the light. He is verbal and logical. The patient's world may be dark, but here are sources of illumination. Within each of us is a spark. Call it a divine spark if you will, but it is there and can light the way to health."[57]

Siegel provides the following account of one patient's victory over HIV disease:

> Exceptional patients have the ability to throw statistics aside, to say "I can be a survivor–even when the doctor isn't wise enough to do so. . . . Hope instilled that kind of courage in William Calderon, who achieved the first documented recovery from Acquired Immune Deficiency Syndrome (AIDS). Calderon was diagnosed in December 1982. His doctors told him he would probably be dead in six months. Understandably, he became depressed and hopeless. Almost immediately Kaposi's sarcoma, the type of cancer that most often accompanies AIDS, appeared and began spreading rapidly on all areas of his skin and throughout the gastrointestinal tract. . . . [This case is reported by Judith Skutch, President of the Foundation for Inner Peace.] With unwavering love and support from her and from his lover, Calderon came to believe in his own survival. By continuing at the job he loved, he refused to give in to the disease. Instead he began meditating and using mental imagery to combat it. He worked to restore strained relationships with his family and achieved peace of mind by forgiving people he felt had hurt him. He loved his body with exercise, good nutrition, and vitamin supplements. And from that point on his immune system showed increased response and his tumors began to shrink. Two years after the diagnosis, Calderon showed no signs of AIDS.[58]

Almost from the beginning of the epidemic, advocates have stressed the necessity to reject the victimized role, which accounts for the use of the term *survivor* rather than victim and the emphasis on living with HIV rather than dying from it.

Whatever life-affirming choices an individual makes should be supported, including resolving conflicted relationships, finding inner harmony, meditation, holistic alternatives, vitamin therapy, or exercise. My concern, however, is that those individuals who do not recover from disease would be judged as *unevolved*. Over the past decade, I have witnessed extraordinary courage and have seen people attempt changes in their lives that had been unimaginable before their HIV-positive diagnosis. Many choose the medical model, others reject it; some combine the medical with holistic alternatives. Norman Cousins' work is both philosophical and practical: "I have learned never to underestimate the capacity of the human mind and body to regenerate–even when the prospects seem most wretched."[59] The link between the threefold nature of human life, the material, spiritual, and emotional is not well understood without the use of scientific knowledge, which has not been fully utilized. Louise Hay, a popular healing practitioner, views HIV disease as a "message from the body, the final attempt of one's own consciousness to communication."[60] Hay rejects the medical model of treating HIV disease, "The people I know with AIDS who are exploring and using alternative healing methods are doing much better than those who are following strict medical procedures that involve putting *poisons* into their body."[61]

Many in the HIV community believe that HIV is not the sole cause of AIDS, that there must be cofactors, suggesting the overuse of antibiotics, poverty, substance use, and the chronicity of other infections. Many believe that the medical establishment aligned with pharmaceutical companies are fraudulent, that antiretroviral therapies are a cruel hoax. Clearly, the medical establishment and holistically oriented practitioners seem in diametric opposition. There is no indisputable answer in this clash of belief systems. My concern has always focused on individuals with HIV disease and I have attempted to realize their potential for self-determination without neglecting their physical, emotional, and spiritual life. From my psychotherapeutic orientation, I have come to believe that individuals who join a support group or seek individual therapy live longer and with some modicum of inner peace.

REFERENCE NOTES

1. Loretta McLaughlin, "AIDS: An Overview," in *The AIDS Epidemic: Private Rights and the Public Interest*, edited by Padraig O'Malley (Boston: Beacon Press, 1989), p. 16.

2. U.S. Department of Health and Human Services, Public Health Service, Centers for Disease Control, *Morbidity and Mortality Weekly Report*, June 1981.

3. *The New York Times*, July 24, 1990.

4. Randy Shilts, *And the Band Played On* (New York: St. Martin's Press, 1987), p. 67.

5. Paula A. Treichler, "AIDS, Gender, and Biomedical Discourse," in *AIDS: The Burdens of History*, edited by Elizabeth Free and Daniel M. Fox (Berkeley: University of California Press, 1988), p. 200.

6. Sander L. Gilman, *Difference and Pathology: Stereotypes of Sexuality, Race, and Madness* (Ithaca, NY: Cornell University Press, 1985), p. 24.

7. Cindy Patton, *Sex and Germs: The Politics of AIDS* (Boston: South End Press, 1985), p. 7.

8. Janet R. Daling, PhD, et al., "Sexual Practices, Sexually Transmitted Diseases, and the Incidence of Anal Cancer," *The New England Journal of Medicine*, October 15, 1987.

9. William H. McNeill, *Plagues and People* (New York: Anchor Books, 1976), 7.

10. Gerald M. Oppenheimer, "In The Eye of the Storm," in *AIDS: The Burdens of History*, p. 268.

11. Paul Starr, *The Social Transformation of American Medicine* (New York: Basic Books, 1982), p. 5.

12. Linda Murray, "Straight Facts About Straight Sex," *Penthouse* 20 (1 September 1988): 206.

13. Jonathan Lieberson, "The Reality of AIDS," *New York Review of Books*, January 16, 1986.

14. Dennis Altman, *AIDS: In the Mind of America* (New York: Anchor Press, 1987), p. 14.

15. *The New York Times*, July 3, 1981.

16. Gary D. Friedman, *Primer of Epidemiology* (New York: McGraw Hill, 1980), p. 5.

17. Katie Leishman, "Letters to the Editor," *The Atlantic*, January 1988.

18. Loretta McLaughlin, "AIDS: An Overview," p. 17.

19. *The New York Times*, September 29, 1985.

20. *The New York Times*, October 28, 1985.

21. Deb Whippen, "Science Fictions: The Making of a Medical Model for AIDS," *Radical America*, Volume 20, No. 6.

22. H. Jaffee and G. Lundberg et al., "National Case-Control Study of Kaposi's Sarcoma and *Pneumocystis carinii* Pneumonia in Homosexual Men," *Annals of Internal Medicine*, 1982, 99:145.

23. Janet R. Daling, PhD, et al., "Sexual Practices, Sexually Transmitted Diseases, and the Incidence of Anal Cancer," *The New England Journal of Medicine*, October 15, 1987.

24. Robert S. Wilden, MD, Correspondence, *The New England Journal of Medicine*, April 14, 1988.

25. Arthur N. Gilbert, "Conceptions of Homosexuality and Sodomy in Western History" in *The Gay Past*, edited by Salvatore J. Licata and Robert P. Petersen, (New York: Harrington Park Press, 1985), p. 66.

26. June M. Reinisch, PhD, *The Kinsey Institute New Report on Sex* (New York: St. Martin's Press, 1990), p. 10.

27. David P. Fan, PhD, and Gregory McAvoy, "Predictions of Public Opinion On The Spread Of AIDS: Introduction of New Computer Methodologies," *The Journal of Sex Research*, May 1989.

28. Helen Singer Kaplan, *The Real Truth About Women and AIDS* (New York: A Fireside Book, 1987), p. 48.

29. Venetia Porter, "U.S. Women and HIV Infection," in *The AIDS Epidemic: Private Rights and the Public Interest*, p. 387.

30. *Newsday*, July 8, 1987.

31. Kathryn Anastos and Carola Marte, "Women–The Missing Persons in the AIDS Epidemic," *Health/PAC Bulletin*, Winter 1989.

32. Debra L. Murphy, "Heterosexual Contacts of Intravenous Drug Abusers: Implications for the Next Spread of the AIDS Epidemic," in *AIDS And Substance Abuse*, edited by Larry M. Siegel, MD (New York: The Haworth Press, 1988), p. 96.

33. Stephen Magura, PhD, et al., "Determinants of Needle Sharing Among Intravenous Drug Users," *American Journal of Public Health*, April 1989.

34. Ernest Drucker, PhD, Principal Investigator, "IV Drug Users With AIDS In New York City," July 20, 1988, p. 22.

35. *The New York Times*, December 11, 1989.

36. *The New York Times*, November 14, 1989.

37. Robert A. Hatcher et al., *Contraceptive Technology, 1990-1992* (New York: Irvington Publishers), p. 79.

38. Mitchell Maiman, MD, Kings County Hospital, New York City, as quoted in *Daily News*, April 29, 1990.

39. LaSalle D. Leffall, Jr., MD, "Health Status of Black Americans," in *The State of Black America 1990* (New York: National Urban League, 1990), p. 136.

40. Nick Freudenberg, "Historical Omissions: A Critique of *And The Band Played On*," *Health/PAC Bulletin*, Spring 1988.

41. *Differential Diagnosis and Treatment in Social Work*, edited by Francis J. Turner (New York: The Free Press, 1976), p. 352.

42. Judith C. Wilbur, "HIV Antibody Testing: Methodology" in *The AIDS Knowledge Base*, edited by P. T. Cohen, MD, PhD, Merle A. Sande, MD and Paul A. Volberding, MD (Waltham, MA: The Medical Publishing Group, 1990), 2.1.2-3.

43. Michael Gross, PhD, "HIV Antibody Testing" in *The AIDS Epidemic: Private Rights and Public Interest*, p. 195.

44. Paul A. Volberding, MD, and P.T. Cohen, MD, PhD, "Clinical Spectrum of HIV Infection," in *The AIDS Knowledge Base: A Textbook on HIV Disease*, edited by P. T. Cohen, MD, PhD, Merle A. Sande, MD and Paul A. Volberding, MD (Waltham, MA: The Medical Publishing Group, 1990) 4.1.1-3.

45. Ibid., 4.1.1-8.

46. Katherine S. Jacobs, RN, BSN and Mariann R. Piano, RN, MSN, "The Clinical Picture of AIDS: Underlying Pathological Processes," in *The Person*

with AIDS: Nursing Perspectives, edited by Jerry D. Durham, RN, PhD and Felissa L. Cohen, RN, PhD, FHAN (New York: Springer Publishing Company, 1987), p. 59.

47. Helen L. Grierson, "Infections of AIDS," in *AIDS: Facts and Issues*, edited by Victor Gong, MD and Norman Rudnick (New Brunswick, NJ: Rutgers University Press, 1986), p. 58.

48. Michael Scoppetulo, "Cancers and Blood Disorders of AIDS," in *AIDS: Facts and Issues*, edited by Victor Gong, MD and Norman Rudnick, p. 81.

49. *Newsweek*, January 26, 1987.

50. Helen Rehr, "The Consumer and Consumerism," *Social Work Issues in Health Care* (Englewood Cliffs, NJ: Prentice Hall, 1983), p. 20.

51. Charles V. Ford, *The Somatizing Disorders* (New York: Elsevier Biomedical, 1983), p. 2.

52. Robert Crawford, "Are You Dangerous To Your Health," *Social Policy*, January/February 1978, p. 11.

53. Steven F. Dansky, "Individual Responsibility and Health Care," unpublished research study, 1987.

54. Steven Locke, *The Healer Within* (New York: E. P. Dutton, 1986), p. 18.

55. Susan Sontag, *Illness As Metaphor* (New York: Vintage Books, 1978), p. 54.

56. William James, *The Varieties of Religious Experience* (New York: Penguin Books, 1982), p 35.

57. Bernie S. Siegel, *Love, Medicine & Miracles* (New York: Harper & Row, 1986), p. 27.

58. Ibid., p. 40.

59. Norman Cousins, *Anatomy Of An Illness* (New York: Bantam Books, 1980), p. 48.

60. Louise L. Hay, *The AIDS Book: Creating a Positive Approach* (Santa Monica, CA: Hay House, 1988), p. 19.

61. Ibid., p. 55.

Chapter 3

Beyond Good and Evil

For us, it is in the confession that truth and sex are joined, through the obligatory and exhaustive expression of an individual secret.*

–Michel Foucault, *The History of Sexuality: An Introduction, Volume 1*

THE MEDICALIZATION OF CONFESSION

In high-prevalence localities, particularly epicenters of the epidemic, HIV antibody testing has been integrated into primary medical care. State legislatures govern testing procedures. Statutes encompass concerns such as patient confidentiality, signing an informed consent for testing, pre- and post-test counseling, authorization for release of confidential HIV-related information, and partner notification programs. While statutes legislate these procedures, there is no adequate surveillance of counseling procedures, only laboratory testing is subject to quality control. There is considerable variance regarding confidentiality compliance and the quality of counseling. Physicians, hospitals, and health settings often have insufficient staff trained to provide counseling, so a patient's signing the informed consent fulfills the minimum requirements. HIV-tested patients may not know primary disease prevention issues, such as the constituents of high-risk and perinatal transmission.

---

*Michel Foucault, (New York: Vintage Books, 1990), p. 61.

When patients test HIV-positive, many experience difficulties with accessing quality health care. For disenfranchised individuals, due to poverty, homelessness, and even for those who are the working poor without insurance benefits, the options are limited. While Medicaid programs provide HIV-related care, patients have difficulty accessing infectious disease clinics or may wait up to several months before obtaining appointments, particularly in clinics in high seroprevalence communities. Individuals without medical insurance endure the financial burden of paying out-of-pocket for costly diagnostic procedures and expensive medications. Individuals with insurance are often limited to selecting physicians who participate in the plan, but are not specialists in HIV disease and lack sufficient expertise about critical early-intervention treatment, such as combination antiretroviral therapy and prophylaxis against *Pneumocystis carinii* pneumonia (PCP). In 1993, the U.S. Supreme Court upheld the right of an employer to restrict insurer coverage for an AIDS-diagnosed patient in Texas, and other states are attempting to enact similar restraints for the treatment of HIV disease.

Anecdotal reports suggest extensive obstacles to receiving quality HIV-related health care. A female with lymphadenopathy, a familiar symptom of HIV disease, was referred by a physician to an oncologist and was not assessed for risk of HIV transmission. She had a history of intravenous drug use and sex with partners having drug histories. A lymph node biopsy will not indicate HIV infection, so the medical interventions did not diagnose antibodies to the virus. Troubled by her health, she went to a New York City Anonymous Test Site and discovered her HIV-positive serostatus. A male with a T-cell count below 200, which fits the criteria for PCP prophylaxis, began a course of therapy that is the third alternate–which is more complex to administer, time-consuming, and expensive.

In this, the second decade of the HIV disease epidemic, inclusive HIV clinical education initiatives for primary-care providers are essential. Human Resources Services Administration (HRSA), a federal agency, funded a consortium of institutions and organizations to offer training targeted to physicians, nurses, dentists, and other health-related professionals. The programs range from general overviews, advanced training, and mini-residencies, and they draw on a large, multidisciplinary expert faculty.

The Center for Disease Control (CDC) recommends sex and needle-sharing partners to notify their partners. In New York State, a partner notification program maintains the anonymity of the infected individual by informing the at-risk individual, without revealing the name of the disclosing individual; an HIV antibody test is then recommended because of known contact with someone HIV-seropositive. The American Medical Association (AMA) recommends physicians to persuade the infected patient to cease endangering any others or to notify them.[1]

The New York State Legislature passed an HIV confidentiality law in 1989 that allows physician disclosure under certain circumstances. The law permits, but does not require, physicians to disclose HIV-related information to a known contact of the patient if certain conditions are present. For this purpose, the physician may not disclose the name of the infected individual and must, to a reasonable extent, make all contacts in person. The physician, however, has no obligation to identify or locate any contact. The physician must counsel the HIV-infected patient regarding the need to notify the contact. If the physician believes the patient will not disclose then he or she must instruct the patient of the intent to make such disclosure. If the patient requests the disclosure through the partner notification program, the physician must honor the request.[2] The principle of confidentiality obliges the professional to protect the content of the pre- and post-test counseling sessions and the result of an HIV antibody test.

DISCLOSURE DEADLOCK

When there is considerable risk–unprotected sexual intercourse with an HIV-infected individual–the testing procedure requires a minimum of three tests over a year. The first HIV test establishes a baseline to determine infection before the most recent high-risk event. Occasionally, the test signifies the process of seroconversion (such is the possibility with an inconclusive result). An inclusive occurs with either or both tests–the enzyme-linked immunosorbent assay (ELISA) and the Western blot. A conjecture of seroconversion is not diagnostically absolute. An inconclusive result may indicate another infection because the tests are reactive to other microorganisms, medical conditions, or the use of medications disassociated from HIV disease. The follow-up HIV antibody test is given within six months from the baseline, with more than 95% of individuals showing antibody presence by that time. If the individual remains HIV-inconclusive, a third test is given within a year from the last unprotected, high-risk event.

After Marjorie (a patient of mine) tested HIV-seronegative, a counselor from the New York City Department of Health Anonymous Test Site referred her for psychotherapy. Mark, her sexual partner, a dancer with a well-known company, was HIV-seropositive, diagnosed after a hospitalization six months previous to my initial session with Marjorie.

Marjorie was a 30-year-old white female who had a master's degree in theater from an Ivy League college. She displayed a great deal of rebellious posturing. Her self-assured demeanor thinly disguised her body language of perpetually agitated motion. She habitually fingered her voluminous red hair, which draped a black leather motorcycle jacket. She simultaneously chewed gum, her mouth tilted to one side, while pumping her left foot. A Philadelphian, her soft-spoken, boarding-school mannered voice was evocative of Grace Kelly's. But her manner contradicted the rebellious image she projected. She was a patrician through and through.

She had returned to New York after spending two years in Paris. She had lived in Paris with her husband Carlos, a famous painter from whom she was now divorced. She noted with affectation, "Ah, to be in Paris simply walking by the Seine. Carlos and I would talk about the international art scene. It was all an aphrodisiac, because we'd return to his studio on the Left Bank and fuck our brains. Fucking was the least common denominator. I was only 23 with my degrees and romantic ideas about Europe. I was a Jamesian heroine, and Carlos was my vision of the human experience and European aristocracy.

"I married him six weeks after our first meeting. I made a cross-Atlantic phone call to notify my family, who were horrified. Haughtily, I told my mother, 'It's a leap of blind faith. I've arrived home in Paris. This is where the real work is done.' I became an artist through marriage. Carlos dominated me from one drink to another, but I refused to be anybody's victim. I adored him as any sensible, sensitive person would do, and became an efficient engine. A fuck machine.

"Even so, I couldn't restrain his erotic energy, which really wasn't about sex anyway. I found out he was sleeping with many other women. It wasn't sex he wanted, but power. After my epiphany, I was enraged. He couldn't escape the onslaught of words I hurled, because they were coming at him so fast. I turned around and ran as fast as I could, finding myself running toward the words. The entire past opened, with memories of my father. I couldn't remember precise events; they appeared dream-like. I think my father sexually abused me.

"I escaped the marriage, hurriedly packing a couple of bags, leaving behind most of my belongings. When I returned to New York, defeated and depressed, I entered my blue period, the anoretic phase. I grasped at an opportunity to become a performance artist in Soho with a multi-racial group called The Gorgeous Mosaic. They got the name from New York City's Mayor David Dinkins' 1989 inaugural speech, when he attempted to promote racial and ethnic harmony within a divided city. The drinking got out of hand, and I was sleeping with a couple of the members of the group. When I met Mark, he offered me to move into his Lower East Side tenement apartment. Within months, we discussed marriage; then I found myself pregnant."

For weeks, Mark noticed swollen lymph nodes in his neck and groin. After reading a medical dictionary, he made the association to HIV disease and became frightened. He attempted self-treatment–through a complicated holistic regimen designed to strengthen his immune system–but the nodes continued to enlarge. He wore turtleneck sweaters and scarves in dance class to escape notice and withdrew from sexual intimacy with Marjorie. The nodes became painfully swollen, and he made an appointment with a physician. The physician mentioned HIV in passing, and Mark denied that he was at risk for contracting the virus. The physician suggested a biopsy to determine malignancy. The biopsy was benign, and the physician recommended surgical removal of the node.

Marjorie said, "I remember being in the room seeing him in pain both from the surgery, and the anesthesiologist bruised his windpipe. He lay in pain and they didn't bring any painkiller. I began to think they were treating him strangely, differently. After the surgery, his doctor recommended the HIV test, and it frightened him. It came back positive. I asked myself, 'How is this possible?' Then, when he was well enough, I asked him, 'How?' He resisted, bristling with irritation at my interrogation. His refusal enraged me, and I thought, 'Doesn't he have a conscience?' I hated the role–like a judge holding him in contempt."

She spoke with her head bowed, self-controlled emotionally, rarely looking at me directly. She arranged a pair of black-framed Ray Ban sunglasses atop her forehead, unveiling reddish eyes from lack of sleep or crying. She wore outlandish fluorescent-colored tights, outstretching her long limbs as if to occupy space. With her eyes shut, she said, "I walked around the block a couple of times before coming up. It's like a terrible dream that won't go away. I'm going around with a baby inside my belly, afraid all the time. I wonder what will happen after it's born? What else is going to happen and change?

"Mark amazes me when he says, 'Everything will be okay.' We've grown apart as two strangers. His back is against the wall, choosing to be silent and suffering. He has no strength. Oh, I should feel sorry for him, looking at his poor face. As I told you last week, this waiting period to get my test results is tortuous." Marjorie was breathless.

She continued: "In the distance, I heard his footsteps when he came home this morning at daybreak. I saw his figure framed in the dim light. He knelt at the foot of the bed, stretched on the floor, muting the sounds of crying. He got to his knees, seeing me awake. He bent his head over me, and I felt revulsion, inhaling the musty scent of his rain-soaked clothes. 'There,' he said, 'I really don't want to hurt you. When you stare back I realize that you're so angry I can't help you.' I said, 'Yes, I'm angry, but more than that, I feel hurt by the deception.' He needs forgiveness [and] begs me not to leave. I have so many questions. At times, I feel my heart hysterically beating, and I want to escape."

She continued: "You see, I love him, so there aren't any authorities to notify–to pressure anyone into believing me. Each is saved by love, if there were a convincing change of heart. His T cells are about 198, and it would be a violation of some code to let anyone know. He won't tell me how he became infected. It wasn't drugs, so it has to be sexual. It's so familiar, it's frightening."

There's no place in society for Marjorie's embittered honesty. Her mind will have to be dulled; she will have to be treated as an invalid or, worse, a lunatic. She felt a moment of epiphany beyond an agonizing self-consciousness. Her words have a whispering unimportance, counting on her to be docile and slight as she looked while making life-and-death decisions not the irrepressible woman–the primordial script of the sacrificing–loving and nourishing. She read of the death-dealing, pleasure-besotted underpinnings of a subculture with libidinous hypermasculinity.

EITHER/OR

The signposts on his road to mental health included going to female-strip discos, where his eyes glistened and he giggled in shocked pleasure as the strippers taunted and teased the male clientele. He felt a numbing discomfort contrasted with his bravura.

Bill, the second example, is a 32-year-old computer programmer. He has a nine-year-old son and lives with his fiancée Clara. He came to treatment several months after his diagnosis of HIV-seropositive, asymptomatic. His parents are both deceased. His mother died of cancer; his father died six months later from alcohol-related complications. Bill has two siblings: an older brother who lives in Texas and a sister who lives in New York.

Bill knew very little about HIV: "When my lymphs swelled, I looked it up in a medical dictionary. I have a professional medical dictionary. I don't remember the name; it has a green cover. You know, swollen lymphs result from many illnesses, but I did read about AIDS. It scared me. The test came back positive. The doctors never mentioned HIV." Bill went through a surgery, and they never mentioned testing. "I feel angry. They never mentioned HIV, and the surgery was unnecessary. Yes, I felt angry."

Clara, Bill's fiancée, explained, "After Bill tested positive, he told me immediately. I've known him for six years, and we have been living together for four years since we became engaged. When I tested, the result was negative.

I asked Bill how he contracted the virus. After becoming agitated, avoidant, and attempting to change the subject, he explained.

"We had sex together. I knew what I was doing was wrong. It's a sin. I always knew that. If he were gay or bisexual or using drugs, I'd understand it; but he's heterosexual. I had a lawyer prepare an agreement, but he wouldn't sign it. I wanted him to be financially responsible for my medical care, and if anything happens to me to provide for my son, Bill Jr. He knew he was positive and didn't tell me. I can't tell anyone. Clara asks about him. She said, 'How come we don't see Ron anymore?' We used to go to the gym together to work out, but he hasn't been there. I found out that he moved. I went over to his apartment and there was a note on his mailbox to forward the mail."

Bill did not keep his second appointment, but telephoned that afternoon to reschedule. He said, "I got confused about the date. I think the virus is affecting my memory. I seem to forget things." He didn't keep the rescheduled appointment either, and when I tried to reach him the telephone number he gave me was disconnected. I didn't hear from him for several weeks, and then I got a telephone call. He said in a panicked voice: "I've got to see you. When is the earliest appointment?"

I saw Bill that afternoon. During the session, he was very agitated, rocking back and forth in the chair. Alternately covering his face, then revealing his teary eyes. He said, "My fiancée, Clara, is threatening to leave me. She said that she needs some space. I pleaded with her. She says that she loves me, but she can't stay with me. The night before we had a heavy confrontation."

He continued: "We discussed how I got the virus. I thought it would have been impossible for me to tell her the truth–that I got it from a man–that it was Ron. Actually, she began to guess the truth because the confrontation started with her questioning me by saying, 'We don't see Ron anymore. He never comes around.'"

He asked: "Could you see us together? I think we need couples counseling." I felt reluctant to see them together, because the issues facing Bill would be unresolvable unless he was prepared to communicate more directly with Clara. I agreed, despite my reservations, to see them together because I did not think he would engage in therapy unless I consented.

There was one couple's session. The first scheduled session was missed; at the second, they arrived a half-hour late. During the session, Clara said she was going to move out and that she had already secured an apartment. What became clear in the session was her frustration with Bill's difficulty over making a commitment before his diagnosis. The diagnosis had exacerbated prior existing problems. Clara was attempting to conceal her rage toward Bill at having been placed at risk. I believe she suspects that he had sex with a male, but she no doubt knows that the transmission was sexual. She feels that his continual pleading does not address many problems in the relationship, and she does not acknowledge her anger at feeling betrayed.

During the week, Bill called to say that Clara was moving to a new apartment. I was firm against couple counseling. Instead, I scheduled an individual appointment. We addressed the issues of lateness and missed appointments. Bill has been making his appointment for the past six weeks.

He told me, "Ron was a close friend. We worked together. I knew him for two years. Now, I know he was never my friend. A friend wouldn't have done this. He knew, and he never told me. He watched me go through this, and he didn't say anything. That's not a friend. I went through this surgery, and he didn't say anything. Now, he tells me that I have to live with it."

LITIGIOUS FRENZY

In an era of litigious frenzy, Kermani and Weiss address the legal aspects of HIV disease and confidentiality when a client insists that the therapist maintain confidence of a seropositive status. They cite the *Tarasoff* decision in California, where the court determined a psychiatrist was responsible to warn and protect an intended victim about a patient's threat of murder:

> The phenomenon of reverse victimization further complicates the confidentiality issue in the rare cases when a patient learns about his or her HIV status from a doctor. The senior author had under treatment a bipolar, homosexual patient. At the patient's request HIV testing was done, resulting in a positive

diagnosis. The patient was informed, and was persuaded to inform his partner with whom he had been living for several years. But the patient was outraged by the discovery, since he had been sexually faithful. The patient blamed the partner and confessed planning to seriously harm him. Warning is a two-way street. Clinicians must evaluate the situation thoroughly before selecting a course of action.[3]

HIV activists' skepticism of public-health authorities, compelled them to oppose measures, such as mandatory testing and partner contact notification, without consent that such measures propose complicated strategies to restrict HIV transmission. Medical ethicist Bayer implies that a backlash effect was created due to the frustration of public-health administrators, jeopardizing clear-sighted policy. He suggests an ironical collusion, fueled by fear and frustration, that weakened implementing behavioral modification:

[F]ear by seeking to thwart the implementation of public health policies designed to identify and counsel voluntarily those who could transmit HIV infection, frustration by threatening the infected in ways that would render collaboration with public health officials difficult to attain. Both subverted the prospects for the emergence of a public culture of restraint and responsibility that could affect the course of the epidemic.[4]

Ultraconservatives and Christian fundamentalists–represented in Congress by William Dannemyer of California and Jesse Helms of South Carolina–proceeded from an anti-gay agenda that viewed the principal measure as statutory:

Congress, the state legislatures, and the courts should repudiate the false notion that homosexual practice is a constitutional right. Sodomy laws should be enforced. Those who practice that vice have no right to claim that it be excluded from consideration in determining their eligibility for positions of responsibility, including teaching and government service.[5]

Response, however, requires also the protection of the common good. The first step in that protection is for the law to affirm the objective wrongness of the degraded behavior that has led to the problem:

> In short, if we are going to be able to avoid a nationwide scouring of the homosexuals among us, with all the hatred, anger, finger-pointing, rumor-mongering, and false accusations such a scourge would entail, we must face the fact that homosexual practices have endangered all of us. In the scale of national values, civil liberties for homosexuals rank somewhat below survival.[6]

To the claim that there is any legal or moral right to practice the vices which have generated the disease, the only coherent response a civilized society can make is total prohibition.

Although a woman was not convicted of prostitution, an assistant state attorney said he felt compelled to ask a district court judge in Prince George County to jail her without bond "for the protection of John Q. Public." Two activist attorneys criticized the decisions and filed a criminal charge. The filing of criminal charges against an HIV-infected individual is not unprecedented. A Washington, DC, man with the virus was accused of assault with a dangerous weapon after he allegedly forced a young boy to have sex with him. A soldier infected with the virus was sentenced to 15 years in prison for engaging in sex with women.[7]

There have been 1,000 HIV-related lawsuits filed since 1988; about 300 have involved blood transfusions, according to the AIDS Litigation Project of the Federal Department of Health and Human Services. Other suits deal with such issues as job or housing discrimination against people with AIDS, or mandatory testing of workers by their employers in the government, the military, hospitals, and schools.[8]

In 1991, a federal district judge in Boston ordered the federal government to pay $42.7 million in actual and punitive damages—one of the largest damage awards in an HIV-related blood-transfusion case. The winner of the award was a marine noncommissioned officer who contracted AIDS from his wife after she became infected with the virus when she received a blood transfusion during a Caesarean section at a Navy hospital 10 years ago. The woman later had a son who had the disease and died before he was a year old; she died not long after.[9]

The Washington Post reported that a man with HIV disease filed a lawsuit against two respiratory therapists for violating confidentiality by disclosing his diagnosis. He is suing the hospital and the therapists for $4.5 million, alleging that one of the therapists, an acquaintance from high school who was not involved in his care, obtained his hospital record and then called his friends and relatives to tell them he had AIDS.[10]

In a *New York Times* story, a woman's fiancé collapsed from a heart attack in Martin, Tennessee, and she ran desperately to a stranger, pleading for help. She did not tell the stranger her fiancé was infected with the HIV virus. An off-duty police officer performed mouth-to-mouth resuscitation. The woman faces felony charges of reckless endangerment for not warning rescuers that her fiancé was infected.

The woman said, "Police showed up at my door after the funeral services. They told me they were charging me with reckless endangerment. I just didn't understand because I would never hurt anybody." The woman, an unemployed nursing assistant, was jailed for five days. She was freed last week on $2,500 bond, and her case was sent to a county grand jury.[11]

In a *Newsweek* poll, nine out of ten Americans believe all health-care workers infected with the HIV virus should be required to report their condition to patients. Ninety-seven percent felt that patients should be required to tell health-care workers if they are infected with HIV. Sixty-three percent think an HIV-infected surgeon should be forbidden to practice. Sixty-five percent said they would not receive treatment from a doctor or dentist who was infected. Sixty-five percent believe dentists with HIV should be barred from practicing, and fifty-one percent think medical doctors should be forbidden.[12]

The AMA urged health-care workers to take the HIV antibody test. It recommended the test for patients "consistent with examinations administered for other communicable diseases." The association rejected mandatory testing for health-care personnel, including doctors.

The AMA supported the principle that a doctor has a responsibility to report to a state board or licensing department any "compelling evidence of impaired effectiveness on the part of a colleague. That requirement would include reporting evidence of an AIDS-virus-infected physician engaging in invasive procedures without notifying patients. Nancy Dickey, an AMA trustee, said she expects "hospitals to help enforce AMA guidelines that an AIDS-infected doctor who is engaged in invasive medical procedures should either notify patients or change specialties."[13]

The United States Senate overwhelmingly approved (99-0) two measures regarding HIV disclosure. The first, sponsored by Jesse Helms, would fine or imprison HIV-infected health-care workers engaged in "invasive physical contact" who didn't tell their patients of their infection and continued to treat them. The bill threatens at least ten years in prison plus a $10,000 fine for doctors, nurses, and dentists who know they have AIDS but do not tell patients and keep doing "invasive" procedures, ranging from surgery to throat exams. The second measure, endorsed by the leaders of both parties and the Bush Administration, requires the states to enact testing guidelines.[14] The CDC stated that 6,436 health-care workers nationwide were infected with the virus, including 703 doctors, 47 surgeons, 1,358 nurses, and 171 dentists and dental hygienists.[15]

These procedures characterize modern society with rituals of confession that function within the convention of scientific regularity. This combination of confession with examination, the taking of a personal and sexual history, occurs within the framework whose theoretical underside is the principle of sex as a "cause of any and everything":

> Confession that had to be thorough, meticulous, and constant, and at the same time operate within a scientific type of practice. The limitless dangers that sex carried with it justified the exhaustive character of the inquisition to which it was subjected.[16]

The obtaining of the confession and its effects were recodified as therapeutic operations. Which meant first of all, that the sexual domain was no longer accounted for simply by the notions of error or sin, excess or transgression, but was placed under the rule of the normal and the pathological.

REFERENCE NOTES

1. American Medical Association, "Report of the Council on Ethical and Judicial Affairs, Report:A(I-87), December 1987.

2. Human Immunodeficiency Virus and AIDS Related Information–Confidentiality, Laws of New York, Chapter 584, S.9265-A, Section 2782.

3. Ebrahim J. Kermani, MD and Bonnie A. Weiss, MA, ATR, "AIDS and Confidentiality: Legal Concepts and Its Application in Psychotherapy," *American Journal of Psychotherapy*, Volume XLIII, Number 1, January 1989.

4. Ronald Bayer, *Private Acts, Social Consequences: AIDS and the Politics of Public Health* (New York: The Free Press, 1989), p. 136.

5. Charles E. Rice, "Civil Rights Are Not as Important as Public Health," in *AIDS*, edited by Lynn Hall and Thomas Modl (St. Paul: Greenhaven Press, 1988), p. 117.

6. Tom Braden, *Washington Times*, November 7, 1985.

7. *The Washington Post*, July 24, 1991.

8. *The New York Times*, July 26, 1991.

9. *The New York Times*, July 26, 1991.

10. *The Washington Post*, July 27, 1991,

11. *The New York Times*, July 9, 1991.

12. *Newsweek*, July 1, 1991.

13. *The Wall Street Journal*, June 27, 1991.

14. *The Wall Street Journal*, July 19, 1991.

15. *New York Post*, July 19, 1991.

16. Michel Foucault, *The History of Sexuality: An Introduction, Volume 1* (New York: Vintage Books, 1990), p. 66.

Chapter 4

A Chronology of Exile

It was undoubtedly the feeling of exile–that sensation of
a void within which never left us, that irrational longing
to hark back to the past or else to speed up the march of
time, and those keen shafts of memory that stung like
fire. . . . And when we realized that the separation was
destined to continue, we had no choice but to come to
terms with the days ahead.

–Albert Camus, *The Plague*

BIOPHYSICAL CRISIS

A medical diagnosis across the spectrum of HIV disease–from
HIV-seropositive/asymptomatic through HIV-seropositive/symp-
tomatic and fully diagnosed HIV disease–precipitates an individual
into a life crisis. The diagnosis induces heightened anxiety, homeostatic disequilibrium and compels the individual to adapt through
coping mechanisms they have found successful in other life crises.
A progressive crisis persists when the individual is unable to adapt
to aggregate biophysical challenges and psychosocial stressors.
With HIV disease, the biophysical crisis confronts an individual
with life transitions characteristic of late middle age. Individuals
face agonizing problems and dilemmas concurrent with feelings of
hopelessness; at times, they feel immobilized, overwhelmed, or
lost.

The diagnostic crisis converges within a socially stressful milieu.
The individual may have suffered multiple losses from HIV disease

within their family and community support system. In this second decade of the epidemic, there are cross-generational examples of HIV, with grandparent(s), child, and grandchild all suffering. The devastation in the gay community is well-documented with surviving individuals and spouses left friendless, guilty, and clinically depressed. The intravenous-drug-using community, in treatment or recovery, is surrounded with HIV infection. The medical diagnosis of HIV disease is systemically manifested through the entire support network. The diagnosis precipitates circumstances with numerous socially contextual issues, including gender, race, sexual orientation, class, and age.

The medical diagnosis of seropositivity is a presenting problem, but not exclusively. Focus on the diagnosis is reductionistic and misleading. The individual usually locates the problem as biophysical (emotional disequilibrium). The intake interview should differentially diagnose preexistent functioning. The interview includes an assessment of problems such as depression and anxiety. The individual fears loss of control and pain. The person may present addictive behavior and substance use. They may have low self-esteem and low self-value. They may not be socially adjusted and have interpersonal difficulties. There may be nonspecific fears present before the HIV disease diagnosis–issues of life identity, often combined with substance use.

The cumulative impact of opportunistic infections (OIs) on vital reserves, coping capacity, awareness, and acceptance of bodily changes as physical well-being declines affects an individual's functioning and independence. Individuals struggle for independence rather than rely on services from the health-care workers, family, and friends. The dread of, and then the horror of, being unable to walk, feed oneself, get out of bed, and take care of one's toilet needs is continual, as is the intermittent anxiety about the course of the illness or the fear of the possibility of a slow, painful death. People with HIV disease face loss of control both physically and financially. The rage at the unfairness of the illness and the loss of a future is apparent in treatment, along with depression, guilt, and helplessness.

THE MICROSOCIAL CRISIS

Many people with HIV disease have quality interpersonal relationships with the presence of a significant relationship. Others may face considerable isolation, or the desire to isolate, without the availability of significant others and family to provide emotional support and care-giving. When an individual has HIV disease the diagnosis resonates systemically, so significant relationships and family members–the entire support network–is in disequilibrium. It is a real struggle, in which the conflict enlightens us about the conceptual schemes, results, and purposes of the investigators who present ideas to the complex and chaotic social and psychological inquiries in human sexuality.

A developmental life-span perspective is essential when treating same-sex relationships. Caution is advisable when using a life-stage approach, because certain behaviors considered normative exclude other adaptive strategies. Cultural sexual ideologies profoundly influence our ideas of normality, health, and abnormality. Society condemns lesbian and gay couples because of Judeo-Christian traditional religious views. The model must emphasize the characteristic stages and transitions that reflect biological, social, psychological, physical, and historical events distinct to lesbian and gay couples.

Heterosexual society promotes psychic, emotional, and instrumental bonds between couples with prescribed roles, rituals, and sanctions within a context of the so-called naturalness of marriage. Gay men and lesbians are without social institutions to maintain same-sex relationships:

> In addition, the sense of belonging, identity, sharing, and support that exist for many heterosexual couples and the role many extended family members play in helping the couple resolve conflicts or adjust to difficulties are usually absent.[1]

While challenges to the inevitability and desirability of marriage existed as early as the mid-nineteenth century, the social world changed drastically between the late 1950s and 1980s. For instance, the double standard of premarital intercourse–the dominant norm among caucasian, middle-class males–lost its hold on women, so most young Americans do not condemn sexual intercourse between unmarried men and women who have some established relationship.

THE MACROSOCIAL CRISIS

Most HIV-disease patients experience the physical, financial, legal, and emotional problems that typically result from any chronic or terminal illness. These problems exacerbate an outcast status assigned to persons with HIV disease due to the popular misconceptions about the disease and to the identification of the disease with groups outside the social mainstream. Prejudicial attitudes shared by some health caregivers result in separate, parallel systems of service delivery:

> The social context creates tensions in medical discourse. Periodically, such tensions that derive from troubling social issues erupt into the discourse, or appear at its margins, and create a countertextual reality that cannot be resolved in the framework of a medical encounter. Doctors tend to suppress such tensions by dominance gestures such as interruptions, cut-offs, and deemphases that get the discourse back on a technical track. The inherent hierarchy and asymmetry of the doctor-patient relationship reinforce this pattern of dominance in discourse.[2]

Rarely are all the issues concerning HIV synthesized to reflect the entire spectrum of concerns that confront a person with HIV disease. Only a tripartite conceptual framework can encompass the characteristics that form the gestalt of HIV infection. It requires a perspective including the following: the medical, the psychological, and the social. This requires the formulation of a holistic model, a unique epistemology.

Within social work treatment, the biopsychosocial assessment is paradigmatic, embodying the professional knowledge base. The initial hypothesis of treatment is fundamental. The individual will have profound reactions to medical diagnosis and treatment that will reverberate throughout the social context. The process of therapy, with an assessment, proceeds from a bicameral interaction that abandons the linear assumption that the therapist is a "free-standing agent acting upon a free-standing subject, the client or family."[3] Instead, it is the circularity of inextricable elements (the bio, psycho, and social) and their relationships that characterize the field or therapeutic system.

For instance, a response to diagnosis reflects individual character structure, a person's distinct intrapsychic nature, self-identity, and consciousness. The individual does not live within a closed system outside social interaction. We all live within a social macrocosm, within a grouping of family and community. All individuals are constituents of a body politic and culture, affected by historical precedence, no matter how isolated or disenfranchised the person may be.

The promotion of the doctor/patient relationship sets partnership as the ideal. This goal presents formidable barriers. For the most part, doctors are not trained to be collaborative: in fact, the training emphasizes leadership and the ability to "take charge." Doctors also function within a social structure that places them highest within a hierarchical order, contradicting any notion of partnership. The ability of patients to express their concerns depends on an economic and social context: patients may not be able to comprehend medical terminology, and the physician may not take the time to explain diagnoses or procedures in understandable language. The patient may be intimidated by the authority of the physician. Therefore, the encounter is complex with the variables of class, gender, and race, each affecting communication.

When making a diagnosis, it is critical to establish the following: (1) a client's self-perception of sexual orientation; (2) where the client fits, using the developmental life-stage model for sexual orientation; (3) the ability of the mental-health professional to deal with their homophobia; and (4) to differentiate social and self-acceptance issues from mental disturbances or problems that do not relate to sexual orientation. It is crucial, on the other hand, that medical professionals be able to recognize the need for mental health and psychiatric evaluation.

Medical decisions have massive reverberations for a whole network of people, with consequences to many others than the patient. Social diagnosis is a process, not a single moment. It is not an element in an ordered set of before-after events in time. In the medical model, such a sequence is the ideal, which one tries to approximate in practice: complaint, history, examination, diagnosis, and treatment. Interventions in social situations may have different phases; they overlap, contrapunctally.[4]

THE GRIEVING CYCLE

This crisis is part of an ongoing, often unconscious, grieving cycle. Losses an individual encounters are concurrent disruptions or those that follow in close time proximity. The grieving cycle may encompass changes in drug and alcohol use or behavioral modification in sexual expression, such as adherence to safer-sex guidelines. Persons with HIV infection experience a biophysical crisis that demands coping with many episodes of illness and hospitalization. They become anxious due to the fear of becoming physically helpless or mentally out of control. This stage of crisis may activate unconscious childhood memories of sexual or mental abuse or inadequate parenting and abandonment. The individual confronts present (and conceivable) losses of autonomy, as well as continual accommodation to increased physical debilitation.

Those with HIV infection must cope with the effect of social stigmatization, which has an intrapsychic component. They struggle with social and self-acceptance simultaneously. Often, they are unable to distinguish between their sense of self and the virus. They feel themselves to be the HIV disease incarnate. The individual struggles with the acceptance of their identity.

The HIV disease epidemic has forced social-work practitioners to rethink their methods of working with the terminally ill, which has been traditionally oriented for an older population. The majority of HIV-disease patients are between the ages of 20 and 50, in the prime of their lives; they exhibit reactions and needs different from those of the elderly. Additionally, there has been a philosophical shift in working with persons with HIV disease by emphasizing wellness and coping strategies of living with chronicity and terminal illness. Reflecting this shift is the rejection by persons with HIV disease of the label "victim." Rather, people with HIV disease may lay claim to life by rejecting the victim role.

The individual should be the stimulus during the diagnostic process. The diagnosis may exacerbate preexistent underlying emotional or social conflicts. An HIV-disease diagnosis precipitates a confrontation with mortality difficulties due to a discontinuity of identity (i.e., facing the meaning of one's life). The threats of helplessness and loss stimulated by such transitions remain latent throughout life, unless the developing person can accept feelings of loss through a normal mourning process.

The symptomatology of normal grief is "remarkably uniform," according to Erich Lindemann, with the presentation of the following[5]:

- Somatic distress, such as exhaustion and digestive difficulties.
- guilt: Shame supposes that one is completely exposed and conscious of being looked at: in one word, self-conscious. One is visible and not ready to be visible. . . . Too much shaming does not lead to propriety but to a secret determination to try to get away with things, unseen–if, indeed, it does not result in defiant shamelessness.[6]
- Emotionally, there is a "sense of unreality."
- Socially, there is "distance from others," and preoccupation with feelings of guilt, a tendency to respond with irritability and anger toward others.

Intrinsic to psychotherapy with persons with HIV disease are the formidable occurrences of debilitating illnesses and hospitalizations that interrupt the course of treatment. The therapist must skillfully distinguish between resistance to psychotherapy and the inability to present for sessions due to illness. Treatment of the HIV-related patient by the social worker is initiated by the biopsychosocial assessment that considers the individual and unique histories, life experiences, expectations, socioeconomic resources, and social supports of the patient.

The historical roots of the term "psychosocial" belong fully within the domain of the social-work profession. The psychosocial theory base reflects the tradition of social work to seek knowledge from all sources. Psychosocial casework developed as a distinct modality emphasizing biopsycho development, interpersonal influence, the effect of significant others, and the interaction with the environments and systems. Through such psychotherapeutic techniques as supportive counseling, the social worker will explore with the person with HIV disease the following aspects of diagnosis.

It is of primacy, that whenever possible, the dually diagnosed individual with HIV disease and chemical dependency is enrolled in a substance-abuse program. The patient, particularly those in the earlier stages of disease, will benefit from a substance-abuse program. There are several modalities for treatment: drug-free programs that are nonresidential; methadone maintenance treatment programs; and the self-help programs utilizing the principles of Alcoholics Anonymous. All of these have proven beneficial in helping such persons deal with HIV disease as well as with their chemical dependency.

DONALD

February 28, 1988

Hospitals are among the most distinguished of American institutions, functioning through a hierarchical structure, a pyramid of power, that has patients at the nadir and physicians the apex. The irony is that, within the hospital system, the patient becomes an afterthought, an obstruction to the bureaucracy, whose central purpose is profit-making. The uninsured poor undergo a "wallet biopsy" before displacement to a municipal hospital. One such hospital is in New York's El Barrio, a desparate community *without* adequate health care and *with* the complications of wide-spread drug use and a high incidence of HIV disease, tuberculosis, and other health problems associated with poverty, such as malnutrition.

The hospital was the real-life setting for the television series *Nurse*. The series, rather than community need or any medical milestone, kept this hospital open. When I was talent-agenting, a career before the epidemic, *Nurse* was my account, and often I booked clients on the show. On occasion, I would even watch the show, although hospital melodramas were never my cup of tea. They made me nauseous, in fact. Hospitals made me uncomfortable, and I hated to visit them.

The El Barrio hospital's interior was filthy, with peeling paint and plaster chips falling from the ceiling. I suspected patients were unwittingly lead-poisoned. The almshouses of the last century–where the undesirable poor, the so-called problem cases, received care from the government–foreshadowed this ward. Most of the patients in Ward 6A were substance users. Hospitalized patients suffer depression, as bedridden castaways, powerlessly living the day with limited social or physical contact. They are foreign bodies, poked and prodded by medical providers and support staff.

This municipal hospital ward was low-tech, and it was not even equipped with private telephones for patients. I couldn't set up a prior meeting time. Donald was asleep, and I stood at a distance, considering waking him. Before I decided, his eyes opened, and he looked at me, expressionless. I felt a sense of awkwardness seeing him in a hospital, removed from his environment, my office, or the group meeting room where we met twice a week. Hospital settings transform accustomed clinical boundaries.

Donald, in his early thirties, was 6'3" with impressive good looks and smooth mocha-colored skin. He had elegant, high-arching eyebrows that bridged his broad nose; his brown-black eyes were melancholic, penetrative. His hands were those of a pianist: they expressed temperament and vitality. Passion survived in his hands. His nails, ordinarily impeccably manicured, were long and yellowish (from the spilling of antiseptic solution from the intravenous site on his wrist). His hair was nubby, configured by the bed pillow, a stark contrast to the polish and scent of his usually well-groomed hair. He appeared as a victim, not his distinctive aristocratic self.

I wanted to withdraw, confronted by his distressing vulnerability and the perturbing conjunction of compassion and revulsion I felt. Embarrassed by the impulse to turn away, I felt self-blame, feeling threatened by his suffering and my humanity as a witness. It brought to mind something Martin Buber wrote: "If we knew the secrets of the upper worlds, they would not allow us so much actual participation in true existence as we can achieve by performing, with holy intent, a task belonging to our daily lives." In a millisecond, I was conscious of our interchangeable identities, where each of us is a parable, nothing but a story.

Donald's personal care needs were formidable. I remembered my masculinity being tempered by providing childcare for my friends' child, from infancy through his sixth year. My lack of enthusiasm only lengthened my learning the basics. (Diapering techniques became elevated to the purpose of human excellence–the trigonometry of a diaper, the quintessence of utility). We held our session bedside, discussing everything from his need for grooming to the topology of suffering itself, one principle of life.

During sessions, Donald described his many life stages, from the poverty of the Sugar Hill district in Harlem to the predominantly gay, caucasian subculture of Greenwich Village. His spiritual odyssey from the Baptist faith of childhood led to the exploration of his African origins. He discovered Islam, only to turn from that religion because of its total rejection of his sexual identity. Then he converted to the Bahai faith. He negotiated spiritually from the discernment of metaphysical limbo. This yearning for self-transcendence and sublimity fused with his intense aesthetic musicality (from classical to jazz).

He said, "My lover is the keyboard. I am divine: Me, myself, and my people. My love is the cause." He reminded me of James Baldwin–artistic sensitivity coupled with political integrity and the passion for racial justice, while also suffering the identical torment as a gay man. He found himself in the arms of gay white men whom he considered racist; their racism was even sometimes intensified by their sole preference for African-American men. I once mentioned Baldwin, and he said, "Yeah. I got looks. Jimmy, well, he always doubted that anyone could love him." Then, he paid me a dubious compliment: "You're not other white men. You're interesting."

The following is a dialogue from one of our sessions:

Donald (D): I feel like an innocent, exposed, with the nurse sponging me. It was as if a wall broke through around me. This illness. It's so difficult to stay in control. Sometimes, I can't stand it any more. I want to give up. I don't even know what giving up means. I don't mean suicide.

Steven Dansky (SD): I think you're afraid of becoming dependent and unable to take care of yourself.

D: Sometimes, I think it's too much to expect from anyone. I don't want to ask for help. Whenever I wanted attention, I felt I was too much. I felt rejected.

SD: Who used to do that to you.

D: What do you mean? [Pause] My mother used to say, "You'll be the death of me." I don't know what I was doing when she said that to me. She would scare me. She'd faint. Just fall to the floor. I would run to her. I felt responsible.

SD: You felt responsible for her, and needed to protect her. Do you feel responsible to protect other people?

D: I don't know. Sometimes I feel that I need you too much, and it confuses me. You're my therapist.

SD: What does it mean to depend on me?

D: I don't know what I need. At times, there I feel anger, and I just want it to go away. It's like poison. It's like the virus. I think it can destroy me.

SD: Are you feeling that the virus is punishment?

D: Not consciously. At time, I feel that I am the virus. The virus becomes everything. My feelings. I feel impotent. For several years, I ate healthy, got to a PWA (person with AIDS) therapy group, meditated and visualized, combined holistic approaches with medical ones, kept myself informed. Nothing takes it away.

There's a demon inside me. I pray for it to go away, but it has such a hold on me. It lies in waiting. Before this hospitalization, I was alone in my room. I sent the homecare attendant out on an errand. She was beginning to drive me crazy talking about her problems, her mother this, her son that, and her boyfriend. I asked her to go to the store. I decided I wanted some toast when she left. I was daydreaming, and I smelled the damn toast burning. I picked up the toaster, but I couldn't get the bread to pop up. Smoke was pouring out. Well, I lifted the toaster up and smashed it against a wall. I felt such anger. Then, I began to weep uncontrollably and wanted to smash myself.

SD: As a child, you were given the message that your needs could obliterate.

D: I don't know what I expected from you, some magical result. That you'd make it go away. I expected something magical. I took many risks and relied on you. I hate this depression.

SD: Are you disappointed?

D: No. [Pause] I like our sessions.

SD: I think you expected HIV to go away if you did everything in your power.

D: I don't think so, not consciously. I suppose there was a lot of pressure to feel positive thoughts. Healing tapes and visualizations and meditations and group and therapy and vitamins and rest and trying to have some sense of control of my emotions and body. There were times when none of it worked. When I felt angry and bitter. When I felt alone. I'd think of failed relationships and blame myself. All the anonymous sex: in parks, theaters, back rooms. I suppose that everyone was anonymous, even those I loved. I worry about my T cells when [I'm] debilitated.

SD: You want it to go away, suppress the pain, control it. I feel you're expressing longing.

D: I feel hopeless. My past is inescapable. I don't know what positive value there is to bring it up. I don't want to hate my mother. My father abandoned her. He abused her. They would fight when he got drunk. I remember standing on my bed, begging them to stop. I jumped on my father and hang from his neck. I remember blood. She hit him or stabbed him with a knife, then smeared the blood from her hands on the walls.

SD: You're expressing shame. As a child, you tried to solve the parent's relationship. You weren't responsible.

D: I know. I couldn't sleep with their constant fighting–the horror of it.

SD: You want to express the shame, but when you decide to do so, it involves hurting people. You feel a sense of betrayal.

D: Yes. [Pause] I wanted him to die. I wanted to kill him. You know, I was afraid of being alone with her. There was nowhere to escape.

SD: You said you were hopeless, no safety or peace.

D: Inside me–there's where it is. I know, but I'm bitter. I feel plagued by it.

SD: Plagued?

D: I did it to myself.

SD: HIV?

D: To some extent, not rationally, but I must think on certain choices in my life.

March 6, 1988

During the visit, I concentrated on Donald, transfixed. His isolation within the hospital separated him from the community. Before, I had known Donald in a hospital setting; seeing his helplessness out of the institutional environment was profound. This afternoon, my scrutiny accommodated the totality of the hospital environment, a pivotal shift from the physical fiction of our separateness to the objectivity of Ward 6A. I felt violated. Our previous session was virtually clandestine and its sanctity was a mirage.

Across the room, which has eight patients, a woman, partially in view despite the drawn curtain surrounding her husband's bed, is weeping hysterically while a priest is giving communion. Her husband suffered from renal failure, with his legs swollen beyond identifiable anatomy. She wrapped towels around his head, which excreted a steady stream of perspiration. He is disoriented, moving in and out of consciousness. The priest shook his head, while the sobbing woman persevered with prayers in Spanish.

The patient in the adjoining bed was intent on hearing our conversation. He sized me up. He motioned to speak with me, and I approached him with suspicion, sensing that he was going to ask me to do something I wouldn't do. He said, "There's this dude in New Jersey. What's the town? Something. I can find out. You know. Well, he got something for me. Now, if you get it, I'll take care of you when you get back." I replied, "No. I won't go on a mission for you." Donald silently watched this scene played out–a litmus test for my street smarts.

Donald and I walked to the solarium. He carefully transferred himself from bed to floor, adjusting the tubing of an intravenous pole. His changed physical stature startled me, noticing his considerable weight loss, his fragility. He walked haltingly down the long corridor to the east wing of the hospital, carrying a styrofoam cup to expectorate phlegm.

The solarium overlooked the East River. The 59th Street Bridge and Sunset Place were to the south–the scene of high society and delicate 1930s Hollywood romances. Roosevelt Island was to the right and Manhattan State Hospital to the left. The same river view that elite eastsiders had of the city. The sun glared a tropical intensity on snow-covered city streets. In a cosmic instant, while we bathed in the orange warmth of a setting winter sun, I imagined the healing potential of energy. I remembered a line from an Emily Dickinson poem: "To mend each tattered faith there is a needle fair though no appearance indicate 'tis threaded in the air."

> **Donald:** I wanted to tell you about a dream that I had last night. Before I fell asleep, I had been listening to Glenn Gould's interpretation of Bach's *The Goldberg Variations.* I meditated on the aria–the theme has a peaceful effect on me. I play it often when I'm hopeless. During the interlude of a note, an unmeasurable synapse, I felt quintessence strain toward me, the presence of godliness in the room. It was intelligible. At once, I felt detached and serene. I saw a figure in shadow and felt safety.
>
> In the dream, I remember walking in a field of wildflowers. Many people greeted me and some I knew. I felt profound safety, even [though] the scenery was unknown, though there were people with whom I had many hardships and struggles [with] in life. I saw my father and cousin. Seeing my father was particularly strange because I had always held him in such contempt for abandoning us and his lack of understanding of me. Ryan White was there, and I held his hand and we wandered together in the field.

Suddenly, Donald darted in panic, bringing us to reality. None of the medications could control the diarrhea. The closest bathroom was nearly a city block away from the solarium. He didn't make it. When

I went searching for him, I saw a trail of watery feces covering the hallway floor. I went for the assistance of a nurse, who became furious over the incident. She asked if I knew who had done it.

I found Donald in the shower room, leaning against the tile wall. He expressed remorse and shame and was weeping. He asked me to leave. I said, "It's all right." I'm at a loss for words, not knowing how to reassure and comfort him. My God, there's no bathroom near Ward 6A. Is the threat of losing bowel control constant for Donald? It is infantalizing to have to suffer this humiliation.

March 17, 1988

January 1986 marked the establishing of diagnostic-related group (DRG) system of fee payment, in which a patient is discharged, even after long hospitalizations, without much information on how to maintain his or her health. The DRG is an attempt by the hospital to provide cost-effective service by setting fixed fees. After a patient receives a diagnosis, hospital reimbursement rates are based on a fixed fee reflecting an average cost of treating a particular condition. If the patient is worse than average and requires extra care, the hospital must pay any cost beyond the DRG allowance. If the patient is better than average, the hospital keeps any money left over.

DRGs give the hospital an incentive to discharge patients quickly–to turn over beds. Patients need to know what they can do to help maintain good health, manage disability, or learn self-therapeutic practices. It is unclear to whom this mantle of responsibility should fall. The objective scientific delivery of medical care, no matter how effective or exact, can never substitute for the adequate recognition of the patient as a human being with emotional needs and complex medical problems.

Donald's discharge was after a five-month hospitalization. He checked out with a brown paper bag of personal items, including several prescription forms, a dozen cans of Ensure (a liquid dietary supplement), an egg-crate mattress, and a clinic card with an appointment in three weeks. He had walked into the emergency room with a fever of 105°; during the five months, he lost 60 pounds, ambulatory and coordinative capacity, significant memory, and the discernment of the future. Most of his social supports beside family, though not irrevocable, required networking. It was improbable he could attend therapy group sessions.

March 20, 1988

Donald called to confirm that he would be unable to continue attending therapy group sessions. His voice was almost inaudible on the telephone. I knew that he wanted to ask me something, but was having difficulty asserting himself.

He said, "I find myself in a predicament. I don't want to go back to the isolation that I felt before becoming a member of the group. The group has been very important to me. HIV has devastated me, and the group helped me to stay alive so I didn't feel so alone.

"When I awakened this morning, I lay in this crowded bedroom with my belongings piled in boxes against the wall. The piano [was] crowded into a corner. I felt disenfranchised, crippled, and a part of the bedroom homeless. I couldn't focus any righteous indignation over my dislocation or physical state, and it frightened me. My feelings are less remote than a year ago, so living in my mother's home I know that I'm going to need help to survive."

During the course of an HIV therapy group, coping patterns develop as members became physically ill. Group membership includes people experiencing the spectrum of HIV disease. Several members, while AIDS-diagnosed having had an opportunistic infection, are independent. They manage active professional and secure social lives with only minor modifications. Other members must negotiate the concurrence of manifold and complicated infections and cancers. When debilitated, their attendance at group sessions requires emotional resolve and determination to overcome physical challenges. Some members may withdraw, detaching into the comfort of their support system. For others, a group assumes centrality and represents their security and fulfills the need for acceptance.

For Richard, a long-term survivor diagnosed five years ago, the group actualized a set of values, such as the strenuous rejection of discouragement when faced with continual limitations. He said, "My willpower releases me from conflict beyond obstacles I couldn't cross before. When I suffer, it's because I haven't conceived the instrument of my will. I've always been creative; now, I mold my inner serenity. I have had to become more independent of my body. I grieve materialism, but I've had to accept alternative life creation."

> At any rate, long before my serious illness, I became convinced that creativity, the will to live, hope, faith, and love have biochemical significance and contribute strongly to healing and to well-being. The positive emotions are life-giving experiences. . . . We need look no further than the phenomenon of the placebo to recognize that, both on the conscious and subconscious level, the mind can order the body to react or respond in certain ways. Such response involves body chemistry and not just psychological reactions.[7]

The need to be independent of own's body reflects a twofold process when reconciling a life-threatening illness, distinctly epitomized by HIV disease associated with sexual behavior and identity. Foucault, Illich, and Szasz all insist that medicalization of the body and psychiatrization of the mind created an idiomatic reality to promote social control:

> First, [Michel Foucault] has pioneered the historical research on the process by which the body of the new subject of the welfare state supported through professional discourse about gender, biology, and sexuality. The judicial attempt to observe and control the sexual functioning precedes by more than a century of clinical control over women's genital organs.[8]

Viktor Frankel, imprisoned at Auschwitz when he was 25 wrote in *Man's Search for Meaning*, that he was working on his doctoral dissertation when detained. He put the thesis into an inner pocket in his overcoat. They took the coat from him when he arrived at the death camp. He had nothing material left. Nothing of this world–neither coat, nor his heirloom watch fob, nor dissertation, only his soul and free will. We move through space, this reality. Most of us will never know freedom, self-acceptance, the love of self and others. None of us will ever know freedom–especially our captors. Frankel affirms his spirituality in these terms surrounded by evil in a physical universe.

Richard came to a session the day following his discharge. Facing the uncompromising March winds, he required support from group members. Richard was a theatrical director, having worked in the theater on several prestigious projects; due to deterioration, his once-heroic muscles were now atrophied beyond improvement. During the group session, he sat immobile and still, except when chilling shock waves sent tremors through his body, which was wrapped in a blanket over a winter coat and scarf.

This last hospitalization conspicuously damaged his spirit. He had left his studio apartment door unlocked one early morning, anticipating the arrival of his homecare attendant so he wouldn't have to climb down from the loft bed once again to let her in. He made a pot of tea, and struggled up the ladder of his loft bed and went back to sleep. The sound of an intruder searching through his belongings beneath the loft bed awakened him. He huddled in the corner of his bed, muffling the sounds of a chronic cough in a pillow. Suddenly, the intruder ascended the loft bed, and despite Richard's pleading, he was beaten unconscious with a baseball bat. He must have lain in his blood for a couple of hours before the homecare attendant found him.

Richard had lived in his Greenwich Village apartment for almost ten years, and he was well known to all his neighbors. In fact, he enthralled them, attaining celebrity status because of his extensive theatrical connections. On Christmas Eve, several had enjoyed his hospitality for a small buffet that Richard had provided knowing it would be his last. He had taken a taxi from the Village to Zabar's, a famous Upper West Side gourmet shop, to prepare the supper. Almost fainting in the store, a customer helped him to a taxi. After the break-in, the building organized to have Richard evicted, claiming that he had invited the intruder into his apartment for a sexual liaison. One neighbor, who had helped Richard after the homecare attendant was calling for help, expressed rage at having some blood on her hand. It reminded me of Shirley Cabey, the mother of one of Bernie Goetz's victims:

> At first, she got only hate mail—terrible letters filled with racial epithets and expressing glee that her son was so badly wounded, letters that wished him dead, that threatened his life

if he ever got well enough to walk the streets again. She talks about them with an astonishing calm, given the messages they carry. 'I didn't know people could be so mean, but I made up my mind I wouldn't let them upset me. So after I read it, I'd take all the hate mail and stick it in between the pages of the Bible and say, 'The good Lord will take care of you.'[9]

Another group member, Danny, said his farewell to the group, although we didn't know it at the time. In a passionate account of self-discovery, he said, "You all know how long it took me to tell my parents. God, it must have been almost two years. I was so afraid that they'd reject me. They have been wonderful, and we have spent quality time together. Nothing is more important than the people in my life: my lover, parents, and a small circle of friends." We never saw Danny again. He wandered off into the lap of his support system. Occasionally, he would call to report on his medical progress, which had become very complex due to a number of infections that included *Mycobacterium avium intracellulare* (MAI) and Kaposi's sarcoma that had begun to affect internal organs.

I asked Donald what he thought about therapy. He quickly responded that he'd wanted to continue. I felt challenged by the specialized conditions that he presented, and I responded by suggesting that we construct a therapeutic context in his mother's home. I agreed to make weekly home visits and have bedside sessions.

April 3, 1988

His mother, Lettie, lived in Sugar Hill–the gem of Harlem, rows of well-maintained brownstones on tree-lined streets; at one end was the imposing, detailed, wrought-iron gates of The City College, with its gothic architecture. To the left, facing south, is The Grange, Alexander Hamilton's colonial home, designated a national landmark. Several blocks north was the Convent Avenue Baptist Church, where Donald played organ for five years. Childhood memories filled the apartment. He remarked a few days before his discharge, "My mother's apartment has an awareness. The rooms give testimony to our family history, and the walls metabolized our life together. You can leave my mother's home and days after you can inhale the scent of the rooms."

After Donald moved into Lettie's home during later weeks, the pivotal turning point of his life that bound him to dependency left him depressed and despairing. Of itself, the resolution that he couldn't return to his Bronx apartment profoundly upset him, subverting any hope of recovery or self-sufficiency. His family dismantled the apartment that survived many life transitions, which they had maintained through his previous hospitalizations at Bellevue, Harlem, and Columbia Presbyterian. He described the photograph-covered walls–memories of life passages and lovers, some of whom had died of HIV disease. He grieved in the study, the safe refuge where he nourished himself. He commanded his brother, Eric, to move the upright piano because he could not part with the highly polished mahogany talisman of his childhood. He relinquished most of his possessions, or sold them to neighbors, with personal papers packed arbitrarily into cartons.

Lettie completely rearranged her apartment, changing each room to accommodate her son. He would have the larger bedroom, closer to the bathroom. The piano in one corner of the bedroom had a row of family photographs placed on top, replacing authenticity and reality besides his family. To be home was the reinvention of the wheel because there was no one that guided the empiricism of functional caregiving. Lettie pridefully declined the services of a homecare attendant. They calculated together, negotiating his unsteady physique from the bed to the bathroom. Even sitting on the toilet seat with decubiti-covered buttocks required creativity. Donald wanted to make the effort instead of the convenience of a bed pan, which reminded him of humiliations he sustained when hospitalized.

Communication was extremely difficult because Donald was too weak to speak audibly. You would have to get close, hope to hear enough words to gauge the meaning, interpreting the meta-language of the interior of illness. It betrayed that we were looking in, looking out, at each other. Blood is thicker. Lettie and Cynthia understood him better than I. He was life-threateningly dehydrated and coughing spasms precipitated bowel movements. A lot for a woman in her seventies to handle. Impossible without home health-aid support. We had begun to discuss getting additional support.

Donald knocked a coffee cup from his nightstand, letting out a startled scream that a nurse interpreted as campy self-parody, completely missing the point. She said, "Well at least you haven't lost your sense of humor." He replied with surgically precise anger, "Is that what you think it is?" The depth of his anger startled me. His panic was complete and the helplessness total, so a mere accident was something to negotiate.

All of Lettie's life-anxieties projected onto infection control: disinfecting dishes, glasses, utensils, clothing, linen, hands, air. The smell of bleach saturated the apartment. Fear of death converted into material concerns, making living *clean*. At every turn, she busied herself with Donald, fussing over him always, moving an arm or leg too long unexercised, changing his bedding, bringing him food, always hopeful to his face, and prudent when expressing any doubts of his recovery. She was heroic to me, and then the homophobia would emerge.

Lettie committed herself to Donald no matter what, and said she'd bury him as a proud mother no matter what he'd done. What had he done: Did he make love to a lover or a stranger or an army of strangers? No matter. Many of us had adopted the politics of the sexual counterrevolution. Every sex act was an act of rebellion, reported gay liberationists–the more acts, the more revolutionary. Was it surprising that even those heterosexuals who loved us would be unable to transform their own prejudices about homosexuality and hysteria about disease and contagion and death? Lettie was determined to be with Donald, yet unmovable from her Christian fundamentalism. The two existed inextricably, the contradictions of motherlove.

Lettie opened to me almost immediately, telling me of how often she nursed a loved one to the end–her husband and a sister who died in her arms. She told the same stories several times. The narrative description was peculiarly distinct from her identity.

She told me she had tried to warn him. She said, "I said, 'Donald, If you sleep with men, there'll be a price to pay. Be careful.' I would warn him over and over." She would wave a finger at him with one hand while the other would be straightening a blanket, tucking him in. Who am I to scrutinize her? While stories of abandonment were common folklore in the gay community during the early plague years, here was an example of steadfast, constant love.

Her love for Donald was always central: "Donald was my favorite.

He always cared how I looked. [He] would look after me. Once, he took me to Tavern-on-the-Green. It was so special, something I could tell my neighbors about. He knew what was in my heart." The prospect of caring for someone through a long illness was too much. HIV brought another dimension, and she sought for ways to deny the reality of her son's gayness and the disease he struggled to survive.

What to tell the neighbors so they wouldn't ostracize the family, quarantine the apartment, picket the building? There was one trusted neighbor, Birdy, who ran up and down stairs carrying plates of food. Cynthia's children, particularly the younger immunocompromised, were treated with steroids. There were so many questions when little information was available. The therapeutic situation has opened from a dyadic relationship to a systemic one.

March 30, 1988

Donald was sitting up in bed and Lettie hovered over him, feeding spoonful by spoonful. Lettie finished her feeding task, leaving us alone to conduct a session. He motioned to me, whispering as I placed my ear close to him: "I've marked a passage for you to read in that book." I took the book from the top of a bureau and read the yellow-underscored passage:

> Claustrophobia is a reality, and it is a living hell. Fortunately, the metal door that locks one in is not flush with the floor. There is a five-inch space under it. I know a woman who slept for months on the floor, with her head next to that five-inch space, and her arm partially out in the hall. She kept a small unbreakable mirror nearby, and moving it back and forth under the door she could see up and down the corridor. It gave her some feeling of space.[10]

SD: It's a commanding passage. What personal meaning does it have for you?

D: I'm alone here. Not in this room. Alone in reality. The woman Harris described moved the mirror under space to create an illusion. I used a mirror of denial, to create the illusion, the feeling of space and time, when there wasn't AIDS. There's no fantasy left.

I remember in group, we used to talk about how PWAs want to isolate. I suppose that's true, but you know when you feel constantly ill, alien in your own body. It's so very difficult to communicate. You don't think anyone who's healthy can understand what it's like to be dying. Even when you're not indisputably dying. Not that stage. Imminent. You're dying nonetheless. My body is no longer mine; that is, it can't do what it always could. I have my mind, but at times, I feel disoriented, whirling, as if I could forget. No one can understand. It's not a test, some mental impression about so-called giving up. When real events happen, there's no time for a pause, no time to discuss and analyze dreams.

SD: I feel that you're angry at me.

D: I don't know what to expect from you. What are the boundaries?

SD: I remember after you had been a group member for several months, and you confronted me with anger, saying, "You can't understand. You're healthy." Your compliant self tried to retract the accusation, and I tried to hold you to the feeling.

D: I was upset at you, at my father. I felt anger toward my mother, her self-sacrifice: Lettie, the symbol of martyrdom. I'm less willing to devote myself to her cause, but I feel guilty, as if I'm committing betrayal. I'm not myself today.

SD: You're redefining risk.

D: Maybe. I feel danger. That you might bring me forward, and there would be no time left. That you'll leave me at the brink.

SD: That's what you meant by boundaries.

D: Yes. The session will end. The 50-minute hour, and I'm alone to cope with my feelings. The demons.

SD: You're describing feelings of being traumatized when a session ends. Were you frightened when you joined the group, frightened to connect with group members and with myself? You described struggling not to withdraw, not giving into despair. This was partially due to your diagnosis, but not completely.

D: I have always felt that life has been cruel and ruthless. That I have never had a successful male relationship. I guess that I've always felt guilty. Years of serial relationships. I never understood my father's rejection of me. I came up against an inability to accept his death.

SD: You've never felt held.

D: I know that I have, but at times I don't think anyone can understand what I need.

April 15, 1988

Lettie warned me, "Now you be careful when you leave. Someone got stabbed in the hallway just last week." I can't deny feeling vulnerable walking through Harlem–moreso as a gay man than as a caucasian. Having lived for ten years on the Lower East Side, I had learned how to walk with antennae picking up the slightest nuance from any direction. I was mugged four times, twice with a knife at my throat and once with a gun to my head; but the most frightening was being a hostage and methodically terrorized in my own apartment.

It was during the late 1960s, before the current gay liberation movement, but during the War in Vietnam. I was on my way home from dinner in the Village. Walking down Second Avenue and 4th Street, a young man with long hair approached me, asking for some change. He said he was a war resister trying to escape to Canada. He said he hadn't eaten a meal for two days. I brought him back to my apartment, and told him that I could make some phone calls for him, that I had many movement contacts.

My roommate, John, was asleep. I told him that I would go to a grocery store to buy some food when he pulled a knife, no amateur's weapon. He told me to awaken John, and he proceeded to take and demand anything of value. He even took records, saying how much he liked the Beatles. To make certain that we were aware of his power over us, he called us faggots and told us to kiss each other. He stood over us and sneered. Our holding each other was to him an act of complete humiliation, a punishment, mocking us.

Once, when I was walking on St. Marks Place, someone called me a faggot from across the street. My feelings were similar to those described by Marilyn French:

> The moral price of such oppression is overwhelming. I do not speak here of the oppressed, who are of course deformed,

corrupted or destroyed by such a system, but of the oppressors. . . . Fear leads to hate, which corrupts. But perhaps most important, the character of the dominator is defined by the oppressed. All that the oppressed is, the dominator can deny being: this is symbolic truth, contradicted by reality.[11]

I caught myself wishing that he was dead, and then became appalled at the thought. I wouldn't want to live in that man's head.

April 19, 1988

A certain mystery: the virus has confined itself to a community. Initially, we hypothesized that we merely had contact with the virus first. We were traumatized, but a unity emerged past our own images of self-loathing and homophobia so we could care for our own. Why has this infection remained in our community? Will time answer this question? Do we *have* time?

Donald was readmitted to a hospital. Despite the inherent fears a hospitalization conjures, I felt relief. I intervened on several levels to get the hospital to take him. Donald had faced imminent death several times and was in and out of the medical intensive care unit (MICU). The rhythm and sounds of a MICU are different from those on a medical or surgical floor—the human replaced by the technological. The respirator moans with its own regularity. The MICU of a hospital is the battlefield, the meeting ground of life versus death. It is the precipice.

Donald is on a respirator in a coma. Even when his eyes are open, they don't focus. We stood vigil. There were several PWAs on the unit, and I noticed one women in her seventies passing aimlessly around the floor. This mother was typical—she hadn't known her son was gay. She hadn't known he was sick. Lettie, sensing the women's despair, moved to speak to her and share her experience as one mother to another.

I was alone with Donald holding his hand. I told him, "We all love you. You must know that." It had been a year since his first hospitalization, and I recalled conferring with the physician at the municipal hospital. The first contact at Metropolitan was a Slavic physician who had a limited understanding of English. I introduced myself as Donald's therapist, feeling the conversation slip away even before I could identify the patient and why I was calling.

Why am I calling? It makes exquisite and logical sense to be in touch with the physician, and of course to get a diagnosis. She says, "Why are you calling?" I try again to explain, "I'm Donald's therapist. Might we sit for a moment?" She replied, "Let me suggest that you call Dr. R. at 2453." She's gone. Dr. R. agrees to meet me, and we sat together in a small, borrowed office. He's Puerto Rican, and speaks little English, but we're able to communicate. He lists acute diarrhea, cryptosporidium, tuberculosis, herpes, salmonella, prostatic abscess, and candidiasis. "By the way, I'm the intern and I leave this case today. There'll be someone else tomorrow." I thanked him for his time.

With physicians overwhelmed by medical practice in the hospital environment–particularly in underequipped, poorly staffed city facilities–it takes tenacious negotiation to get what you need. Most often, what you need is a moment. Time. As simple as that. Time spent with a patient follows from accounting principles. For example, surgeons average about $1000 per hour. An internist who spends an hour counseling a patient to alter his lifestyle to avoid future surgery will be lucky if he can bill $60.

You mustn't ask for what you need. Instead, you negotiate an agreement without giving in, which is best achieved by putting yourself in their shoes. Interns receive insufficient supervision, lack of support, and are underappreciated; but most crucially, they are learning how to practice medicine. They are also learning about their patients. America spends $425 billion on health care, but few understand why it costs so much and why it is changing so fast. Most often, malpractice is a direct outcome of profiteering by insurance companies, lawyers, various cottage industries (such as expert witnesses), and increased awareness by the consumer of professional accountability of services rendered. However, the rise in malpractice suits are also a result of the increased strain in the relationship between doctor and patient.

Added to the complexity of the hospital system is the homophobic stigmatization of the person with HIV disease within the institution. The notion of confidentiality of hospital records is a misnomer: records are accessible to most of the health-care workers within the hospital. Doctors, nurses, and social workers routinely request the chart of any patient who is currently within the hospital, or they may request the records of past patients. They may examine records of patients who are not under their professional jurisdiction, and the information contained in those records is summarily relayed to agencies of federal, state, and local governments, as well as to insurance companies.

Homosexuality is notated on the records of a patient with HIV disease. Sexual orientation is not referenced for any other patient within the hospital. The classification does not facilitate any medical diagnosis or treatment; it only serves to label the patient. Assumptions are then unconsciously made about the way(s) in which the patient with HIV disease contracted the disease. During interdisciplinary rounds at a major New York hospital, an intern said, when referring to a gay male HIV disease patient, that she couldn't recall the patient being discussed. Then a flash of recognition crossed her face. She said, "Oh yes. Now I remember him. I took a bone marrow sample from his back once." Remarking on the irony of knowing a person by a part, she continued, "I only knew him from the rear." The chief resident of the oncology unit, not to miss an opportunity to express his disdain toward the patients he must serve, continued, "You and about another several dozen men." I recollect a physician noting on a patient's medical chart: "This unfortunate woman with AIDS performed fellatio on rooftops."

April 30, 1988

Donald hadn't attended group for several months, but nonetheless his presence endured, and a couple of members undertook to remain in contact. It is commonplace that the illness of a group member reverberates to the extent that other members consider themselves mirrored by the ailing member, and they feel urgency and defenselessness. For two-and-a-half years, I had been the co-therapist for the HIV disease therapy group, and there was no one left alive from the original 12-member group configuration. The long-term members observed the debilitation and later death of many of the participants.

Elemental to an open-ended HIV disease group is the cyclical and recurrent episodes of disabling medical complexities, dying, and death of its members. The group undergoes progressive stimuli associated with traumatic circumstances. Even nonanxious members suffer distress confronted with the recurrence of disturbing circumstances and experience the incessant potentiality of danger and cope with adaptation to uncertainty. Individuals may pursue a group with omnipotent thoughts, magical thinking, and equate therapy with protection from the progression of HIV disease. A member feels conflict when attempting to resolve fear when confronted with existence juxtaposed against the emphasis placed on so-called positive thinking by practioners:

> If you have AIDS or an AIDS-related disease, don't just make your goal to get back to where you were before you got ill. This was not a well place to be, or you would never have been able to get this disease. With the incubation period being so long, it is as if, after you have been exposed to it, the disease sits around patiently in your system waiting for you to run your immune system down so it can then take over.[12]

The intrapsychic repercussion to group members frequently manifests with resistance to atypical group attendance. Debilitated members experience shame, feeling responsible for a relapse in their condition, or they believe they have an unspoken moral obligation to protect other members.

May 2, 1988

Ram Dass warns that there are intrinsic contradictions within helping:

> We define boundaries of time and space for our involvement. . . . Careful boundaries assure that suffering won't spill over into the rest of our lives. These may be necessary; we all have other commitments. As often as not, however, they are artificially contrived to ward off that loss of control which so threatens and frightens the mind.[13]

My role as therapist included hospital sessions, touching, and a changed therapeutic situation and environment.

Donald remained on the respirator for two weeks, before a transfer from the MICU to a single-bed room the previous week. I felt helpless to ameliorate Donald's life-threatening circumstance. The therapeutic method primarily involves language, so the process without verbal communication is enigmatic. Treatment of critically incapacitated individuals is discomfiting, because it transcends language interpretation. The system appears phenomenological in the immediate experience of the therapist. The therapist who works with the very ill or dying need not yield when confronted with the barriers that demand the reconstruction of experience without language. Phenomenology is not talking about reality; instead, it is the restructuring of reality into experience. The transferential context is recast into the phenomenological, and I had to assure myself that my presence in the MICU was meaningful, though Donald was often unconscious or disoriented.

Without a doctor to consult, it was almost impossible to balance my fears for Donald's health against the progression of the disease or to know what action would be appropriate. He was deteriorating, but I had no previous experience by which to judge. During this critical interlude, Dr. Norman and I became confidants, and I manipulated my schedule so hospital visits coincided with his late-afternoon shift. I became conscious of my rescue fantasies with Dr. Norman assuming a white-knight role. I refocused my attention to support his work, commenting on the difficulties of providing care for desperately ill people. I felt guilty, concerned that Donald noticed the burgeoning friendship, especially since Dr. Norman was important to his care.

May 7, 1988

I read this passage from James Baldwin today:

> It is a very grave matter to be forced to imitate a people for whom you know—which is the price of your performance and survival—you do not exist. It is hard to imitate a people whose existence appears, mainly, to be made tolerable by their bottomless gratitude that they are not, thank heaven, *you*.[14]

June 28, 1988

Today was the Gay Pride march.

The particular use of language, let alone concepts, is a principal method exercised to indicate power. When one group dominates another–as in the family unit, in public, or in corporate life–language metaphorically conveys approval or disapproval, which can be subtle or evasive. Extended to their logical conclusion, disapprovals can be life-threatening. Therefore, during the early development of an oppressed people's consciousness, the *word* assumes a position of centrality: self-definition is the process that uses language as one of its most vital expressions, representing historical development–the initial awakening from powerlessness to political movement. Language becomes the analysis of a person's history into affirmation and myth-making; in its purist sensibility, it leads to self-criticism and activism.

Numbers of gays suggested the term "faggot" as our identification, and the reasons were twofold:

1. Taking an epithet hurled against us and making it suit our purpose. The affirmation of "faggot" would have shock value for gays who would have to think through and experience emotionally, transforming the negative into the positive.
2. Using the term "faggot" would be the historic recognition of our having supported women's rebellion against the patriarchy during the Middle Ages, when gay men were used as kindling and mixed with bundles of wood bound together (i.e., faggots) and burned at the feet of witches. However, "gay" became the term of self-identification; imperfect as the word may be, it was the result of our collective "town meeting."

We began to tell our gaystory by digging into our personal unconscious and combining it with theory. Many gay men aligned themselves with patriarchal definitions of gender; masculinity as "power-over" became the ideal. Others, aligning with the feminist interpretation of sexism as the root of oppression, brought their experience to different conclusions. Their writing attempted to experiment syntactically with the feminist axiom that the personal is political.

Syntactical experimentation attempts to represent experience in a nonlinear, nonmasculinist way. Syntax in most Western language represents a power relationship: a doer does to a done-to. Syntax (along with the pronoun) is the part of language most resistant to change. Yet there have been periods in history in which reflective, meditative, associative writing was popular–writing that did not so much narrate as convey experience.

July 2, 1988

Until today, I've been hiding, unable to face my feelings, my mortality. I stubbed my toe in a rage and felt I did it to myself.

> It has been advocated that patients be given credit for the possible discernment of intercurrent instances of physical or emotional involvements in the life of the psychiatrist. It should also be kept in mind, however, that patients are people absorbed in their own troubles who are trained to look upon the psychiatrist as a participant observer of their difficulties. The attention given by the patient to the life and the problems of the psychiatrist should therefore not be overestimated, either.[15]

It's too painful to acknowledge the deep disappointment. Curt is doing poorly. Tom's funeral was yesterday. Donald wrote in his journal:

> On a wall in my hospital room is a pencil and charcoal drawing of Jesus at the crucifixion given to me by my dear friend Charles. I've often identified with this picture: the suffering, his mystical depth, his Semitic blackness, all project many aspects of myself.

Bob's been hospitalized again. Donald was transferred out of the MICU, only to be transferred back after a day. My relationship with Mark is untenable. No job prospects. I'm feeling there's something wrong with me. Something wrong with everyone else.

July 12, 1988

Sitting in St. John the Divine. There are memorial headstones of Whitman and Dickinson. I overheard two women say that this wing of the Cathedral will not be complete in our lifetime, much less the entire structure.

I haven't wanted to think of Donald today. His presence has changed my life and there's no going back to before. Bed sores cover his body. Pure weight. His 6'3" tall and slender presence must have once graced a disco floor.

I have to make a trip to Bloomingdales to buy Curt, a friend, a pair of pajamas–he's going into NYU Medical Center tomorrow. In addition to KS, they suspect he may have PCP. (Eudora Welty describes the moment as a "feeling awaiting a gesture." Life is full of these moments). Curt wept in my arms today, saying, "Nobody understands. No one can hear me. It's as if I were somewhere else already." We walked through the Village and brought back a couple of bunches of lilacs, filling several vases in his living room.

August 15, 1988

My health is off. It's been a week-long virus. I imagine it's terminal. I thought caregivers were exempt. A more accurate diagnosis would be HIV-disease anxiety. I joined the ranks of the worried well.

August 20, 1988

I went to a shiatsu lecture/demonstration. It was an introduction to a philosophic and practical holistic approach to reality. An old CCNY classmate ran the session. It was in his apartment. There were pillows on the floor, and the walls were covered with bits of madras, wood, and relics–all symbolic and filled with meaning. He ran a crystal pendulum over my body, using a quick circular motion. If he reached a trouble spot, the pendulum would slow down. Then he could identify a particular organ as potentially diseased. It was hokey, but the demonstration was impressive, and, of course, entirely accurate.

From there, I went to see Donald. He's eating solid foods. Mitchell died last week. We spent some time together on Fire Island last summer. In his drinking days, he must have been able to shine a cocktail party. His wit could slice paper.

August 30, 1988

Isn't it true that one of the most potent romantic icons of this culture–that of Rhett and Scarlett going up the mansion steps–is essentially a rape scene? Take me away from all this. Indeed! The answer will come. Something. Just listen. Feminist theologian Mary Daly said: "It is the creative potential itself in human beings that is the image of God."

September 3, 1988

Donald's sister, Cynthia, and I struggled for one hour changing Donald's shit-soaked sheets. We pushed and pulled, exhausting Donald. Why didn't I take the Red Cross training?

There was a memorial for Tom tonight. I miss him.

September 15, 1988

I had coffee with John, a friend. A friend of his is HIV-infected. He spoke with tears running down his cheeks, his coffee cup shaking on its saucer. He described his friend in detail: "We'd had sex many years ago, before I got sober. I stopped hearing John, trying to recreate the scene, to recall the event through an alcoholic haze, a blackout. What did we do sexually?"

October 1, 1988

Cynthia asked me, "Will you see this through to the end?" I responded without hesitation, "Yes."

October 17, 1988

Donald's gaining some weight. It's been a week since I've seen him, and he told me about his loneliness. It's rare for him to express an emotion so directly. Something is beginning to grow between us, a connection. It isn't that mystical.

His knowledge of classical music is extensive. The radio station WNCN is always on. I have this image of Donald coming out of a coma, turning to me and his first words are: "Beethoven had a revolutionary importance in the transition from the classical to romantic movements." I think that actually did happen earlier, when last rites had been said for him the last time.

October 31, 1988

Donald is lying under the Metropolitan Museum of Art's Van Gogh Arles poster, which a friend hung on a bare wall. His room is another part of the planet, some other reality.

> This time it's just simply my bedroom, only here color is to do everything, and giving by its simplification a grander style to things, is to be suggestive here of rest or of sleep in general. In a word, looking at the picture ought to rest the brain, or that the imagination. . . . I shall work on it again all day, but you see how simple the conception is. The shadows and the cast shadows are suppressed; it is painted in free flat tints like the Japanese prints.[16]

We look at each other for long periods, and I try to communicate nonverbally. Most of our contacts have been nonverbal over the last several months. It's very difficult for Donald to speak. When he makes the effort, I often have to ask him to repeat himself.

He asked me to butter his bread. Without his glasses, it's hard for him to do anything, he explained. The hospital lost his glasses when he was transferred back and forth from the MICU. A tooth was also lost in the transfer from one floor to another. He asked me to butter his bread—as if it were an intimate request and performing it would be a symbol of openness.

There's no future in this room. We don't speak of going to the movies together or catching an exhibition at the Metropolitan Museum. It's only the present, each day. The future is the next visit, the plan of it. The future is dim.

November 6, 1988

Donald's Gay Men's Health Crisis (GMHC) buddy gave him a haircut. The buddy, Bob, told me: "Nothing's easy in that hospital.

Nothing. He's able to turn his head. He feeds himself with effort; most else is impossible. The front of his haircut looks okay, but I'm afraid the back is choppy. It was hard to lift his head and cut simultaneously, but there had been no one to help. It reminded me of how I paint rooms around furniture. I never moved a refrigerator. I once painted my living room with the piano in place. I want to change. God, this is painful.

"He wanted to get into a chair for the haircut, and I felt badly that I didn't acquiesce, but I thought of an earlier time when it had taken three of us to get him back into bed after a spell in the chair. I was so afraid he'd fall. He'd done that once, breaking off another front-tooth cap. I'm used to the spaces between his front teeth. I think of him all the time."

November 25, 1988

The intrapsychic life of gay men has been tempered by HIV disease, so images of suffering, death, and dying are universal during post-epidemic existence. I ran into an old friend, Ron, outside Donald's room. Ron was comforting a friend whose lover was dying. The friend starting singing a parody of Leslie Gore's song "It's My Party": "It's my party and I'll die if I want to. . . ." Ron's friend admitted, "Jim's ready, but I can't let go."

December 23, 1988

It's an unusual group session. One member said of a new boy-friend, "He's to die for."

> Sex is worth dying for. It is in this (strictly historical) sense that sex is indeed imbued with the death instinct. When a long while ago the West discovered love, it bestowed on it a value high enough to make death acceptable; nowadays it is sex that claims this equivalence, the highest of all.[17]

The room was calm, as if silence equals death. Sex equals death. The members spoke of sex and sexual addiction.

> Within the addictive system, sexual experience becomes the reason for being–the primary relationship for the addict. For

the addict, the sexual experience is the source of nurturing, focus of energy, and origin of excitement. It is the remedy for pain and anxiety, the reward for success, and means for maintaining emotional balance.[18]

I think the dictionary definition of compulsion has to do with constant preoccupation, self-absorption, self-preoccupation. Frankel calls narcotization "spiritual anesthesia":

> Suffering and trouble belong to life as much as fate and death. None of these can be subtracted from life without destroying its meaning. To subtract trouble, death, fate, and suffering from life would mean stripping life of its form and shape. Only under the hammer blows of fate, in the white heat of suffering, does life gain shape and form.[19]

It will pass, this latest fantasy of being rescued.

June 8, 1989

My friend Linda and I saw Diana Ross get out of a black Corniche and slink into the Sherry Netherlands Tower. She glanced once in my direction, almost crossing my path. It was the look of someone who checks danger when a stranger gets too close. The paranoia is reserved for those who walk city streets or for celebrities anywhere.

We had seen a production of Eugene O'Neill's *Moon for the Misbegotten*. When we passed through Rockefeller Plaza, walking home on a summer night, it had become the war zone. DMZ. Cops. TV cameras. A gunman was shooting from a window, holding his ex-girlfriend hostage in a deserted office building high above the skating rink. Prometheus Unbound.

June 10, 1989

Donald's taken a turn–he's running a fever of 106°. An ulcer on his hip had become abscessed. Pam, a nurse on the floor, cares for Donald with extraordinary love. They knew each other as children. Went to the same church. May have dated once.

She said that he wasn't receiving proper care, and I decided to take some action. I would meet the intern, the resident, and their superiors in the hierarchy. To make my presence known. To walk the corridors with a sense of ease and authority. To pace conspicuously on the floor. To find out where things are kept: paper towels, pads, tape. To let it be known there were those who cared for this man–this gay, black man with HIV disease.

June 12, 1989

I awakened Donald to let him know I was in his room, but he couldn't visit. He fell back to sleep. I feel so powerless.

June 14, 1989

Donald has pulled through this one. They debrided the infected ulcer on his hip. It required several transfusions. A severed nerve. He almost bled to death. Once again, the priest said last rites.

> The medical establishment has become a major threat to health. The disabling impact of professional control over medicine has reached the proportions of an epidemic. *Iatrogenesis*, the name for this new epidemic, comes from *iatros*, the Greek word for 'physician,' and *genesis*, meaning 'origin.' . . . Although almost everyone believes that at least one of his friends would not be alive and well except for the skill of a doctor, there is in fact no evidence of any direct relationship between this mutation of sickness and the so-called progress of medicine.[20]

Donald can barely move his head or raise his arms. He can't move his legs at all. The room looks like afterbirth: there are signs of struggle everywhere. The transfusion apparatus is still on the bureau top. Tubes and bottles and blood.

I'm in a rage that they haven't cleaned up the room. I reported it to the patient representative's office.

June 16, 1989

It's been months since Donald's seen daylight. When will he go home?

June 18, 1989

I'm feeling very militant. I want to learn to be more assertive at the hospital. To create a new awareness that will get the job done. That's Ron's phrase: "To Get The Job Done."

June 20, 1989

A message from Curt tonight on the answering machine: "I love you." KS is spreading to his internal organs, a very dangerous development.

June 15, 1989

The complaints I made at the hospital have brought some results. The room is meticulous. The transfusion apparatus has been cleared out of the room after being there for a week. Some nurse had the audacity to tell me they were letting it sit there until it was no longer infectious. He's even got a new covered waste disposal, in chrome no less.

Lettie brought a pair of eyeglasses for Donald. One homophobic nurse said to her, "What's the use of making him new glasses?"

I must keep Pam in view; she approaches Donald with patience, dedication, dignity, and a sense of responsibility. I'm learning to question, trying to balance each decision and take appropriate actions.

I think romance–falling in love–has little to do with the ethics of love–responsibility and choice. The act of love. How exciting. It can redirect the course of my actions and change my feelings. Even if we are powerless to change our sexual responses and attractions, we can make choices.

Donald is doing better, but I can't imagine what that means in the literal sense. HIV disease is an enigma. Often, someone will ask me how Donald is, and I never know how to answer. I brought him tissues, several issues of *GQ*, magic markers, a drawing pad, and an alarm clock.

He has no coordinative ability. It's very frustrating. When he couldn't get the cap off the magic marker, he lost control–first anger then tears. He began his first work of art: some scribbling in a corner of a page. He signed it with his initials. I suggested that he might want to date the work. He's going to have to relearn coordination. There really won't be time for that, though; this disease won't reverse itself. Living will. Should he draw a living will?

I remembered a scene in his room, with Lettie and the patient representative. We stood over his bed; he was barely conscious. I explained that the cards from the bank, when signed, gave Lettie power of attorney. He understood. I asked him to sign the cards. He refused. We all stood in disbelief. Donald gave no explanation, only an adamant refusal. I tried to explain to him that giving his mother power of attorney was merely a convenience, so she could have access to his bank accounts (especially since we anticipated the receipt of his first Social Security check–with retroactivity). He was emphatic: "No!" Finally, he gave in. But he was unable to steady his trembling hand to sign the cards. I held the pen and cards for him, guiding him through a signature.

June 18, 1989

Donald said to me, "I must be boring." I burst into laughter. "You may be many things, but boring isn't one of them." A little test. It's his version of Cynthia's "Will you see this through to the end?"

June 20, 1989

Donald said, "If I can't accept myself, then I can't accept God."

June 25, 1989

I marched with three friends in the Gay Liberation Day parade. Many marchers carried signs bearing the names of deceased friends and lovers, bearing them down Fifth Avenue to the Village.

June 27, 1989

I've been sick with a cold all week and haven't been able to see Donald.

June 30, 1989

A client in Alcoholics Anonymous (AA) pointed out to me that the organization's meditation book says miracles are changes in our personality.

July 4, 1989

For Donald, freedom is being taken off the IV.

August 12, 1989

Donald was taken out to the solarium on a stretcher. It's the first time since March that he's felt a breeze on his skin, sun in his eyes. To smell the air. To see Gabriel on St. John the Divine a few rooftops away. Lettie said it was a joy for both of them.

September 4, 1989

The world is no longer of any consequence to Donald, and he spoke of quiet acceptance of death. He's been separated from his possessions so long that he doesn't know whether some items survived the move from the Bronx to Harlem. When was the last time he stroked the keys of the upright piano, playing Beethoven's Sonata No. 4?

Life is letting go.

Donald spent hours waiting to be X-rayed, sitting uncomfortably on a cold metal table. His body is in rebellion. When we spoke of the wait, he shuddered. Then with a smile, he said, "I want to be buried in a large, comfortable coffin with satin cushions." I said, "I want to be cremated and my ashes thrown over Christopher Street– the Village as homeland."

September 16, 1989

The GMHC buddy washed Donald's hair. He told me later, "I didn't want to visit, but despite the feelings, I showed up. I stood at the 79th Street bus stop, wanting to return home. I almost called Donald from a pay phone and gave him some outrageous excuse: a ceiling collapsed, a pipe burst, I pulled my back, I'm locked out, I'm locked in. I don't want to visit.

"The air is clear and smells fresh and I can conjure the hospital smell. 'Fuck this,' I tell myself, 'you don't have to do what your feelings dictate. Feelings are not fact.' I boarded the bus."

September 17, 1989

After many months, Donald has an erection. He's been visited by Angel, a mythical companion. He unburdened himself by telling me sexual anecdotes.

November 11, 1989

Each time I walk down the street by the hospital, I'm reminded of the miracle of the unexpected. Even if I'd sent a scout ahead to chart the territory, there would be no way to prepare for the journey to Donald's room, except to make it.

Donald and I listened to Al Jarreau together. We closed our eyes, and we went to some other place. At first separate, then together. Away from red plastic bags, antiseptic smells, catheters, and despair. Away.

I decided to walk along the park when I left, rather than take the direct route to the subway. It was raining, a fine mist, and damp leaves covered the street.

April 7, 1990

It's Easter Sunday, and I took a volume of Walt Whitman off the shelf, deciding to carry it with me to the hospital. I had not read him in years–never fully appreciating him or accepting his importance as the gay poet laureate. I began reading *Calamus* on the bus ride to the hospital. My God, the beauty of the poetry was astounding. The work was appropriate to our time–particularly the sense of deep yearning and disappointment–and there were moments of loving triumph, the recognition of the "love of comrades" as a bold revolutionary gesture.

It has only been twice during the year that I've known Donald to

wear anything other than hospital pajamas. Today, he wore a blue-
and-gold-striped t-shirt; it made a profound difference. He looked
handsome. Less like a victim.

I asked Donald if I could read him some Whitman. He took the
book from me with a hungry gesture. He turned to "Song of Myself," and said that he'd read to me. He let out a bellowing sound
and began to chant the poetry from a section he knows well.

The sound is musical–and in a style that I'm certain Whitman
would approve of. Donald looks at me for approval, feeling a moment of self-consciousness, but he went on chanting. I asked if I
could read some to him. My style is different. I read the short poem
"Of You Whom I Often and Silently Come": "Little you know the
subtle electric fire for your sake is playing within me."

June 6, 1990

A nurse called me outside Donald's room and said he is depressed this week. She asks, "Isn't there anything positive about
AIDS you can tell him?" She is genuinely concerned. She's heard a
tape by Louise Hay. Another patient was listening to the tape until
his Walkman was stolen from his room. I felt such ambivalence
speaking to her, knowing that the nurses on this floor are known
throughout the hospital as being burned out. And yet, I wonder if
there are some changes in Donald's attitude. I begin to question
him, to draw him out. He was himself. I wonder what the nurse saw.
Lettie was short with the nurse when the depression was mentioned:
"He's got a lot to be depressed about."

The Ancient Craft of Caring for the Ill. Again at the Cathedral of
St. John the Divine. When, at the end of the nineteenth century,
plans for the Cathedral began, that part of upper Broadway became
known as the home of three great institutions: St. Luke's Hospital,
Columbia University, and St. John the Divine.

The Cathedral is stone upon stone, unsupported by any steel
infrastructure. It's being built by community labor, using the medieval apprenticeship method, with stonecutters taught the ancient
craft. The basic building blocks of the Cathedral are intricate cor-
nices.

I sat in the Cathedral to wait.

Hospital waiting, on the other hand, is like no other. It must have been hours turning to days. The doctors are characteristically vague–not unlike the Wizard of Oz working the scene from behind a puff of smoke; but they have been notably absent from my experience with Donald. They've always required persistent tracking down. When they're newly on the case, their knowledge is sketchy and they're unwilling to offer much. When you track them down, weeks have already passed, and you forget the crisis that warranted your seeking help.

June 17, 1990

It occurs to me that the one question I've never asked Donald (and God knows I've asked many) is, "How do you stand it?" What gives you the courage? The situation, the absolute confinement, the isolation, the burden of guilt, the responsibility. What psychological adjustment has given you the strength? Enduring the unendurable. The subject of art. Or, on second thought, is it the action beyond despair that makes the subject? What could be the purpose? Struggle rests outside, in the realm of fantasy projection. It can't be. There must be something uniquely human at work here.

June 23, 1990

Donald dies.

August 1, 1990

It's 3 a.m. on Fire Island. I'm listening to the ocean, not an environmental compact disc, but the authentic ocean.

REFERENCE NOTES

1. Travis L. Peterson and Josephine H. Stewart, "The Lesbian or Gay Couple as a Family: Principles for Building Satisfying Relationships," in *Lesbian and Gay Issues: A Resource Manual for Social Workers* (Silver Spring, MD: National Association of Social Workers, 1985), p. 28.

2. Howard Waitzkin and Theron Britt, "A Critical Theory of Medical Discourse: How Patients and Health Professionals Deal with Social Problems," *International Journal of Health Services*, Volume 19, Number 4, p. 595.

3. Lynn Hoffman, *The Foundations of Family Therapy* (New York: Basic Books, 1981), p. 4.

4. R. D. Laing, *The Politics of the Family.*

5. Erich Lindemann, "Symptomatology and Management of Acute Grief," *American Journal of Psychiatry*, 101: 141-148, 1944.

6. Erik H. Erikson, *Childhood and Society* (New York, W. W. Norton & Company, 1963), pp. 252-253.

7. Norman Cousins, *Anatomy of an Illness* (New York: Bantam Books, 1979), pp. 86-87.

8. Ivan Illich, *Gender* (New York: Pantheon, 1982), p. 109.

9. Lillian B. Rubin, *Quiet Rage: Bernie Goetz in a Time of Madness* (New York: Farrar, Straus & Giroux, 1986), p. 154.

10. Jean Harris, *Stranger in Two Worlds* (New York: Zebra Books, 1986), p. 306.

11. Marilyn French, *Beyond Power: On Women, Men, and Morals* (New York: Summit Books, 1985), p. 137.

12. Louise L. Hay, *The AIDS Book: Creating a Positive Approach* (Santa Monica: Hay House, 1988), p. 114.

13. Ram Dass, *How Can I Help?* (New York: Alfred A. Knopf, 1985), p. 59.

14. James Baldwin, *The Evidences of Things Not Seen* (New York: Holt, Rinehart & Winston, 1985), p. 44.

15. Frieda Fromm-Reichmann, *Principles of Intensive Psychotherapy* (Chicago: The University of Chicago Press, 1960), p. 213.

16. "Van Gogh's Bedroom," *Van Gogh in Arles*, The Metropolitan Museum of Art.

17. Michel Foucault, *The History of Sexuality* (New York: Pantheon Books, 1978).

18. Patrick Carnes, PhD, *The Sexual Addiction* (Minneapolis: CompCare Publications, 1983), p. 17.

19. Viktor E. Frankl, *The Doctor & The Soul* (New York: Vintage Books, 1973), p. 111.

20. Ivan Illich, *Medical Nemesis* (New York: Pantheon, 1976).

Chapter 5

Hocus Pocus Is Coming

Dilegua, o notte! Tramontate, stelle!
Tramontate, stelle! All'alba vincero!
Vincero! Vincero!

Giacomo Puccini, *Turandot*

THE HEN CROWS (OR, THE CONSTRUCTION OF SEX AND GENDER)

Although research on sexual identity dates back to the nineteenth century, the Kinsey studies of the late 1940s brought revived attention to the issue. Currently, the HIV disease pandemic invigorated new scientific research into questions concerning the etiology of same-sex identity. During this century, many theorists proposed biological arguments such as genetic transmission or hormonal imbalances; others advanced sociocultural arguments; and some offered a configuration that included a sequelae of each developmental and genetic constituents. American culture subscribes to a masculinist doctrine of resolute gender stereotypes, which have been increasingly disputed by women. An amplified meaning of homophobia is the postulate that diminished masculinity correlates with homosexuality. The expression of gay-male sexual identity is not a pro forma contradiction of, or in opposition to, stereotypes of gender-defined roles. Instead, confronting masculinism is an informed political declaration and a personal commitment.

The characterization of same-sex relatedness as psychopathological and the corollary presumptions of secondary personality disorders and negative characterizations of functioning is not astonishing to nearly all gay men and lesbians who have been submitted to therapies of cure or tacit acceptance. What is incredulous, however, is the fascination–within Western, particularly American, culture– with the subject. All questions that introduce an etiological theory of sexual identity are dispiriting, because as Sedgwick recognizes:

> Advice on how to make sure your kids turn out gay, not to mention your students, your parishioners, your therapy clients, or your military subordinates, is less ubiquitous than you might think. By contrast, the scope of institutions whose programmatic undertaking is to prevent the development of gay people is unimaginably large.[1]

Physicians, psychiatrists, psychotherapists, and scientific researchers practice homophobic assumptions, at times conscious, often unconscious, as the guardians of the psychological and physical well-being of gay men particularly during the HIV pandemic. Many gay men have not unconditionally reconciled their sexual identity, and they are psychologically vulnerable. Medically, they face a frighteningly difficult disease to manage and are forced into a constrained alliance with biomedical institutions that have life-and-death authority over their lives.

The heterosexist culture largely subscribes to a fundamentalist, ecclesiastic/sociopolitical dictum whose mission is the eradication of an authentic lesbian or gay-male identity. During the twentieth century, a concomitant obsession with same-sex relatedness accompanied the steadfast ascent of medical and psychiatric institutions. The principal reason for research into causality was to impose curative interventions and treatment. Unquestionably, there is no analogous investigation into the etiology of heterosexuality.[2]

The examination of medicine and psychiatry in relation to its view of same-sex relatedness occurs within a historical continuum that has seen decades of intense and increasing questioning by such oppressed peoples as women, gays, lesbians, and African-Americans. Lewes criticizes the psychoanalytic failure in interpreting homosexuality "at least partly [as] the result of an initial gynecophobic stance."[3] He attributes gay men with similar psychic characteristics as women, which is a mistake politically. The ferment challenged white heterosexual male domination of medical sciences and generated new theories of human development, sexuality, gender, and relationship. These pioneering second-wave feminists included Phyllis Chesler, Mary Daly, Kate Millet, Shulamith Firestone, Robin Morgan, Adrienne Rich, and Naomi Weinstein. Nearly all of them disputed the so-called diagnosis and therapeutic that dismissed women's oppression:

> Unalterably born into one group or another, every subject is forced, moment to moment, to prove he or she is, in fact, male or female by deference to the ascribed characteristics of masculine and feminine.[4]

Actually, anatomical experimentation to determine the morphological boundaries of sexual bipotentiality date back to the eighteenth century, when John Hunter transplanted the testicles of a cock into the abdomen of a hen. The vivisection demonstrated "masculine morphological traits of a rooster, and presumably, also, the brain-mediated behavioral trait of crowing, could be induced to appear in a hen."[5]

In 1989, an autopsy study conducted in Amsterdam examined 16 male brains–six heterosexual and ten gay. All subjects had died from HIV disease. Scientists measured the suprachiasmic nuclei from the anterior hypothalamus (the hypothalamus, located in the forebrain, contains a nerve center linking the nervous and endocrine systems that control emotions and sexuality). They discovered the hypothalamus was larger in the brain samples from the gay-male subjects than those in the heterosexual men. These early findings appeared to vindicate biological or congenital determinism as an etiological theory of same-sex relatedness. Gender developmental theorists made immediate counterclaims to the research finding, proclaiming the unlikelihood of suprachiasmic nucleus as the sole factor in sexual identity: "It is more likely that it might be a locus of male/female bipotentiality, the resolution of which is governed ultimately by input from other sources."[6]

In a similar study in 1991, Dr. Simon LeVay, a neurobiologist, confirmed an identical finding during an investigation conducted at the Salk Institute in La Jolla, California. In this research, LeVay examined thin slices of autopsied brain tissue from 19 homosexual men, 16 presumed heterosexual men, and six women also thought to have been heterosexual. He focused on a particular segment of the hypothalamus known as the interstitial nucleus of the anterior hypothalamus, which previous studies had shown to differ significantly between men and women. Measuring the volume of cells in the region, he found that in the heterosexual men, it averaged about the size of a large grain of sand; but in the women and the gay men it was almost undetectable.[7]

During the 1950s and 1960s, endocrinologists submitted hormonal imbalance theories to account for same-sex relatedness. They hypothesized that the hormone testosterone, a physical substance, is the psychological embodiment of masculinity. The assumption rests with the premise that gay males are less masculine than heterosexual males because they have decreased testosterone levels. This proves not to be the case, since hormone measurements demonstrate no variance between gay males, heterosexuals, or bisexuals.[8] Further, masculinity is not observed within, or defined by, measuring physical substances in the body. Due to the failure of studies of prenatal neuroendocrine influences on sexual orientation and biological determinism, researchers about-faced, returning to the importance of a model based on interactions between nature, nurture, and sexual orientation.[9]

During the decade before the modern gay liberation movement, which began in 1969, numerous institutions–such as the American Psychiatric Association (APA)–became the focus of political protest. Activists challenged the APA because it categorized homosexuality in psychiatric nomenclature as "pathological," a sociopathic personality disturbance. For three years, intense struggle ensued to eliminate homosexuality from the *Diagnostic and Statistical Manual* (DSM). The controversy raged among factions within membership of the APA, and protest persevered from the lesbian and gay community.

The DSM-III retained homosexuality diagnostically, distinguishing ego-syntonic and ego-dystonic adjustment. In 1987, with the publication of the DSM-III-R, the APA expunged homosexuality as a diagnostic category. The Final Task Report on Homosexuality endorsed by the APA, stated: "Homosexual orientation is no more related to mental illness or psychological problems in general than is heterosexuality."[10] The report described any therapeutic attempt to proselytize lesbians and gay men into heterosexuality as "ethically questionable." This decision was not well-received. Some claimed–from a well-motivated, humanitarian effort to protect the homosexual person from legal and social repression–that the APA's Nomenclature Committee *has cast doubt on the entire procedure of psychiatric diagnosis* [emphasis added]."[11] The question of designating lesbian and gay men as inherently neurotic and pathological is crucial for obvious sociopolitical and ethical reasons. Such definitions guide the therapeutic choices of professional and client alike, and determine the options available.

By 1972, a movement of Effeminists, male pro-feminists, formed to "urge all such men as ourselves (whether celibate, homosexual, or heterosexual) to reject masculinist standards, whether expressed as physical, mental, emotional, or sexual stereotypes of what is desirable in a man."[12] Even as early as 1970, one year after the beginning of the gay liberation movement, I wrote in *RAT* newspaper:

> Male homosexuality could be the first attempt at the non-assertion of cultural manhood. It could be the beginning of the process by which we can reach a gender redefinition of Man: the "non-man." Homosexuality from this standpoint is the first step in the process of "de-manning."[13]

RAT was a New York male-left weekly that was taken over by feminists. "Hey Man" was the sole article written by a male during the history of the liberated newspaper. I was concerned because of the male domination of the gay movement that compelled lesbians to accomplish their political self-interest within the ranks of the feminist movement or in the separatist movement. The impact of Effeminism was extensive from the faltering male left, the political underground (exemplified by the Weathermen), and the gay movement. Lesbian/feminist Johnston, observing the fleeing of lesbians and women from male-dominated movements, wrote of effeminism:

> The first authentic Western male revolutionaries. The first men to confess the inappropriateness of their manhood and to withdraw the classic male demand of support from the female.[14]

Duberman reviewed gay political theory in the *New York Times Magazine*:

> The gay movement is, to be sure, barely three years old, and fertile if fragmentary material is beginning to emerge elsewhere. . . . While Revolutionary Effeminism may seem "adventurist," violence-prone and opaque, it is formulating basic questions on gender.[15]

He also declared the effeminist question of gender-typed roles as basic to gay polemics.

An assault from the institutions of psychiatry and psychology emerged, as if anticipating the upheaval of the feminist, lesbian, and gay movements. During the 1950s and 1960s, homophobic and gynephobic theoreticians and practitioners questioned the authenticity of a gay and lesbian identity, so they supported the preservation of gender stereotypes. When reviewing the psychoanalytical, vernacular terms betray an inundating bias toward same-sex relatedness. Same-sex identity, as a diagnosis, became contained within a quantifiable system of measurement; gradients and degrees of pathology correlated with prognostication for treatment outcome. The following classifications defined inexorable homosexuality: absolute inversion, chronic, congenital, innate, narcissistic variety, obligative, passive, object-homoerotic, and spurious. The following varieties were considered more responsive to treatment: dystonic, episodic, temporary, transient, transitory homosexuality–each less resolute, almost a form of pseudohomosexuality. See the work of such homophobic psychoanalysts as Bergler, Bieber, Kernberg, and Ovessey.

Recently, a New York City psychoanalytic institute offered a course focusing on countertransferential therapeutic complexities when treating clients with HIV disease. Contention developed when the well-meaning therapist members discussed homosexuality. The case presented involved a mother whose son developed a cluster of HIV-related medical complications and became severely debilitated. The mother was distraught, expressing divergent and conflicting emotions, such as anger toward her son for being gay and for becoming ill, and for not assuming responsibility for his sexual identity and the subsequent illness.

One member of the class suggested a therapeutic approach to exonerate the mother from culpability for her son's sexual identity. The reasoning for the intervention flows from an ontogenetic premise that same-sexual identity is not the confluence of the constellation of family, environment, culture, or biology any more than is heterosexuality. The rage the mother carries reflects a twofold complementary proposition: 1) she is responsible for, or influenced by, the organization of her son's essential and authentic sexual identity, and 2) sex identity is reversible, a preference, lifestyle, or a choice made by volition. All members of the class disagreed with the intervention, subscribing instead to psychoanalytic training, although it was a posture they determined to be altruistic.

Stoller's work on the development of gender identity proposed male identity as a *secondary phenomenon*. He states that male identity (i.e., masculinity) actualizes through the rejection of the primary identification with the mother. For a boy to become masculine, he must resolve the infant symbiotic affinity through rejection:

> If we put aside biologic factors, such as CNS/hormonal influences, the longer, the more intimately, the more mutually pleasurable is a mother-infant son symbiosis, the greater the likelihood that the boy will become feminine; and that effect will persist if the boy's father does not qualitatively and quantitatively interrupt the merging.[16]

For masculinity to develop, each infant boy must erect intrapsychic barriers that ward off the desire to maintain the blissful sense of being one with mother. In Erikson's schemata, human development occurs in stages where autonomy first exhibits when an infant "wriggles his hand free when tightly held."[17] This model depicts male development as a contradistinction from the female infant. The representation of feminine experience is a preoccupation with "inner space," which is gender-stereotyped as receptive and passive. Female development is about being and self-discovery, with depersonalized biologic drives subordinated. In Baker Miller's innovative approach to the psychological development of women, she characterizes autonomy as defined by women as an extensive, not lesser, potential to extend relationships to others simultaneously with the development of oneself.[18] Chodorow disclaims the pervasive

psychoanalytic argument that proposes that a child must relinquish
the primary identification with the mother because of the "devaluation of relational qualities." Chodorow "allied to this suggestion
that it does not need to be, and often is not, relationship to the father
that breaks the early maternal relationship."[19]

> Psychoanalysts often claim universality for the content they
> have found, when this is in fact developed in the psychoanaly-
> sis of patient populations drawn almost entirely from people
> living in Western industrial capitalist societies. These people
> have grown up in one kind of family and one culture. Psycho-
> analysis assumes that "the family" is nuclear, and that in an
> intense mother-child bond and parenting by the mother alone,
> possibly aided by one other woman, is natural and even neces-
> sary to proper development.[20]

Some psychoanalysts consider homosexuality an aspect of the
paranoid personality type within narcissism. It manifests through
the compulsion to reunite with an authority figure capable of nour-
ishment. The narcissist struggles against the desire for reunion because of shameful feelings and fear of humiliation. The narcissistic
self is terrified of shame and fears obliteration from the omnipotent
object so this conflict is experienced as life over death. The diagnosis of pathological narcissism has played a major role in the anomalous treatment of homosexuality. In Kernberg, the treatment prognosis for a homosexual cure falls within three categories:

- The severe type (most neurotic)
- The more severe type (who are capable of loving their objects
  with motherly concern)
- The most severe type (who presents better surface functioning
  but who is pathological)

For Kernberg, the most extreme category is innate homosexuality–which includes those who claim that at no time in their life has
their sexual instinct followed a different course. He rejects the
possibility of a biological or congenital basis to sexual identity
because of a construction that includes two other classes. The third
class is especially difficult to reconcile with the assumption that

inversion is congenital. Hence, the desire of those holding the view to separate the absolute inverts from the others results in the rejection of the general conception of inversion. Accordingly, in a number of cases, the inversion would be of a congenital character, while in others it might originate from other causes. Kernberg claims gay men have an essentially neurotic personality organization. Object relations reflect "an unconscious submission to the oedipal father related to guilt over their oedipal longings for the mother and castration anxiety." He terms this as a *negative Oedipus complex*:

> On the contrary, by far the large majority of male patients we encounter who present casual homosexual behavior or casual bisexual orientation belong the to the borderline spectrum of pathology. Thus, from a clinical viewpoint, there is a discontinuity between neurotic male homosexuality and normality, and male orientation toward one or the other sex does not seem to follow the usual distribution of polymorphous perverse sexuality.[21]

Many psychoanalysts and psychotherapists treat gays and lesbians who have requested help because of impulsivity, compulsivity, and driven, frantic sexuality. Often, the symptomatic behavior is attributed by the analyst–and sometimes by the patient–to homosexuality. The clinical and psychoanalytic literature on homosexuality often suggests, subtly or openly, that patients' homosexuality causes extensive associated psychopathology. In scientific language, homosexuality is often treated in the literature as an independent variable, and disorders of sexual and personal relationships are treated as dependent variables. There are no studies, however, comparing patients of similar levels of ego integration and opposite points on the Kinsey spectrum. Edelman states that clinical evidence suggests that the etiology of nearly all pathological sexual behavior is integral to disordered ego and superego functioning and disordered object relations:

> To understand sexual pathology, then, one must understand character pathology. There is no homosexual or heterosexual character type. In fact, it would appear that homosexuality,

bisexuality, and heterosexuality are distributed across the entire range of character types and character structures.[22]

Bergler creates a character study, a personality structure of so-
named *tell-tale indices of homosexuality*–some conscious, other
unconscious–including injustice collecting; provocation; pseudo-
aggression; self-pity; fugitive from women; narcissistic safeguards;
constant dissatisfaction with partner; sexual mass consumption and
prowling; inordinate malice masking masochistic depression; meg-
alomaniacal conviction of being special; jealousy; inner guilt; com-
pensatory hypernarcissism; hyper-superciliousness; flippant cynical
outlook; pathologic parasitic tendencies; conspiratorial attitude; artistic posturing; and superficiality. Bergler concludes with the statement that "the homosexual's whole personality is neurotically
sick."[23]

Gender theorist Green, a neo-Stollerite disciple, propagandizes
heterosexism by claiming that, within the evolutionary hierarchy,
human behavior pursues heterosexuality with uncompromising vig-
or. He submits a sophistic childhood anecdote to buttress his argument, remembering guppies being devoured by a voracious mother.
He nourished a sole survivor in isolation, and when it was fully
developed, he introduced the guppy into a tank with adult male and
female guppies:

> Like a horse out of the starting gate, he made for the closest
> female guppy and "penetrated" her. The young mind of this
> researcher was not unimpressed with that single-mindedness
> of heterosexual purpose.[24]

Although the expression of same-sex relatedness does not portray a
single-mindedness of reproductive purpose, the behavior is intrinsic
to animal and human behavior, cross-culturally:

> Intercourse is commonly written about and comprehended as a
> form of possession or an act of possession in which, during
> which, because of which, a man inhabits a woman, physically
> covering her and overwhelming her and at the same time pene-
> trating her; and this physical relation to her–over her and in-
> side her–is his possession of her.[25]

When questioned about the male infatuation in classical Greek culture with virility, nonreciprocity, and the repudiation of pleasure for women and the man/boy in sex, Foucault replied:

> The Greek ethics of pleasure is linked to a virile society, to dissymmetry, exclusion of the other, an obsession with penetration, and a kind of threat of being dispossessed of your own energy, and so on. All that is quite disgusting.[26]

Dworkin maintains "all forms of dominance and submission, whether it be man over woman, white over black, boss over worker, rich over poor, are tied *irrevocably* to the sexual identities of men [and] are derived from the male sexual model."[27]

French suggests that the nearly universal obsession with upholding an authoritarian identity corrupts male relationships, withdrawing them from many forms of human fellowship and affection:

> [T]he male drive to transcend is not merely a drive to subjugate women and men not of one's immediate group; it is at root a drive to demonstrate that men are not bound to nature and necessity.[28]

There is no similar research into the extremist expression of the masculinist principle represented by cultural heroes such as Arnold Schwarzenegger, militarists such as Colin Powell or Oliver North, political leaders such as George Bush (who was humiliated by the appellation of *wimp*, a term with decided gender coloration) or religious leaders such as Cardinal John O'Connor.

Green conceived of the so-called Sissy Boy Syndrome, a repugnant appellation, examining mothers of male children who were interested in doll-playing, cross-dressing, and female role-playing. These sissy boys, he determined, had a unique bisexuality, a *psychological androgyny*. His research into the mothers of sissy boys disclaimed Stoller's earlier findings. Stoller concluded that these mothers competed as equals with males when their sons were young. In the Green study, "the mothers of the 'feminine' boys did not report early girlhood sex-typed behaviors that were statistically different from those reported by the mothers of the 'masculine' boys."[29]

Green believes that an *incubation period*, a value-laden term implying insidiousness, explains latent expression of same-sex relatedness even when there is early developmental interruption of cross-gender behavior:

> As long as the boy's behavior is cross-gendered during this period, homosexual arousal will emerge years later, irrespective of the patter of gender-role behaviors during the intervening years. The atypical boys may not have changed internally but were merely conveying a *veneer* of 'masculinity.' Perhaps they modify behaviors to the point of reducing stigma.[30]

Green erroneously associates cross-gender behavior with a gay sexual identity when, in effect, many behaviors stigmatized as cross-gender are elements of heterosexual male identity. Allegedly gender-appropriate behavior proceeds from a sequence of events in early child development: cultural indoctrination and meanings the sexed body assumes.

In psychosexual development, gender-regulated behavior is pre-phallic, discernible during the first year of life and determined by the third year. The designation of gender-specific behavior fixed by biologic sex in the early years of life becomes delineated by core gender with the parental function that has unconscious and conscious components. Person claims the organizing principle of gender in the psychic structure is comparable to other modalities of cognition such as space, time, causation, and self-object differentiation.[31] She believes gender, through the process of acculturation, dictates sexuality. She refers to so-called anomalous genetic males who were misdiagnosed female at birth. These males raised as female dream the dreams of women, therefore, Person hypothesizes that gender, rather than biology compels the self into a distinct psychosexual sequence.

The controversy about same-sex relatedness persists without resolution because not all psychiatrists, psychoanalysts, or psychologists agree that homosexuality is an authentic sexual identity. As Bayer suggests, the classification of behavior as pathological relates to the question of deviance and "the appropriate scope of psychiatry, its modes of explanation, and its targets of therapeutic intervention."[32] This is a critical distinction from value judgments about what is desirable or undesirable because of therapeutic interventions and the approaches of psychiatry.

The premise of sexual identity choice dates as early as 1919, when Freud wrote that psychoanalytic research contributed to the theory "that everyone, even the most normal person is capable of making a homosexual object-choice, and has done so at some time in his life, and either still adheres to it in his unconscious or else protects himself against it by vigorous counter-attitudes."[33] Freud quotes from Leonardo da Vinci's essay *Conferenze Fiorentine*, where the artist states, "No one has the right to love or hate anything without the thorough knowledge of its nature."[34]

Downing comments that same-sex relatedness, manifest or latent, expressed or sublimated, is prominent in each of Freud's case studies, both in those devoted to actual persons in analysis and in those focused on figures he only knew indirectly, such as Schreber, Leonardo, and Dostoevski.[35] Sexual identity and gender are fundamental to Freud's work:

> As I have looked anew at all the relevant texts, I have been surprised to discover what a central role homosexuality plays in Sigmund Freud's work–and how different what he says about it is from what he is generally taken to have said. I have also been struck by how when Freud writes of the importance of homoerotic impulses in human life, he writes of *us* not *them.* [Author's emphasis][36]

In an unpublished letter to Ferenczi on October 17, 1910, Freud wrote the following:

> You probably imagine that I have secrets quite other than those I have reserved for myself, or you believe that my secrets are connected with a special sorrow, whereas I feel capable of handling everything and am pleased with the greater independence that results from having overcome my homosexuality.[37]

Freud had intense and passionate collegial relationships: one of which was with Wilhelm Fliess. Fliess was probably Freud's closest friend and the two corresponded for 17 years, during which time, Freud wrote several of his most important psychoanalytic works,

including *The Interpretation of Dreams* and *Studies on Hysteria*. On
the following December 16, again in an unpublished letter to Ferenczi, Freud mentions Fliess for the last time: "I have overcome
Fliess, about whom you were so curious." The implication of
Freud's concern with his sexual identity is unrefutable. Outing the
father of psychoanalysis is taboo, and his reputation remains intact
with dubious interpretations, such as Becker's:

> Knowing Freud's lifelong tendency to reduce vaguely anxious
> feelings to specific sexual motivations, we are entitled to as-
> sume that his "unruly" urges could just as well have repre-
> sented the ambivalence of dependency needs.[38]

VINNIE

I hadn't seen Barbara for two decades. No doubt, we would have
passed each other on the street without recognition. Still, the inflection of her voice and the breathless, staccato rhythm of her speech
during the late-evening telephone conversation was immediately
familiar. She knew, through a mutual friend, that I had an AIDS
practice and she wanted to refer someone to me. She described her
friend's circumstances as the commonplace predicament during the
epidemic: "John is my friend. I don't really like Vinnie. Well, I
don't mean that. We have an antagonistic relationship. I've known
John more than 25 years, since we were in college together. I've so
much to say, and I'm taking your time. My feelings toward Vinnie
don't matter–he doesn't need to vindicate himself. He has AIDS.
My God, I think he's dying. I don't know what to do."

Basic Stressors of HIV Disease

- Basic threat to narcissistic integrity; separation anxiety
- Fear of the loss of love and/or approval
- Anxiety about loss of control of developmentally achieved
  biologic (bowel or bladder movements) or emotional functions
  (feeling states)

- Dread of inordinate pain and suffering
- Fear of loss of, or injury to, body parts
- Reactivation of feelings of guilt and shame
- Apprehension about retaliation for previous transgressions
- Fragmented sexual identity
- Witness to multiple deaths from HIV disease
- Fear of abandonment
- Anxiety about memory loss or dementia
- Transfigured body image
- Worry about public disclosure
- Loss of livelihood
- Concern for the future guardianship of children
- Fear of death and dying

"John calls me in the middle of the night after Vinnie's asleep, and the essence of death is all-consuming to him. I wonder what goes through his mind. Despite his openness, it feels as if we're communicating in code. I try to protect him, keep some balance, but it's hypocritical. Honestly, I feel helpless.

"Vinnie was hospitalized last month with AIDS-related pneumonia. The hospital staff was understanding. John had legal papers in hand–just in case. He has medical power of attorney. He expected difficulty as the lover, not as a family member. Vinnie was on a respirator in an ICU for two weeks. When he was transferred to a room, we knew that he was going to make it. It was a close call. I remember when he was under an oxygen tent, and he asked for a pencil and wrote 'Home.' We stood over him, knowing his condition was improving. He was unable to focus his eyes, as if staring into the abyss.

"Linda told me that you're working with people with AIDS, and I thought you could help Vinnie. He gets so depressed and afraid."

Barbara wanted to be a passionately impartial ally to the male lovers, to be demonstrably sympathetic, but she felt a combination of frustration and anger. Her self-assured moral neutrality irritated me. Her concern, when juxtaposed against a remoteness to the totality–the experience of social intolerance of same-gender relatedness, medical complexity, and the stigma of AIDS–corrupted her caring stance. I immediately felt self-reproach, overturning my judgments, knowing her concern was genuine. I rationalized that my exhaustion that day had left me with aching paralysis and an extravagant headache.

*   *   *

Four months later, Vinnie made an appointment, and in a distinctly Germanic accent, he was defensively apologetic for not having done so earlier. Vinnie appeared boyish despite his 40 years. It was his transparent blue eyes that communicated innocence. His skin was almost perfect, except pitting in the hollows of his cheekbones. He tossed a U.S. Marine Corps baseball cap on a side table, revealing a salt-and-pepper military-type haircut. When he took off his fashionably distressed, brown-leather bomber jacket, I noticed an ostentatious, pewter-colored belt buckle with the Marines' insignia.

During the initial session, he sat on his hands, thwarting any physical gesture that might insinuate feelings–he was emotionally self-regulated. When he spoke, a scarcely noticeable, defiantly upturned lip communicated his disappointment and skepticism.

"I was in therapy last year," he said. "She didn't understand. When I left, she said, 'You're a hard nut to crack.' I didn't want to be cracked like a nut. Are you gay? Shouldn't I ask?" Without pausing for a reply, he continued, "Are you HIV-positive? I know you're not going to answer. I feel pressured to be here. I'm doing it for John. He thinks I need individual therapy. We're in a couples group, and he's in individual therapy. He doesn't want to push too hard. He's trying to get it out of me."

"What is he trying to get out of you?" I asked.

"I didn't mean that. When I get depressed, it fucks him up."

"What happens when you get depressed?"

"What do you mean? Having AIDS is being on an emotional roller coaster. I make myself into a ball and stay in bed for days. After my diagnosis, I faced the most painful time of my life." (See Figure 6.)

"There were other difficult times in my life, but everything changed when I met John. I became a different person. Even the music I listened to changed. I used to like country-western music, and John loved opera. I discovered that I had almost a perfect

FIGURE 6. Correlation of Biomedical and Psychosocial Stages in Early HIV Disease

Biomedical

EXPOSURE
- Sexual intercourse
- Injection drug use
- Perinatal transmission
- Blood transfusion
- Organ/tissue transplant
- Occupational exposure

SEROCONVERSION

A window period, from six to eight weeks for approximately 97% of individuals, takes place from infection with the HIV virus and detection through antibody testing.

ASYMPTOMATIC

For an indeterminate period of time, in many cases up to a decade or more, an individual presents with no significant symptomatology.

Psychosocial

- Feelings of self-blame
- Inability to adjust behaviors
- Rage toward nondisclosing partner
- Anger toward medical provider or institution
- Denial of feeling exempt and/or omnipotent
- Lack of adequate education
- Victim of sexual abuse or rape
- Fear of battering partner

DIAGNOSTIC CRISIS

INDIVIDUAL AND SYSTEMIC DISEQUILIBRIUM
- Shock and numbness
- Denial
- Anger
- Depression and suicidal ideation
- Relapses of substance use and safer sex
- Injury to self-esteem
- Disclosure to partner
- Stress of relationships
- Anger toward sexual partner(s)
- Fear for family's future
- Disclosure to medical provider(s), social services, agencies, and strangers.

REESTABLISH EGO INTEGRITY
- Adaptation through use of coping mechanisms
- Changes in high-risk behaviors
- Medical self-management
- Use of psychological supports

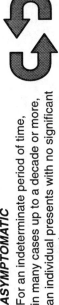

163

musical ear, and I could tell who was singing, what notes they reached. I studied librettos to follow plots.

"John panics when he sees me depressed, walking around the bed with his hands behind his back, and then he gets into bed and holds me. Don't misunderstand me. I have no problems with John. There's nothing I could ask for that he wouldn't do for me. He's my teddy bear–the perfect caregiver. I couldn't ask for more.

"He calls Barbara because he has to bare his heart to somebody, and one night thinking I was asleep, I overheard him talking to her. It was deceitful."

He interrupted himself, alternately looking at his watch and me– vulnerable at the self-disclosure. He hesitated a moment, then reaching into his gym bag, he extracted a large pill container. With bravado, he displayed a handful of pills, saying, "I can swallow them without water.

"I have two T cells left. I've named them Frick and Frack, and I hope they don't take a vacation together. I haven't wanted to know my T-cell count ever since I had my first bout with PCP. There were about 80 at the time, and that was over a year ago. I call it the T-cell lottery.

"I've had PCP at least twice. About two years ago, John insisted that I go to a doctor. I thought about AIDS, but I put it out of my mind. I didn't have the HIV test. Besides, I thought my risk was low: I wasn't into anal sex. I'm an oral type. It got to the point where I had to do something because I was having shortness of breath. I'd come home from work and collapse, and could barely make it up the stairs to my apartment.

"I had insurance, but I had to go to a clinic. I don't think the doctor knew much about AIDS. He did ask me whether I was homosexual. I told him yes, and he took a chest X ray and told me that I had an upper respiratory infection. He sent me home with a prescription for erythromycin. It cleared up in about a week, but I think it may have been PCP.

"I guess that I knew it was AIDS because ever since the previous year the thoughts were almost constant. I would awaken with a cold sweat from AIDS dreams in the middle of the night, and John would comfort me. I knew. I just couldn't face it. I isolated myself from AIDS because I didn't know anyone. Well, that's not accurate, there was no one in my intimate circle, but there were many ac-

quaintances who'd died–even an ex-lover. That's an intimate. Denial. I pushed it away. A year later, the same symptoms reappeared,
but this time I was running high fevers, about 104°. It was about
three in the morning when John had to take me to an emergency
room. It terrified me. I lay on a gurney for two days before there
was an available room, and they had begun pentamidine intravenously. I didn't need an interpreter to see it on John's face. He'd
leave the room when close to tears.

"I don't know how I survived the two days waiting for a room. I
couldn't sleep, though the fevers went down because there was such
chaos. Cops everywhere. All these gunshot wounds. Crack addicts.
I saw a patient rip the IV lines out of his wrist and get up to leave. A
doctor tried to stop him, and the patient punched him in the jaw. A
security guard had to restrain the patient. A nurse told me the
patient was having a psychotic episode induced by angel dust. He
had been there several times before, and they'd pump him with
tranquilizers. He left the next day without remembering anything.

"That week they did a bronchoscopy, and, of course, they diagnosed PCP. I knew that meant AIDS. I was in the hospital for three
weeks. It was the most depressing time of my life. When I returned
home. I just wanted to sleep. I felt such anger. No. *Rage.*

"It scared John because I couldn't respond to anything; no comfort he offered mattered. I felt he was there for me, but I was so
afraid of dying–I wanted to die. When John was at work, I just
rolled into a ball. Sometimes, I listen to music: I love opera. There's
an aria that Pavarotti sings in *Turandot*: I would play it over and
over. I knew that I had to control myself. The music satisfied the
emptiness, the feeling of physical enslavement. I had to use all my
intelligence.

"My health has been okay for the past year, but what's okay
when you've got AIDS? It's a constant adjustment to deterioration.
If I look back to the hospitalization, I couldn't have predicted that
I'd make it, that I'd survive. I don't recognize myself emotionally. I
look in the mirror and wonder who am I. Physically, I've aged, with
the weight loss and the greying of my hair.

"My doctor took me off AZT because of peripheral neuropathy,
which has been a problem for several months. I'm waiting to get
DDI. My doctor applied for it a couple of months ago, but there was

a problem with the application. I'm getting angry because it's taking so long. John's furious about it. He wants me to confront the doctor. I have full trust in my doctor. He spends a lot of time with me. He told me that hundreds of his patients had AIDS and boasted he hadn't lost one. John thinks it's a ridiculous statement. I want him to let me alone about it.

"Last month, I had a scare. I was seeing floaters and thought that it was CMV retinitis. They don't know what caused the floaters, but I was tested for CMV and was all right. I can't imagine losing my sight, although they have medication that prevents blindness. The medication is DHPG, given IV. God, I don't want to have a Hickman catheter. Can you imagine me at Fire Island, walking on the beach with tubes hanging from my chest?

"I still have some vanity. I feel guilty saying that because members of my PWA group have dealt with such extraordinary medical difficulties over the years. I've been fortunate. There's a member of my group, Mike, with the most disfiguring KS I've ever seen. It's all over his face. The lesions produced edema, and his face was so swollen that it took a while in the morning so he can see. Mike goes to work every day, rides the subway. People stare at him. They know it's AIDS. I remember this radio commercial with an announcer who drones, 'You don't look like you have AIDS.' Going to work is important to his sense of purpose."

*   *   *

Vinnie continued: "Smoking grass has helped me." He paused momentarily, anticipating a comment from me. "And it got me through the second PCP hospitalization. I smoked in the bathroom. I always wondered if they could smell it in the hallways. Once, John and I smoked together. We had sex. We hadn't had sex in months—not orgasmic sex. It was great."

Vinnie had been in treatment more than eight months, but had been unable to attend sessions for almost two months after a six-week hospitalization for PCP. He was using a cane to support himself after several occurrences of falling.

He said, "I joined a PWA support group and John and I go to a couples group, and I've learned to live with AIDS. The groups have helped me, though it has been very painful; most of the group members when I first came in have died. I'm very self-protective about the AIDS group, and I don't see anyone outside the group. I'm afraid of making a connection only to lose the person. We mirror each other, and when I see the serious debilitation of a member I think that could be me. I remember Greg, who hadn't been to group for two months, and then he returned for a session, dying the following week. He was almost unrecognizable, a skeleton, looking so old. Even his voice was different; he sounded ancient. He came to group to say goodbye to us, but it wasn't clear to us at the time."

It was not easy for him to tell all this, Vinnie confessed, biting his lips and nervously fingering his drawn and ashen cheek. "I believe my world is ending."

He continued: "Greg only spoke once during the session despite the physical pain, but, mentally, he was reflective, almost meditative. Each of us knew that he was dying, and I remember experiencing him already in the past tense, an expatriate returning from a strange country.

"He said, mind-reading my thoughts, 'I didn't really see anything, anything at all. You know, I never would have chosen David. He wasn't my rescue fantasy man, not Mr. Right. He's my flesh and blood. One afternoon, I thought that I was going crazy. It was exhausting, as if I had been shouting at the top of my lungs in an empty house. Then I fell asleep, passed out, and when I awoke, David was in bed next to me. He was crying with the intense taste of grief on his lips, 'Oh, my darling.' I recognized the privilege in knowing him. People are all that matter. It's as simple as that.' We sat in silence and there was a chill in the room.

"I had experienced this before when a [group] member was close to death. They'd come to group and leave us with an epiphany, an ending."

Clinical Stressors of HIV Disease

- Capability to regress adequately in the service of recovery
- Capacity to maintain adequate defenses against the stressors evoked by illness and/or hospitalization
- Access to feelings and fantasies

- Skill to communicate needs
- Services of empathetic and flexible caregivers, such as physicians, nurses, counselors, and support system

He began: "Since our last session, I thought about my courtship with John. If you can call it a courtship since it began ostensibly with what could have been a one-night stand. We met in a West Village bar, and he took me home to a loft building in Soho that looked more dilapidated than any tenement I'd ever seen. I panicked during the elevator ride. When he closed the accordion metal gate, it was claustrophobic, a space barely large enough for two. The elevated grunted ascending to the top floor. The loft was probably enormous, but it was impossible to see because of cartons piled from floor to ceiling, several rows deep. It looked like a warehouse, windowless, and smelled musty with plaster flakes that had fallen from gaping holes in the walls as the ancient building settled over time. A radiator rhythmically blasted scalding steam against another wall.

"I asked him, 'What's in the cartons?' John said he had a hobby of making miniatures: 'I began during the Bicentennial—George Washington and the revolutionary army, a colonial town, an interior. I made many myself—I would find a piece of scrap metal, a button, a filing. I would sculpt it into the perfect shape, or it would be as simple as turning it on its side and painting it.' It wasn't until months later that I discovered he had a porno mail-order business, made amateur video and audio tapes. Yeah, the miniatures were a hobby, but the porno business supported him. I suspected something, even that first night, but I didn't really want to know.

"We walked through a narrow passage into an area at the north end of the loft that served as an apartment. This area was in distinct contrast to the rest of the loft. John transformed the space into small rooms overflowing with art nouveau objects with a large comfortable sofa and overstuffed chairs. He clearly had taste, was a collector, and each comforted me. There was something hallucinatory about the loft—nothing appeared as it was. I thought of John as an illusionist. The miniatures were a fantasy movie set.

"He asked me, 'Would you like to see the garden? I have a rooftop garden.' We scaled an outside metal staircase to the roof. It must have been about three in the morning, and John turned the electric switch and flooded the garden with light. The garden had everything that could grow, without any design or sense of color, just pots and boxes or any container that could hold soil: day lilies, mums, orchids, pansies, tomatoes, basil, cacti, bonsai. Row after row, flowers and plants covered the entire roof, hardly a space to put a chaise, [or] for that matter a stool.

"John passed me a joint, and we must've smoked for hours. I found myself absorbed by a cyclamen–the dark cores of pink and the purple circles, the petals turned back, the leaves mottled in many shades of green. I got stoned and remember thinking that these plants' leaves and flowers are perfection without consciousness, design without nerves, or pain. Put a handful of seeds and dirt into a pot, and they come up with this beauty. We had sex on the rooftop until morning, and I don't remember when we crept into bed.

"John told me that during the night I uttered sounds, indistinguishable animal noises. Now, after these ten years he's attuned to me that if I'm running a fever–maybe a couple of points–he awakens."

*   *   *

"My parents have never accepted John and don't acknowledge our relationship. After we were together for five years, we decided to invite them to spend Christmas with us. By that time we'd moved to a small apartment on Bank Street in the Village, keeping the loft strictly for business. We were going to sleep in the living room, giving my parents the bedroom, which would be comfortable with a king-sized bed. I remember wondering if we could keep Petunia, our dog, out of the bedroom. She used to nuzzle between us, fighting for pillow space.

"I brought my parents to the apartment from JFK and discussed an itinerary with them. They knew of John, had spoken to him, and I guess they knew we were lovers. They, I mean my mother, would always send cards and gifts to both of us. She'd say, 'Send my love to John,' after every telephone call. I was 35 years old and never mentioned a woman, so I just assumed they knew. I remember her expression when I showed her the bedroom, and she said, 'Where does John sleep? There's only one bed.' I replied, 'Are you joking, Mother? With me. Where else?' She hadn't even taken her coat off when she turned, picking up her valise, she said to my father, 'John, we're leaving.'

"I didn't speak to them for a year until my sister telephoned. She told me they found my younger brother, Ben, in my parents' basement. He shot himself in the head, committed suicide. I went home for the funeral, and we never spoke about the Christmas visit. Ben was a cocaine addict for several years, in-and-out of programs, jobless, and without family. His wife left him with their infant son in the middle of the night, fearing that he'd beat her again, and there was a court injunction against him.

"I grew up in the Bronx after World War II; my parents emigrated. The neighborhood was the center of our lives. It was difficult as a boy, being the neighborhood 'sissy,' taunted unrelentlessly. It was mostly a Jewish neighborhood, and many had come from having been holocaust survivors. My next-door neighbor had lost her husband and five-year-old child. They shunned us for being German, called us Nazis; but we had lost family. My mother's sister was a radical who resisted the Nazis and was beaten during a rally and died in the streets–her head bashed almost beyond recognition.

"My mother told stories of the war. She would sit on the windowsill all night as the planes would fly overhead. We would hear them very close to the rooftops. Sometimes they would use chemical bombs, anti-civilian, phosphorous. It would coat your skin like napalm. There wasn't anything you could do to get it off. Not water. Nothing. It would eat through a person's flesh to the bone. On January 16, when the bombing of Iraq began, I was home sick, couldn't go to work. The entire week was stressful, and I thought every vibration was overhead bombing. Often, I use environmental, white noise, for relaxation, and I've got a CD of the sound of the ocean, but I couldn't listen to it that day. The roaring of waves was too violent, and [it] affected me as if it were the sound of bombing noises.

"Under occupation, we were busy scrounging, keeping ourselves alive in the sadness of the aftermath. My parents were against the Reich. The government would use very sophisticated techniques to frighten people. When I was a child, there were posters everywhere warning people one against the other. We were afraid that our conversations could be overheard, that they tapped the telephones. We were consciously paranoid. Even now I'm not prone to conversations on the telephone because I fear that the conversation is being overheard. I'm accused of being abrupt.

"It was difficult to immigrate to the U.S., and it was through the vigilance of family that we came here. My father's brother had become a citizen after he married an American.

"My childhood memories are often vague, and it was difficult for my previous therapist to get much from me. She called me resistant, and that made me angry. She may have been right, but I didn't want to hear it because those memories were painful. I suppose that I didn't want to deal with my past. I was seeing her to discuss HIV– how this damn virus was destroying my life. She wanted me to talk about my parents and was dragging it out of me.

"My father drank a lot, was alcoholic, and he could be abusive. He did the best he could. Why dwell on it? Now, he has emphysema, and, at times, I feel that we're in competition with each other about who's going to die first. He came to visit during my hospitalization, and he had strep throat, running a high fever. What was he trying to prove? Showing me how sick he was? I felt that he was placing me at risk, and I had to ask him to leave; the incident made me angry. My mother's a nurse and should know better. I try to explain my illness to them, but they're in such denial, they don't understand. She's so passive about her health: can you imagine, a nurse–she lost so much weight and doesn't do anything about it. She looks anorexic.

"I feel so weary, and when I resist the conditions they place on me, when I don't jump when they say jump, then all hell breaks loose. I know the bottom line is my being gay, which they accept on a surface level, but I know that they don't understand me. They don't want to hear about my life because it causes them pain, so I'm forced to protect them. Protect them from me."

* * *

Adjustment to Threatening Events[39]

- A search for meaning in the experience
- An attempt at mastery
- An effort to restore self-esteem through self-enhancing evaluations
- An ability to form and maintain a set of illusions

"I had this dream last night," Vinnie continued. "I don't remember details, but when I awoke, I wrote this on a pad." He took a folded piece of paper from his T-shirt pocket and handed it to me. Initially, it mystified me because he chose not to read it aloud. When I opened the paper and saw characters written arbitrarily and scribbled on the page, then immediately, I appreciated his purpose by showing it to me. I asked for his interpretation.

"It took me a while to decipher it, but I knew there was a sentence. I wrote it with my left hand because, my right was numb from having slept in a fetal position with it squeezed under my body. It says, 'Hocus pocus is coming.'

"Years ago before I met John, I used to be into the Tarot, and I thought of the Magician card, sometimes known as the Juggler. I found my deck and looked at the card that pictures a juggler standing beside a table on which are paraphernalia–trinkets, thimbles, dice, cups, coins, and a knife. The Juggler is satisfied, playing with them and using them as a distraction. It's the Juggler's impersonation, the ultimate stratagem, as an illusionist.

"I've conjured all the ill blood from my body. Yes, it's about HIV, but it's also the continual sham of self-rejection. No more. I've juggled different roles, with little or no identity of my own–unaware of potential greatness. When I die it will be in wholeness instead as an everyperson [sic] between heaven and earth.

"I try to make light of it, but I feel that I'm anguishing between heaven and earth. I'm aware of the metamorphosis. We all sense there are powers that make the world we see when we look at it–and other powers that unmake it. People get used to it. And when people express incomprehensible fears, they feel that they're expressing this truth, somehow, one that may be otherwise inexpressible in our present condition. The part of the proposition is that human wickedness is absolute, a public health problem, and nothing but."

* * *

An individual's adaptation to illness can be characterized not only by the specific nature of the disease process but also by the meaning of the illness to the individual. (See Figure 7.) Gay men encounter a lifelong process of information management about their sexual identity. The diagnosis of HIV infection brings in a different

FIGURE 7. Correlation of Biomedical and Psychosocial Stages in Advanced HIV Disease

SYMPTOMATIC
- Consistent decline in T4 cell count
- Chronic gynecological infections
- Lymphadenopathy
- Weight and muscle tone loss
- Dermatological infections
- Oral candidiasis or chronic vaginal candidiasis unresponsive to treatment
- Persistent fever and/or night sweats
- Profound fatigue
- Shingles caused by herpes zoster virus (HZV)

ADVANCED HIV DISEASE
- At risk for opportunistic infections (OIs) with T4 cell count below 200
- Occurrences of hospitalization
- Complexity of medical management with multiple infections or cancers, and chronicity
- Mobility impairment
- Eyesight loss

TERMINAL STAGE
Usually, the configuration of several OIs and a totally debilitated immune system.

REACTIVATION OF CRISIS
Life Transitions
- Issues of sexual identity
- Changes in support systems
- Reliance on medical treatments
- Financial instability
- Work/career alteration

Emotional Flooding
- Guilt
- Anger
- Helplessness
- Feeling loss of control
- Suicidal ideation and depression
- Substance use relapse
- Safer sex practice slippage

Social Isolation
- Stigmatization
- Abandonment
- Withdrawal

GRIEVING CYCLE
- Emotional adjustment to changes in body image, e.g., lesions, weight loss, vision impairment, lack of mobility
- Progressive debilitation and loss of independence
- Reliance on caregivers, medical providers, social services agencies, and volunteer organizations
- Kubler-Ross[1] five stages of dying: 1. denial, 2. anger, 3. depression, 4. bargaining, and 5. acceptance
- Near death experiences
- Detachment
- Noncommunicative

173

manner–the crucial struggle with the essence of core identity. Crisis is integral to the theory of psychosocial development as a predictable part of growth:

> At every life stage we can anticipate that some tension will arise from the discrepancy between the skills that are developed at the beginning of the stage and the expectations for growth during the stage. In addition to these predictable crises, any number of unpredictable stresses can occur during a lifetime.[40]

One prognostication of an individual's adaptation or modes of survival when challenged with a life-threatening illness is found in assessing their history. During the initial sessions, it is meaningful to ascertain the individual's strengths when they have undergone pivotal circumstances in their life, such as parental loss or other deaths. Life transitions, along with the achievement of developmental tasks for gay or lesbian clients, are distinctive.

Assessing Adaptation to Stressors

- Individual's history of reaction to stressful events
- The ability of the individual to fulfill new developmental tasks
- Distinguishing coping behavior when managing principal disappointments and losses
- Reactions to previous medical illnesses

The discovery of same-sexual identity precedes sexual expression so that a prepubescent child often experiences a profound and perturbing comprehension of unacceptable difference within the heterosexual nuclear family and heterosexual culture. Adolescent sexual expression for gay men is frequently experimentation with friends or with strangers. It is typically concealed, without discussion; the event may be recanted, and one individual may be rebuked or blamed. During this phase of development, adolescents are singularly at risk for HIV infection because safer-sex guidelines directed toward gay men do not reach adolescents during this transitory phase since they do not self-identify as gay. Coming out is a process consisting of separate perpetual, lifelong phases.

The Developmental Process of Coming Out

- Sexual coming out with the acknowledgment of same-sex object orientation
- Intrapsychic coming out as the manner of self-discovery and acceptance
- Social coming out with the disclosure of same-sex relatedness to family system and society
- Political coming out as the recognition of the necessity to extend self-esteem and struggle against discrimination macrosocially

The integration of sexual identity is decisive to adjustment through the spectrum of HIV disease. Commonly, the disclosure of HIV serostatus is a twofold process coupled with an affirmation of same-sex identity. The therapist must appreciate the intersection of an integrated or fragmented same-sexual identity in sustaining an individual through the sequence of adjustments to HIV infection. The therapist cannot merely position a nonhomophobic stance. The therapist should be knowledgeable of the developmental stages of gay or lesbian clients and of the culture of gay and lesbian identity. Any gay or lesbian individual must withstand the sociopolitical ramifications of the continuous struggle to validate authenticity when confronted by a society that minimizes and deprecates the centrality of sexual identity by declaring it sinful and depraved at one point of the homophobic continuum. Through minimization implied by terms that define core identity as a choice or lifestyle. Through annihilation that declares identity is merely a sexual act that should exist in privacy.

REFERENCE NOTES

1. Eve Kosofsky Sedgwick, *Epistemology of the Closet* (Berkeley: University of California Press, 1990), p. 42.

2. James P. Krajeski, "Psychotherapy with Gay Men and Lesbians" in *Contemporary Perspectives on Psychotherapy with Lesbians and Gay Men* (New York: Plenum Medical Book Company, 1986), p. 13.

3. Kenneth Lewes, PhD, *The Psychoanalytic Theory of Male Homosexuality* (New York: Simon & Schuster, 1988), p. 237.

4. Kate Millet, *Sexual Politics* (New York: Equinox, 1970), p. 233.

5. John Money, PhD, "Androgyne Becomes Bisexual," *Journal of The American Academy of Psychoanalysis*, 18(3), 392-413, 1990.

6. Ibid.

7. *The New York Times*, August 30, 1991.

8. Richard Green, *The "Sissy Boy Syndrome" and the Development of Homosexuality* (New Haven, CT: Yale University Press, 1987), p. 403.

9. Richard C. Friedman, MD, *Male Homosexuality: A Contemporary Psychoanalytic Perspective* (New Haven, CT: Yale University Press, 1988), p. 11.

10. Jose Gomez, *Demystifying Homosexuality: A Teaching Guide About Lesbians and Gay Men* (New York: Irvington Publishers, 1984), p. 159.

11. Norman Cameron and Joseph F. Rychlak, *Personality Development and Psychopathology* (Boston: Houghton Mifflin Company, 1985), p. 492.

12. "The Effeminist Manifesto," *Double-F: A Magazine of Effeminism*, No. 2, Winter/Spring, 1973.

13. Steven Dansky, "Hey Man," *RAT* Newspaper, New York, May 8, 1970.

14. Jill Johnston, *The Village Voice*, New York, July 6, 1972.

15. Martin Duberman, *The New York Times Book Review*, December 10, 1972.

16. Robert Stoller, *Presentations of Gender* (New Haven, CT: Yale University Press, 1985), p. 182.

17. Erik H. Erikson, *Identity and the Life Cycle* (New York: W. W. Norton & Company, 1980), p. 56.

18. Jean Baker Miller, *Toward a New Psychology of Women* (Boston: Beacon Press, 1986), p. 95.

19. Nancy J. Chodorow, *Feminism and Psychoanalytic Theory* (New Haven, CT: Yale University Press, 1989), p. 233.

20. Nancy Chodorow, *The Reproduction of Mothering: Psychoanalysis and the Sociology of Gender* (Berkeley: University of California Press, 1978), p. 53.

21. Otto Kernberg, "A Theoretical Frame for the Study of Sexual Perversions," in *The Psychoanalytic Core*, edited by Harold P. Blum, Edward M. Weinshel, and F. Robert Rodman (Madison, CT: International Universities Press, 1989), p. 255.

22. Friedman, *Male Homosexuality*, p. 81.

23. Edmund Bergler, MD, *Counterfeit-Sex: Homosexuality, Impotence, Frigidity* (New York: Evergreen Books, 1961), pp. 204-206.

24. Green, *Sissy Boy Syndrome*, p. 386.

25. Andrea Dworkin, *Intercourse* (New York: The Free Press, 1987), p. 63.

26. *The Foucault Reader*, Paul Rabinow, Editor (New York: Pantheon Books, 1985), p. 346.

27. Andrea Dworkin, *Our Blood* (New York: Harper & Row, Publishers, 1976, p. 13.

28. Marilyn French, *Beyond Power: On Women, Men, and Morals* (New York: Summit Books, 1985), p. 262.

29. Green, *Sissy Boy Syndrome*, p. 68.

30. Green, Ibid., p. 388.

31. Ethel Spector Person, "Sexuality as the Mainstay of Identity: Psychoanalytic Perspectives," in *Women & Sexuality*, edited by Catherine R. Stimpson (Chicago: University of Chicago Press, 1980), p. 50.

32. Ronald Bayer, *Homosexuality and American Psychiatry* (New York: Basic Books, 1981), p. 181.

33. Sigmund Freud, *Leonardo da Vinci and a Memory of His Childhood* (New York: W. W. Norton & Company, 1964), p. 49.

34. Ibid., p. 23.

35. Christine Downing, *Myths and Mysteries of Same-Sex Love* (New York: Continuum, 1991), p. 51.

36. Ibid., p. 13.

37. *The Complete Letters of Sigmund Freud to Wilhelm Fliess, 1887-1904*, translated and edited by Jeffrey Moussaieff Masson (Cambridge, MA: The Harvard University Press, 1985), p. 4.

38. Ernest Beck, *The Denial of Death* (New York: The Free Press, 1973), p. 117.

39. S. Taylor, "Adjustment to Threatening Events: A Theory of Cognitive Adaptation," *American Psychologist*, 45:1161-1173.

40. Barbara M. Newman and Philip R. Newman, *Development Through Life: A Psychosocial Approach* (Homewood, IL: The Dorsey Press, 1984), p. 518.

Chapter 6

The Silent Epidemic

They thought death was worth it, but I
Have a self to recover, a queen.
Is she dead, is she sleeping?
Where has she been,
With her lion-red body, her wings of glass?

–Sylvia Plath, Ariel

WOMEN AND HIV DISEASE

Women constitute the fastest growing group at risk for HIV infection. (See Figures 8-10.) In 1989, they represented 10% of the cases reported to the Centers for Disease Control (CDC). However, epidemiological data skew the risk to women from intravenous-drug-using (IVDU) partners because the CDC defines risk hierarchally. If there is IVDU in the woman's history–regardless of whether the drug use is years into the past–the CDC delegates her transmission risk into the IVDU category, notwithstanding any risk from heterosexual contact. Of course, there is no certain method to determine how she became infected. This fact depreciates the transmission risk through heterosexual intercourse. The public and media must reconcile the incongruous warning of hazardous, unprotected heterosexual intercourse with the CDC percentages detailing the "secondary" risk through heterosexual intercourse. Tema Luft was one such woman who slipped through the statistical cracks: "Look at me. I'm an average heterosexual woman; I had regular sex with a few guys and I got it."[1]

Epidemiologically, more than half of women infected with HIV are active or former IVDUs. Thirty percent contracted HIV from

FIGURE 8. Female AIDS Cases by Race/Ethnicity (of 22,056 Cases Through February 1992)

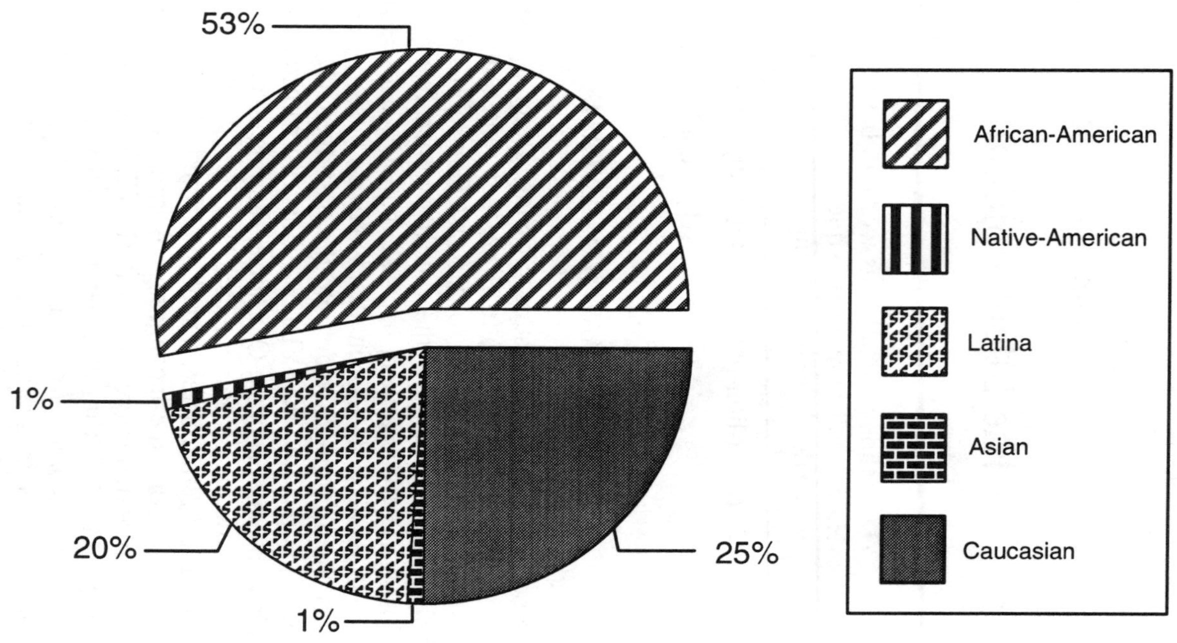

African-American
Native-American
Latina
Asian
Caucasian

53%
25%
20%
1%
1%

FIGURE 9. Female Exposure Categories (of 22,056 Cases Through February 1992)

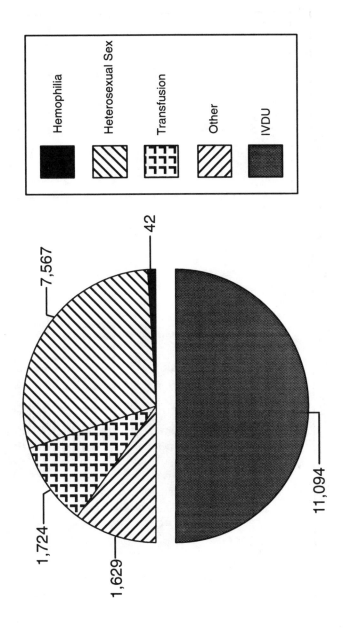

Hemophilia

Heterosexual Sex

Transfusion

Other

IVDU

7,567

42

1,724

1,629

11,094

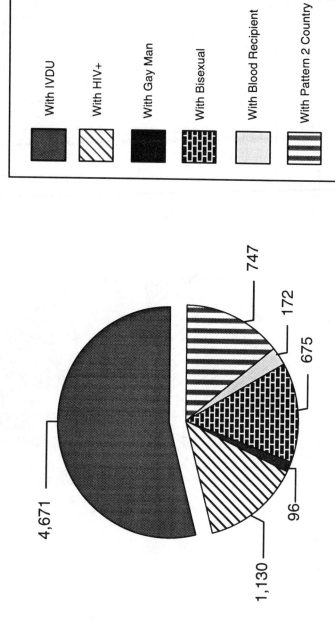

FIGURE 10. Female Heterosexual Contact (of 22,056 Cases Through February 1992)

With IVDU
With HIV+
With Gay Man
With Bisexual
With Blood Recipient
With Pattern 2 Country

4,671

747

172

675

96

1,130

their sexual partners, of which 67 percent were active or former IVDUs. Four percent of HIV-infected women contracted the virus from heterosexual male partners, and 16 percent from bisexual men. Eleven percent contracted HIV from a blood transfusion. Although the CDC does not keep statistics on lesbians with HIV infection, the documentation of several cases among lesbians who are not IVDUs suggests that sexual transmission between women is possible.

In 1989, only 5 percent of women were enrolled in AIDS clinical trial groups (ACTGs) conducted by the National Institute of Allergy and Infectious Diseases (NIAID). Often, physicians do not assess women for risk of HIV infection. Common somatic complaints in HIV-infected women remain undetected symptomatology that are most likely diagnosed as vaginal infections such as pelvic inflammatory disease (PID), vaginal candidiasis, and chronic vaginitis. (See Figure 11.)

> In some areas, right-wing elements have used AIDS to further their political agenda. In Vermont, for example, some conservatives attempted to discredit the reintroduction of the Equal Rights Amendment by tying it to the AIDS issue. The logic was equal rights means man hater, which equals lesbian, which means homosexual, which equals the spread of AIDS.[2]

As Kaspar notes, although lesbians are believed to be low-risk, they are susceptible to the disease. Besides risk of infection, many lesbians have devoted their professional, personal, and political lives to HIV activism, suffering the loss of many friends and colleagues and incurring political backlash:

> The lesbian community has seen its limited financial resources siphoned off to a relatively more affluent gay men's community. At the same time, gay men have not invested time, money, or energy back into the lesbian community.[3]

As HIV-infected individuals, women negotiate the dual obligation of managing their self-care; as primary caregivers, they must meet the needs of infected partners and children. (See Figure 12.) Variant configurations of infectivity and disease progression coexist

FIGURE 11. Gynecological Manifestations of HIV Disease in Women*

MENSTRUAL IRREGULARITIES
- irregular period
- heavier or scantier periods
- increase in premenstrual symptoms: breast pain, swelling, anxiety, depression, cramps

VAGINAL CANDIDIASIS
While vaginal candidiasis (yeast infection, thrush, or vaginitis) is common to most women, in HIV-infected women it is recurrent and persistent.
- thick, odorless, white or yellow discharge
- vaginal and vulvar itching or burning
- pain during urination
- raised white and gray patches on the vaginal skin

PELVIC INFLAMMATORY DISEASE (PID)
While common, in HIV-infected women it is more chronic.
- stomach pain or tenderness, lower back pain, pain during and after sex
- frequent need to urinate
- persistent cramps, fever, chills
- abnormal pain during bowel movements or urination
- fatigue or weakness
- cramping or stiffness of stomach muscles
- swelling of lymph nodes
- nausea, vomiting, headache, rapid pulse

HUMAN PAPILLOMARVIRUS (HPV) AND CERVICAL CANCER
HPV has been reported in 31-95% of HIV-positive women. In HIV+ women, cervical cancer is treatment resistant, recurs frequently, and progresses rapidly.

SEXUALLY TRANSMITTED DISEASES (STDs)
SYPHILIS
In primary syphilis, the following symptoms may present: painless, hard, red sores on or around skin or genitals, anus, or mouth. In secondary syphilis, there may be hair loss, sore joints, wide-spread rashes, swollen lymph nodes, and weight loss. In tertiary syphilis, there can be heart disease, eye disease, and neurosyphilis.

HERPES SIMPLEX VIRUS (HSV)
HSV can cause sores in or around the following:
- mouth, genital area, vagina, rectum, and anus.

CHLAMYDIA
Symptoms include the following:
- yellow vaginal or cervical discharge
- painful urination
- bleeding or pain with sex
- irregular menstrual periods
- spotting between periods

GONORRHEA
Symptoms, appearing within 3 to 11 days, include:
- increase in vaginal discharge
- uncomfortable and more frequent urination
- conjunctivitis
- menstrual irregularities
- swelling of vulva
- spotting after sexual intercourse

TRICOMONAS VAGINALIS
Symptoms, when present, include the following:
- itching and irritation
- yellow-green odorous discharge
- painful intercourse

* Adapted from *Treatment Issues*, Volume 6, Number 7, GMHC, New York, 1992.

within identical families, and this uniquely influences the mastery of family systems to surmount crisis events of disequilibrium and maintain homeostatic balance:

> Although the AIDS crisis and the gay response to it has opened the door to overcoming this invisibility and legitimizing the health needs of gay men, the attention it demands has set lesbians even further back from having our health care needs recognized–even when we have AIDS, are dying in astounding numbers from breast cancer and other cancers, and neglect our health care needs in order to care for others. And while AIDS has disproportionately affected gay men, the increase in anti-gay violence that has accompanied the epidemic affects gay men and lesbians equally.[4]

The late 1980s marked the development of prevention strategies and outreach efforts to reach new and diverse populations by several HIV-related agencies and hospital-based programs–several of which addressed the needs of women, people of color, and immigrant populations with insufficient funding sources, and within communities having complicated health quandaries:

> The situation in Harlem is extreme, but it is not an isolated phenomenon. We identified 51 health areas (of 353) in New York City, with a total population of 650,000, in which there were more than twice as many deaths among people under the age of 65 as would be expected if the death rates of U.S. whites applied."[5]

The questions of substance use and recovery is a central concern relating to HIV disease. Female IVDUs are thought of as more deviant than males and are consequently stereotyped and stigmatized. The drug industry is male-dominated both in the production and distribution of drugs. Women have less socioeconomic access to the drugs (particularly injection-needle drugs) that they are most frequently introduced to by men. Gender discrimination is prevalent in substance-use treatment programs that conform to the needs of male IVDUs:

> Treatment programs not only fail to address women's needs for female-oriented vocational training, child day care, asser-

FIGURE 12. U.S. AIDS Cases: Pediatric, Children, Adolescents, and Young Adults
(Reported Through August 1991)

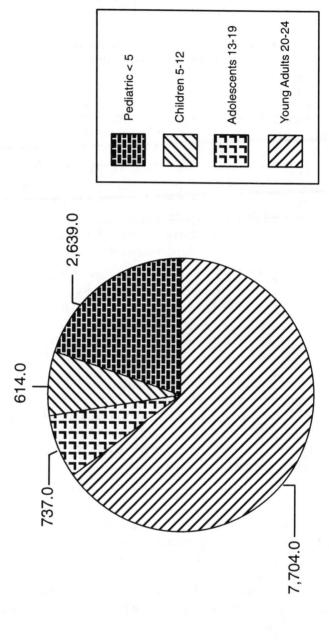

Pediatric < 5

Children 5-12

Adolescents 13-19

Young Adults 20-24

2,639.0

614.0

737.0

7,704.0

tiveness training, educational support and training, and health and social services, but they are hierarchal in nature, structured to require acceptance of an external locus of control.[6]

The concerns of women of color and those women who are HIV-seropositive often focus on the essentials of food, money, and shelter, so that access to appropriate HIV-related medical care is subsumed with women receiving early-intervention care later. These life-sustaining issues are urgent, and without attention, a sense of powerlessness becomes prevalent for the majority of HIV-infected women:

> For some women, the homeless environment was likened to a pit called limbo where no one wanted to be. One woman was ashamed for putting herself in the situation and reported being very lonely. This woman felt her life was wrecked by doing "unrepairable harm to myself physically, in terms of sex."[7]

The crisis predisposition reinforces this demoralization, so that precipitating events are insoluble in the immediate future. This internal tension exhausts coping mechanisms beyond an individual's customary problem-solving methods. The crisis reactivates unresolved problems from the past as well as those that are more current. Crisis theory defines this disequilibrium as an upset in a steady state with three sets of interrelated factors.

Factors That Precipitate Crisis[8]

- A hazardous event that poses some threat
- A threat to an instinctual need that is symbolically linked to earlier threats that resulted in vulnerability or conflict
- An inability to respond with adequate coping mechanisms

A WOMEN'S SUPPORT GROUP

Many of the earliest organizational responses to the epidemic recognized the significance of group intervention as an effective therapeutic strategy for individuals with HIV disease. HIV-related support groups were organized in communities throughout the United States, particularly in urban centers with considerable demographic incidence of HIV disease. Sponsoring organizations servicing the HIV-related population utilized several contrasting modalities. By 1991, congruent with epidemiological demographic modifications, support groups had to confront the emergent needs of women, people of color, and IVDUs. The synthesis of crucial issues of gender, race, culture, class, substance use, and geographic locale became essential to both the therapeutic approach and to organization of support groups.

The consequences of the HIV pandemic on service providers is particularly evident in metropolitan localities having considerable HIV-positive seroprevalence. Rural communities encounter challenges for which they are ill-equipped. The National Institute for Drug Abuse estimates that 350,000 to 400,000 people regularly inject heroin intravenously and that another one million inject the drug occasionally. Of these, slightly more than 500,000 are women. Awareness of effective education strategies and comprehension of the particular requirements of a target population are essential components for HIV prevention programs. There are myriad, but often predictable, ways that community-based multiservice organizations, medical, mental, and dental health providers, and substance-use treatment programs provide assistance for the shifting priorities of the populations they service.

A positive serostatus may be *the* presenting problem when an individual applies for support group membership, but there may also be a complex array of psychosocial problems. HIV-infected individuals are not a homogeneous group, though they experience many similar biomedical, psychological, and social difficulties. Nonprofessional voluntary staff often conduct the intake assessment interview, confining information-gathering narrowly to HIV-related concerns. The mental-health professional uses the intake interview as a pertinent diagnostic component. The dyadic intake interview, even under optimal circumstances, cannot prognosticate interpersonal group behavior. A possible clinical method is observation of a potential group member's interpersonal behavior in an intake or waiting list group that simulates the actual group–this method is known as pretherapy.[9] The purpose of the screening process is manifold, and it should not exclude information about the psychological life and functioning of the individual in favor of an exclusively social interpretation of a potential member.[10]

The refinement of the intake process is necessary because of the complications of substance use and impaired mental status frequent among HIV-positive individuals. These complications affect the interpersonal capacity, group dynamics, and the ability of the facilitator to conduct a successful group. Potential group members often present a tripartite diagnosis.

Tripartite Diagnosis

- Complex biomedical conditions
- Chronic or intermittent substance use
- Premorbid psychiatric disorders, often undiagnosed

Impaired mental functioning may be a consequence of underlying HIV-related neuropsychiatric organicity–for example, HIV dementia complex (HDC) or toxoplasmosis–or may develop during the course of illness. When this takes place, the clinician attempts to neutralize the effect of the cultural stigmatization of HIV disease by maintaining a committed, positive, nonjudgmental posture that might underestimate the appropriateness of a thorough diagnostic assessment.

The eventuality of complicated and debilitating illness (particularly during the terminal phase of illness) and of the death of individual group members is a notable concern within an HIV support group. Anticipatory loss threatens the transaction of individuals within the family system and continually threatens equilibrium. Within support groups, for instance, members experience a communal passage during various phases of membership illnesses and deaths. Feeling fundamental uncertainty, they struggle to maintain hope, often redefining their beliefs while simultaneously coping with preparedness for loss. The prosaism "giving up" symbolizes values laden with fear.

A partner's death causes enormously painful grief, with symptomatology that manifests psychologically and physically over considerable duration. Bowlby emphasizes the necessity of differentiating between healthy and pathological states within the mourning process. He points out that most of the clinical literature on grieving focuses on pathological variants, not on the normal process. This occurs because healthy and pathological responses to loss are complex and intricately related to each other. Bowlby proposes five categories or conditions that affect the course of mourning. The course of grieving is mediated by the personality structure of the bereaved:

> Perhaps some of them, acting in conjunction, could lead even a relatively stable person to mourn pathologically; but more often, it seems, their effect on a stable personality is to lead mourning to be both more intense and more prolonged that it would otherwise be. Their effects on a vulnerable personality, by contrast, are far more serious.[11]

The negative impact of bereavement on health has been called the *loss effect*:

> One of the most plausible alternative interpretations of the association of poor bereavement outcome and low social support is that it is due to some personality trait, such as neuroticism. Thus, neurotic persons might be more likely both to have (or perceive themselves as having) nonsupportive social environments and, at the same time, to be more likely to have breakdowns under the stress of bereavement.[12]

Within support groups, there are often unresolved bereavement issues for members who have joined the group shortly after the death of partner, family member, or other significant person.

Bowlby's Variables Affecting Mourning[13]

- The identity and role of the person lost
- The age and sex of the person bereaved
- The causes and circumstances of the loss
- The social and psychological circumstances affecting the bereaved about the time of and after the loss

• The personality of the bereaved, with special reference to his/
her capacities for making love relationships and for responding to stressful situations

Most HIV patients experience the physical, financial, legal, and
emotional problems that typically result from any chronic or terminal illness. Women have to reconcile their gender-typed role as a
caregiver with their HIV-seropositive diagnosis. Most often in our
culture, across racial and class distinctions, women are sole caregivers. Women are responsible for life-giving, nurturing, and the outcome of the infant's life into adulthood. Within single-parent households, women fulfill this role alone or with female support from
their extended family. Rather than being a noteworthy achievement,
the single-parent family has become disreputed.

In her germinal book on gender bias in the professions of psychiatry and psychology, Chessler noted that these male-dominated
professions accounted for the continuation of traditional myths
about abnormality, sex-role stereotypes, and the belief in female
inferiority. Traditional psychoanalytic and therapeutic theories and
practices participate in a misogynistic view of women, with sex-
role stereotypes defined as scientific alongside curative interventions that promote a male balance of power. She accuses the institution of private psychotherapy as a promoter of sexist ideologies, a
mirror of the female experience in patriarchal culture.[14]

Since the earliest theoretical formulations of the second wave of
feminism during the 1960s, a woman's basic right of sovereignty
over her body has been predominant. Therefore, women's health
concerns have been primarily to establish female-oriented and -ad-
ministered medical facilities. Politically, this has been compelling,
because male-dominated medical institutions have not provided for
women's health care without the imposition of sanctions and beliefs
contrary to the self-interest of women. The patriarchy has historically imposed itself into the most fundamental sphere of the female
gender, such as sexuality, mothering, childbirth, birth control, and
abortion. Again, during the 1990s, the issue of a woman's right of
choice–whether to become pregnant or to terminate a pregnancy–
has assumed center stage in federal and state legislative and judicial
branches of government.

Masculinist thought and art, on the other hand, have openly conceived, worshipped, and promulgated the *love-death*.[15]

Over the past several decades, feminists have scrutinized the underlying theories of psychiatry, psychology, and social work. Many aspects of the mental-health professions have been suspect because of male bias and the misinterpretation of women's experience. It is important to know what type of clinical treatment these psychiatric patients receive, how many clinicians there are, the theories on which the clinicians draw, and how these psychiatrists and psychologists view their patients. Until recently, the diagnosis of behavior difficulties is practiced without a discrete female developmental theory, so psychiatric categories are gender-biased.[16] Often, mental health professions treated the women's needs without regard to the distinctive cultural realities their lives and psychology, their life patterns, psychological processes and personality development.

THE FAMILY

Intervention efforts require development of gender and culture-specific strategies. There is insufficient knowledge on the mores of a community, such as social class, neighborhood, education, drug-use status, and other social and cultural variables–all of which have significant effects on sexuality.[17] For instance, women of color often integrate HIV into their traditional beliefs about illness:

> The most common patient complaints among Puerto Ricans are depression, anxiety, somatic concerns, hallucinations, and actual or feared loss of control. Patients rarely report depression as such but rather complain of symptoms of insomnia, eating problems, fatigue, headaches, body aches and feelings of weakness and exhaustion. Similarly, anxiety, in and of itself, may not be recognized by patients although manifested in reports of heart palpitations, dizziness, and fainting.[18]

Disease is viewed within a spiritual context because of evil influences, as punishment from God, or the disturbance of natural harmony. Prayer is curative. Laxatives, such as castor oil, are believed to keep the body healthy.[19] People also differ in their experience of pain, symptoms, the cause of illness, attitudes toward helpers, and treatment choices. There are also prototypical examples of HIV disease within families.

Examples of HIV Disease Within the Family System

- Seropositivity of each partner and child
- One partner with advanced HIV disease; the other, HIV-symptomatic
- Each partner HIV-infected with noninfected children
- Cross-generational representation of HIV disease, with grandparent, daughter, and child
- One child or sibling infected, not the other(s)
- One partner infected, not the other
- Multiple deaths within family and extended system
- New guardian of child(ren) also HIV-infected

McGoldrick and Pearce differentiate the definition of family cross-culturally, rejecting the dominant American meaning of family as the two-parent (mother and father) nuclear family. Diverse racial and ethnic groups determine the boundaries of a family through kindred and community. For instance, African-Americans define family through a combination of an extended network of kin and community. Several ethnic groups, such as Italians, determine a family multi-generationally, across three or four generations, including godparents and old friends. The Chinese include ancestors and descendants into their definition of family.[20] Lesbian families may include the children of each partner and an extended family of friends.

Factors of cultural variability guide revised conceptual models of clinical intervention, such as the definition of families that are racially or ethnically mixed or have same-sex pairings. As McGoldrick and Pearce write, the dominant model centers on the intact nuclear family, but African-American families, for instance, employ an extended network, including kin, community, and religious affiliations. Italian-Americans consider family across three or four generations, including godparents and old friends.[21] The gay or lesbian family includes a network of family, friends, and community. In Latino families, the *compadres* are sponsors or godparents participating in baptism, communion, and confirmation. This role is seriously undertaken and is not a formality. With death or disability of parents, *compadres* automatically assume parenting responsibility. Children of upbringing (*hijos de crianza*), foster children, are taken into the home and raised as one's own. No stigma is attached to a parent for surrendering the child, nor to the child who is given up.

Any illness, particularly HIV disease (with its negative value-laden assumptions) is a stimulant that creates conflict within the extended family system. When attempting to sustain the family unit, it is not uncommon to find a disorganized or dysfunctional support system. There is acute alienation from familial relationships. In their caregiving role, familiar responsibility is delegated to women, who are then blamed when difficulties arise.

The American family unit is characterized by an abnormal level of physical and sexual aggression. In incestuous families, maternal culpability is assigned when "the problem lies with the excessive power of the father" who feels it is his "prerogative to seek sex from his daughter."[22] Wife-battering, present in many marriages and relationships, is often viewed as part of the myth that holds the victim responsible for abuse. Women experience intolerable and self-destructive guilt.

Latinas experience a unique combination of power and powerlessness. The idea that personal problems are best discussed with women is very much a part of the culture:

> There is widespread belief among Hispanic women of all social classes that most men are undependable and are not to be trusted. At the same time, many of these women will put up with a man's abuses because having a man around is an important source of a woman's sense of self-worth.[23]

Although Latin women have the opportunity to exercise their power in some areas, they also receive constant cultural messages that they should be submissive and subservient to males in order to be seen as "good women." Suffering and being a martyr are characteristics of a "good woman." The high incidence of somatic complaints presented by low-income Hispanic women in psychotherapy might be a consequence of this emphasis on martyrdom, in which self-sacrifice is often a somatic expression of needs and anxieties.

Families have a cross-generational history of coping patterns to negotiate with disruption and the disequilibrium of serious illness and death. An assessment–or, if possible, a genogram–of a family system discloses the following.

Assessing Illness in the Family System[24]

- Time of the death or serious illness in the life cycle
- Nature of the death or serious illness
- Openness of the family system
- Family position of the serious ill, dying, or dead family member

Extended families often confront difficulties by allocating responsibility and several vague boundaries that create confusion and stress, so caregiving responsibilities might become contentious. The nonsupportive extended family creates further a caregiver's social isolation due to severe restriction of leisure and recreational time.[25]

HIV disease within a family system has important consequences for children who are protected from illness-related information and who may be isolated and excluded from major family decisions. A "web of silence"[26] surrounds the family, and children observe parental anxiety, preoccupation, physical absence, and illness, and death with poor information, so they lose confidence in their parents and become anxious about their future.

Roles within a family are recast when a member has HIV disease. Often, children are "parentified," assuming demanding roles as caregiver and confidantes, attending to the demands of parents:

> As the family adapts to the behavior and presence of the chronically ill member, this need for attention may be handled primarily by one member, who becomes a "rescuer." Given the traditional role expectations of women in our culture, the member is often the mother or wife of the PWA (Person with AIDS).[27]

The integration into the family of a member with HIV disease creates multiple dilemmas because, in and of itself, the caregiving for a chronically ill person is demanding. Yet frequently, family members with HIV disease stimulate unresolved and underlying problems surrounding sexual identity and patterns of substance use. Families that have been avoidant or hostile to the sexual identity of the person with HIV disease confront this concern during caregiving. As well, when there has been mistreatment by family members, resulting from the effect of substance use, the family is compelled to reconcile formerly unsurmountable difficulties. For instance, the primary caregiver mother might say "I remember one Thanksgiving, and I went to get the turkey to begin the dinner. It was gone. Tommy sold it on the street to get drugs." Domestic violence and wife-battering also exist in many American marriages:

> The sense of body power as human and healthy and a women's rejection of all forms of physical abuse. . . . Women's current attempts to exchange powerlessness and submissiveness for an internal sense of body power and enjoyment are causing reactions which range from surprise to disgust and rage.[28]

The consequence of marital violence is a severe and traumatic experience frequently precipitating depression and other related disorders. The phenomenon of self-blame has attracted considerable attention in recent years, particularly in relation to depression and self-esteem:

> There is a significant relation between early repeated abuse and types of attribution when in the violent relationship. When self-blame was reported, those with early abuse tended to blame their character and women without abuse tended to blame their behavior.[29]

Not only is marital violence associated with a greater risk of concurrent depression, but rates of depression for women no longer in violent relationships are high or higher than those of women currently still in such relationships.

Pribor and Dinwiddie found psychiatric correlates between sexual abuse and incest in childhood, and they suggested that patients who present with psychiatric disorders should be queried about childhood sexual abuse during history-taking:

> As expected, compared to general population rates, women in treatment who had a history of incest in childhood reported higher prevalence of virtually every psychiatric disorder investigated other than anorexia nervosa, mania, pathological gambling, and schizophrenia. Much of the higher rate could be attributed to sampling from a treatment population; however, even when compared to age- and race-matched treated comparison subjects, incest victims still demonstrated higher rates of anxiety disorders (agoraphobia, panic disorder, PTSD, and phobias), depression, and alcohol abuse and dependence.[30]

The persistence of episodes of depression after the point of separation from a violent partner may be explained in a number of ways, not the least by the continuing existence of social stressors or deprivation:

> Borderline patients did experience a significantly higher rate of sexual abuse in their childhood years, including abuse by family members as well as nonfamily individuals, than did the depressed group. Seventy-one percent of the borderline patients but only 22% of the depressed patients reported a history of sexual abuse. Although we used a broad definition of sexual abuse, including exhibitionism and fondling, over 40% of the sexual abuse involved penetration.[31]

The experience of sexual and physical abuse in childhood often results in the development of borderline psychopathology.

THE METAETHICS OF CAREGIVING

Frequently, the life necessities of women become subsidiary to those of men. Professional psychological treatment becomes reinforced into gender-typed distorted cultural definitions of behavior, attitudes, and values. Approximately, 90% of psychiatrists and more than two-thirds of psychologists are male; often, they have not received adequate training about women's needs.[32] Feminists suggest that a radical shift of primary ego-identity is necessary for women's survival as strong individuals.[33] The presentation of depression by women is often rooted in powerlessness.

By itself, caregiving has influences deleterious to the physical, social, and psychological well-being of the caregiver.[34] When there is no provision of respite for the caregiver, it affects physical, emotional, and spiritual well-being. Physically, caregivers may present progressive somatization with complaints of headaches, dizziness, back pain, and the inhibition or alteration of sleep patterns. Psychologically, caregivers deny, displace, conceal, and suppress anger; they feel depression, guilt, resentment, and self-blame. When the care-receiver's condition worsens, increased demands compel blame; the caregiver is filled with new foreboding about the future. The range of emotional distress for a caregiver becomes exacerbated when a central concern may be the mode of viral transmission. Self-blame, in particular, is precipitated when perinatal transmission is the risk factor for an infant or child. A mother's self-censure is a significant emotional stressor whether or not she knew her serostatus during pregnancy.

Transmission by a nondisclosing partner who engaged in extra-relational sexual behavior, drug use, or had an unrevealed history of either, or both, is a principal issue within families. Underlying transmission issues intensify anxiety, creating predicaments for women as caregivers because they feel it is inappropriate to express anger to their ill partner. Anger, however, surfaces in numerous indirect ways.

Often, male partners relinquish responsibility, so female partners must negotiate with medical providers, social service agencies, and schools. For instance, a dyadic subsystem is supported between female caregivers and physicians. Dysfunction results for both the care-receiver and the caregiver, when biomedical concerns such as diagnosis, medical care, and medication instructions and compliancy occur with a patient who is nonparticipatory.

Within the family system, women are socialized to attend to the needs of others, so women "have been led to feel that they can integrate and use all their attributes if they use them for others, but not for themselves."[35] As sole or primary caregivers to HIV-infected individuals, women contend with the dual uncertainty of their biomedical condition and that of a family member, a partner, a parent, or child. An analysis of caregiving role requires an ecosystemic framework to include extrafamilial interactions.

REFERENCE NOTES

1. Tema Luft, "Going Public," in *AIDS: The Women*, edited by Ines Rieder and Patricia Ruppelt (San Francisco: Cleis Press, 1988), p. 68.

2. Barbara Kaspar, "Women and AIDS: A Psycho-Social Perspective," *AFFILIA*, Volume 4, Number 4, Winter 1989, p. 15.

3. Deborah Stone, "A Selfish Kind of Giving," in *AIDS: The Women*, edited by Ines Rieder and Patricia Ruppelt (San Francisco: Cleis Press, 1988), p. 148.

4. Risa Denenberg, "Invisible Women: Lesbians and Health Care," *Health/PAC Bulletin*, Spring 1992.

5. Colin McCord, MD, and Harold P. Freeman, MD, "Excess Mortality in Harlem," *New England Journal of Medicine*, June 18, 1990, Volume 322, Number 3.

6. Dooley Worth, "Minority Women and AIDS: Culture, Race, and Gender," in *Culture and AIDS*, edited by Douglas A. Feldman (New York: Praeger Publishers, 1990), p. 114.

7. Adeline M. Nyamathi, RN, PhD and Charles E. Lewis, MD, ScD, "Coping of African-American Women at Risk for AIDS," *WHI*, Volume 1, Number 2, Winter 1991.

8. Lydia Rapoport, "The State of Crisis: Some Theoretical Considerations," in *Crisis Intervention: Selected Readings*, edited by Howard J. Parad (New York: Family Service Association of America, 1965), p. 25.

9. Irvin D. Yalom, *The Theory and Practice of Group Psychotherapy* (New York: Basic Books, 1975), p. 259.

10. Francis J. Turner, *Social Work Treatment* (New York: The Free Press, 1986), p. 305.

11. John Bowlby, *Attachment and Loss, Volume III, Loss: Sadness and Depression* (New York: Basic Books, 1980), p. 173.

12. Wolfang Stroebe and Margaret S. Stroebe, *Bereavement and Health* (New York: Cambridge University Press, 1987), p. 225.

13. Bowlby, *Attachment and Loss*, p. 172.

14. Phyllis Chesler, *Women & Madness* (New York: Avon, 1972), p. 61.

15. Robin Morgan, *The Demon Lover* (New York: W. W. Norton & Company, 1989). p. 102.

16. Chesler, *Women & Madness*, p. 57.

17. Mindy Thompson Fullilove, MD et al., "Black Women and AIDS Prevention: A View Towards Understanding the Gender Rules," *The Journal of Sex Research*, Volume 27, Number 1, February 1990.

18. Sandra Samaniego, PhD, "Cultural Considerations in the Psychotherapy of the Puerto Rican Patient," unpublished paper.

19. Jacquelyn H. Flaskerud and Cecilia E. Rush, "AIDS and Traditional Health Beliefs and Practices of Black Women," *Nursing Research*, Volume 38, Number 4, July/August 1989.

20. Monica McGoldrick and John K. Pearce, *Ethnicity and Family Therapy* (New York: Guilford Press, 1984).

21. Ibid., p. 75.

22. Kathleen Koch and Carolynne Jarvis, "Symbiotic Mother-Daughter Relationships in Incest Families," *Social Casework*, February 1987.

23. Olivia M. Espin, "Psychotherapy with Hispanic Women: Some Considerations," in *Handbook of Cross-Cultural Counseling and Therapy*, edited by Paul Pedersen (Westport, CT: Greenwood Press, 1985), p. 169.

24. Fredda Herz, RN, PhD, "The Impact of Death and Serious Illness on the Family Life Cycle" in *The Family Life Cycle: A Framework for Family Therapy*, edited by Elizabeth Carter and Monica McGoldrick (New York: Gardner Press, 1985), p. 125.

25. Salvador Minuchin, *Families and Family Therapy* (Cambridge, MA: Harvard University Press, 1974), p. 95.

26. Patricia McKeever, MScN, "Siblings of Chronically Ill Children," *American Journal of Orthopsychiatry*, 53(2), April 1983.

27. Jim A. Cates, Linda L. Grahman, Donna Boeglin, and Steven Tielker, "The Effect of AIDS on the Family System," *Families in Society: The Journal of Contemporary Human Services*, Family Service America, 1990, p. 196.

28. Helen V. Collier, *Counseling Women: A Guide for Therapists* (New York: The Free Press, 1982), p. 210.

29. Bernice Andrews and Chris R. Brewin, "Attributions of Blame for Marital Violence: A Study of Antecedents and Consequences," *Journal of Marriage and the Family*, Number 52, August 1990.

30. Elizabeth F. Pribor, MD, and Stephen H. Dinwiddie, MD, "Psychiatric Correlates of Incest in Childhood," *American Journal of Psychiatry*, 149:1, January 1992, p. 55.

31. Susan N. Ogata, PhD, Kenneth R. Silk, MD, and Sonya Goodrich, PhD, "The Childhood Experience of the Borderline Patient," in *Family Environment and Borderline Personality Disorder* (Washington, DC: American Psychiatric Press, 1990), pp. 93-94.

32. Collier, *Counseling Women*, p. 3.

33. Chesler, *Women & Madness*, p. 299.

34. Ronald W. Toseland, PhD, et al., "The Effectiveness of Three Group Intervention Strategies to Support Family Caregivers," *American Journal of Orthopsychiatry*, 59(3), July 1989.

35. Jean Baker Miller, *Toward a New Psychology of Women* (Boston: Beacon Press, 1986), p. 61.

Chapter 7

Another Voice

The dependency of all the luminous bodies, of all the heavenly powers and gods, on the Great Mother, their rise and fall, their birth and death, their transformation and renewal, are among the most profound experiences of mankind.

–Erich Neumann, *The Great Mother*

THE FORMATION OF A WOMEN'S GROUP

An HIV-related women's group was organized in the borough of Brooklyn, New York, where there is a statistically high seroprevalence of HIV disease. The needs of the population, particularly as they relate to women, were underserviced since the majority of HIV community-based organizations were located in Manhattan. The group met weekly for a one-and-a-half-hour session. The group's membership had eight members, who were referred and interviewed for membership.

Phases of Group Development

- Pregroup phase
  - –private pregroup phase
  - –public pregroup phase
  - –convening phase

- Group Formation Phase
  –integration
  –disintegration
  –conflict reintegration
  –reorganization
  –synthesis phase

- Group Functioning and Maintenance phase
- Termination Phase
  –pretermination phase
  –termination
  –posttermination

The topology of the host agency engendered typical institutional conflicts on the nature of organizational mission, which was not HIV-specific, so the agency struggled with its response to the HIV pandemic. Without the support of institutional sponsors and the larger community, the programmatic goals will be difficult to achieve. Factors blocking these goals include (1) integrating HIV prevention into existing services (for example, sex education, health counseling, or prenatal care); (2) issues of staff burnout, leading to high turnover and low morale, varying staff responsibilities, and providing staff with adequate supervision, training, and support; and (3) allowing staff to play a role in setting their own workplace. To develop effective preventive campaigns, HIV educators need to understand the specific behaviors and social environments that put women at risk for HIV infection:

> Many factors can prevent administrators from wanting to put HIV prevention high on their agenda: denial that HIV is a problem in their setting, fear that the agency will be stigmatized by its association with HIV; unwillingness to offend those who oppose public health (as opposed to moralistic) approaches to prevention.[1]

Sometimes, more progressive institutions scrutinized their mission to augment direct-service specifications with consequent intra-agency disputes. The pandemic outbreak is simultaneous to federal withdrawal of financial allocation.

Agencies persevere with limited funding resources, and crisis-driven rationale supersedes well-planned program development. Some agencies opportunistically respond to funding allocation without setting goals, thus creating structural problems such as fragmentation of services, with antagonistic and competitive rivalries toward expansion preferences. This occurs especially within organizations that have irresolute and uncreative leadership and that lack sound policy-setting mechanisms. Program expansion occurs even when there are inadequately and insufficiently trained staff. HIV-increased obligations on existing staff takes place without critical additional training, supervision, and support. Many agencies with non-HIV programs are located where HIV development faces barriers due to executive, administrative, and staff resistance to providing services to populations most affected by the pandemic (and where hidden prejudicial attitudes emerge frequently in unpredictable behaviors).

The HIV-related women's group was initiated within an ambiance of unresolved policy, considering the impact of the pandemic on the population it services and on the expansion of its mission to incorporate services. The agency administered confidential HIV-antibody testing with pre- and posttest counseling in its clinic, and during the second year there was a fourfold increase of self-referrals for testing. The group responded to the availability of funding through the New York State Department of Health AIDS Institute to establish a comprehensive HIV case management program.

The program included evaluation of clients regarding their biomedical knowledge of HIV disease, including treatment options, clinical trials, benefits, the routes of viral transmission, and safer-sex procedures. Salient issues of antiviral and prophylaxis treatments were delineated, and the client receives biomedical education about T4 cell testing procedures. An assessment of the client's medical status is critical, so she may be referred for appropriate medical intervention and further evaluation. Clients received assistance to access primary medical care. The program provided psychological support services using several mental modalities to address the psychological repercussions of an HIV-seropositive diagnosis, including crisis intervention, psychoeducation, supportive counseling, group services, couple counseling, and extended individual psychotherapy.

Integral to the program is the social services component for clients who are homeless, without financial entitlements, have no medical insurance coverage, have never been medically evaluated, have poor dietary habits due to poverty, have unplanned pregnancies, are socially isolated, have experienced many losses due to HIV disease (including the death of life partners), have been discriminated against due to race and sexual orientation, have limited understanding about HIV disease, or are debilitated from long histories of substance use.

Prevention and educational inreach strategies were developed for intervention in the clinic, particularly during clinic sessions for the treatment and diagnosis of sexually transmitted diseases. With volunteer support, video showings on HIV were presented in the waiting areas. Patients have been voluntarily participating in self-administered risk assessments, as well as risk assessments one-to-one. Case-finding, a social-work tool, provides patients with more than the distribution of condoms or brochures, which by themselves cannot provide complete information or help people with techniques to modify behavior.

Most waiting-room patients were attentive to the videos, but those patients who are not interested have the option to move to a different waiting area. The program provided training for interns and volunteers, covering a full complement of HIV-related issues. Interns and volunteers have been a cost-effective method of providing continuing education for patients, as well as for those who accompany patients for services. A staff inreach worker stationed in clinic waiting areas presents a continuous video loop, condom demonstrations, and is available for individual consultations.

The program began with a dedicated telephone line to serve as a resource for HIV-related questions from the community. Telephone and in-person counseling sessions are conducted with individuals who are not ready to proceed with the antibody test, but who are worried or suffering stress from an inability to conform with sexual behavior modification that would help prevent contracting HIV.

Several organizations applied the technique of mutual peer support originated by Alcoholics Anonymous (AA), a self-help prototype adapted to meet the requirements of many diverse anonymous programs. Positives Anonymous (PA) conducts open membership meetings for people with HIV disease by using circumscribed nonhierarchal organizational structure. Members share their experience, strength, and hope to encourage fellowship and commonality through identification with a speaker. The sharing process is noninteractive, although reference to content can be made by a later speaker.

New York City-based Body Positive initiated a program of support groups in many communities to address the requirements of diverse populations. These are peer-facilitated groups adhering to the paradigm of self-empowerment through mutual support. The agency has an extensive volunteer base from which facilatators, most of whom are HIV-positive, receive training after participation in a support group. The support groups are time-limited (usually lasting 12 weeks) and closed, with members screened through an interview process. Gay Men's Health Crisis (GMHC) implemented closed, open-ended AIDS therapy groups (ATG) facilitated by voluntary mental-health professionals. GMHC requires therapists to be members of a supervision group directed by staff. The agency does not impose adherence to any one theoretical approach, so the therapists—with their varied training—practice differing techniques.

The HIV-related women's group met for a year and a half in an easily accessible, centrally located women's reproductive health clinic in the business district of Brooklyn, New York. The group membership was organized from two family-planning clinic populations in New York City. Additionally, a New York City Department of Health Anonymous HIV Test Site provided group referrals through the efforts of two counselors, Sarah Ramirez and Philip Melendez. Several newsletters that service the HIV community announced the formation of the group, and flyers were posted in various settings where women receive a variety of health-related services.

Returning to this concept of circularity and oneness that preceded patriarchy, racism, class systems, and other hierarchies that ration self-esteem—and that create obedience to external authority by weakening belief in our natural and internal wisdom—is truly a revolution from within.[2]

CONFLUENCE OF THERAPIST AND GROUP

The issue of gender was a fundamental consideration during the planning stages to initiate the group. The suitability of a male therapist to facilitate an all-women's group seemed speculative. Feminist orthodoxy challenges male eligibility to comprehend the distinctive needs of women present, and that male presence, of itself, inhibits the therapeutic process and consciousness-raising. My personal and political allegiance as a profeminist directly contradicted the appropriateness of facilitating a women's group. I struggled with a serious dilemma. For more than two decades, since I first became conscious of the women's movement and its politics and philosophy, feminism influenced many of my life decisions.

It was inconceivable to facilitate a women's group. In fact, my profeminism and awareness of the extent women suffer in patriarchal systems seemed to make me more of a unsuitable candidate than a therapist with less consciousness of women's issues. This does not indicate that a professional who supports theories that reinforce male supremacy, including most psychoanalysis, would be preferable. My reticence to facilitate a women's group was not shared by the agency.

GROUP MEMBERSHIP

Many members of the group are in substance-use recovery. The women are mostly symptomatic or fully HIV-disease diagnosed. Two women have been pregnant; one has an HIV-seropositive infant, another has an infant who seroconverted to negative; and several are struggling with pregnancy concerns. Most of the women have children. Several members are grandmothers. Many members of the group come from families multidiagnosed, such as HIV-seropositive partners; three of the women's husbands have died from HIV within the last year. Several have partners who are critically ill from HIV disease. Most of the women live on fixed incomes and are below the poverty level. The racial component of the group was caucasian, African-American, and Latina. The following are bio-psychosocial descriptions of the group members.

* * *

Carmen is a 27-year-old Latina who has used drugs since adolescence. She is HIV-positive, symptomatic, with a T-cell count of 170, which constitutes risk for several opportunitistic infections, such as *Pneumocystis carinii* pneumonia (PCP). She was hospitalized throughout the past year for drug-associated infections, principally endocarditis and chronic hepatitis.

She has a history of supporting herself and her addiction through sex: her john first introduced her to intravenous drug use (IVDU). Before being jailed, she lived on the streets–in abandoned cars, on rooftops, and in apartment hallways. She has three children: Tito, 9, Marisa, 3 (who's in foster care), and Annette, 10 months. Annette has HIV disease, and is cared for by Carmen's sister, Maria. Carmen's mother, also named Carmen, is incarcerated for armed robbery. Her mother's husband, Juan, is an alcoholic who sexually abused Carmen and her oldest sister when she was 11.

Carmen said: "I want my kids back. They're mine. Even Annette; I want to take care of her. My mother don't let me know what's happen'. When she has tests, she don't tell me. When she was in the hospital, I didn't know nothin'."

Carmen, forced to leave her mother's apartment due to her continued drug use, had been homeless, sleeping in hallways and basements.

"I used to steal from her," Carmen told the group. "I remember once she went to cook the Thanksgiving turkey, and I had sold it.

"I've been clean for three months in a program. I go to NA [Narcotics Anonymous] meetings, too. I've been through a lot. Seen things that I wish I didn't. I had to prostitute myself to survive. I remember once, a doctor threw me out of the hospital because he found out I split one afternoon to cop drugs. I came back, but he told me I had to leave. He called it a 'disciplinary discharge.' I found out he wrote on my medical chart that I was 'performing fellatio' on rooftops. I didn't even know what fellatio meant, but I found out. I got pissed."

Multiple marriages are usual in Carmen's extended family, and her father, Enrique, now deceased, was married five times.

"He got killed for selling bad stuff," Carmen said. "I didn't really know him. After he left, I didn't see him again until I was 12.

I was about eight when he left. I didn't give a shit by then. I guess I was curious though."

There is a pattern of attempted suicide in the family, including her mother, who is her father's second wife (his first wife committed suicide). Carmen's brother, Pedro, attempted shooting himself. A few months after Enrique separated from Carmen's mother, her mother attempted suicide, taking antidepressants with alcohol. She had discovered that he was living with his soon-to-be third wife.

There is an extensive history of substance use in the family, including both parents and her brother Peter. There is also mental illness: Carmen's mother was institutionalized after the suicide attempt. The family has a pattern of keeping secrets, and Carmen discovered as an adult where her mother had been: "I was eight, and both of them were gone. He with another woman and she in a mental hospital. I didn't know what had happened. I was being taken care of by my mother's sister, my aunt. But she didn't tell me nothin'."

Carmen discovered that her husband Ernesto, from whom she is separated, was hospitalized for pneumonia: "I didn't know what PCP was, but I got afraid. I'd seen many people I did drugs with get sick, get AIDS. I went to see him. I didn't know that was him when I went into the room. He used to be so big. When I left I was angry and in shock. How could this happen? He introduced me to IV drugs. We'd shared needles many times. I knew that I was pregnant. I didn't know what to do. I knew a social worker from one of the hospitals where I had been. I called her. I wanted to get into a program. Then, I decided to have an HIV test. I wasn't prepared for the results, so I never went back to get them. I found out when Annette was born."

                              *   *   *

Donna is a 29-year-old Italian-American female who was diagnosed with AIDS during a hospitalization when treated for PCP.

"Man. I didn't know what was goin' on," she told the group. "They said I got pneumonia. So I thought, 'Big deal.' I had so many close calls in my life. But I knew this was different. Well, you don't need a degree. They moved me to another ward with these precaution signs everywhere. I felt like a leper. I didn't want to think it was AIDS. Ya know what I mean? But they'd look at me funny. And even the nurses who tried to be nice. . . . I knew it was serious. They didn't tell me it was AIDS. This social worker kept comin' to talk with me. Well, she musta thought I was in big denial. I guess she put it together, that I didn't really know it was AIDS. She made the doctor come and talk to me, and she stayed in the room with me. I was freaked. Even with my drug history. I didn't wanna believe it."

Donna had led a double existence, having snorted cocaine for six years, without her family's knowledge.

"At least I thought no one knew. I thought they were stupid. I'd be at work. They must've thought I had a bladder problem. I was always in the bathroom. I sit at my desk stoned. I was this secretary on Wall Street. High all day. When I began to shoot drugs, I'd keep my works stuffed in my boots. I'd ride the subway with the other nine-to-fivers with needles stuffed in my boots. I'd sit on the train, feeling like a fraud, a junkie, and I'd put my makeup on.

"One day at work, I was so high I walked into a wall. You could hear it across the room. Crack! I had to go to an emergency room to get stitched up. They began to look at me different. So I quit. Said that I needed rest. Said my father was dying of cancer."

When her common-law husband, Tommy, discovered she had AIDS, he beat her with a tire iron and refused to be HIV-tested. She has a ten-year-old son, Kenny, with a learning disability and a pattern of truancy from school.

"I can't tell him. I've been clean for almost two years. It was enough that his mother was a junkie. I used to neglect him. I can't put this on him. Sometimes, though, I think he knows, and I feel that's why he's truant. One time I had a friend [Cookie] from NA over. Cookie looks ill. When she left, Kenny says to me, 'She got AIDS. Don't she?' I says, 'Yes,' but I don't tell him about me.

"Ya know, I know Tommy's positive. He's got symptoms. He got lymph nodes out to here. But he don't do nothin' about it. I know he's scared. Nothin' I tell him matters. I think he's usin' again. He disappears for hours. Don't tell me where he's gone. I know he's usin'."

* * *

Rhonda is a 48-year-old African-American woman whose husband of 17 years was diagnosed with PCP. She was unaware that her husband, a pastor, was having sexual relations outside the marriage. During her interview, she explained her religious faith, stating that she felt that God would protect her. When she continued, however, she expressed that her greatest fear was focused upon pain. During her husband's hospitalization in an AIDS unit, she witnessed the death of a patient in an adjoining bed. The patient hadn't received sufficient medication to manage pain. This had a profound effect upon her. Also, she saw numerous examples of the process of HIV disease. Despite the security of her faith, she feared the possibility of a slow, painful death.

After diagnosis, persons with AIDS (PWAs) feel a loss of control, both physically and financially, with rage at the "unfairness" of the illness and the "loss of a future." A PWA may become depressed, feeling guilty and helpless. They deny that this could happen. There is a loss of self-esteem and control.

*   *   *

Harriet was diagnosed with PCP over a year ago, and she has not been hospitalized since this episode. Harriet has a limited support system, except a friend committed to helping her. Her sister died of AIDS two years ago. The friend is the only member of her social supports who knows her diagnosis. Harriet is terrified of rejection, and the emotional burden of her AIDS diagnosis is unshared with anyone else. Harriet was a former IVDU who began using when in high school and continued through two years of college (at the time of her first pregnancy). Her husband was arrested and imprisoned in an upstate prison facility, where he has been more than ten years. She said, "I'm in prison too. Those on the outside aren't free. Prison inside and out."

Knowing that her daughter is ill, Harriet's mother, who lives in a retirement community in Florida, arrived to stay with her daughter and offer assistance. Harriet's mother accompanied her to an AIDS clinic, sitting in the reception room, looking very troubled and lost, feeling at a loss to help her daughter, whose debilitated condition was evident. Apparently, she did not disclose to her mother.

The initial session with Harriet centered upon two areas: arranging with an AIDS Center attorney to arrange custody papers for her children. This constituted a major step for Harriet by involving another professional, other than medical, in planning her life. The second intervention was to encourage Harriet to share the stress of her diagnosis with others who can offer support.

She was admitted to the hospital in a state of delirium. A nurse, attempting to reach her said, "Do you know Steve?" She replied, "Of course I know him. I love him." Those were her last words to me.

* * *

Tonya is a 37-year-old African-American whose husband died a month and a half ago. At the time of his death, she discovered that he had AIDS, and she went to be HIV-tested. She was HIV-seropositive. She has no symptoms. She said, "I collect my hair each day and put it in a drawer."

Tonya's teenage daughter, Alice, has begun substance experimentation, including alcohol and marijuana. One early morning, several patrons found her outside a dance club, missing one of her shoes and leaning against a wall in a drunken state. Tonya's son, Jamal, has been sexually provocative toward Alice, making seductive comments and touching her. Tonya's youngest son, Scott, tried to intercede, threatening to kill Jamal if he touched her again.

Tonya had been in treatment with another clinician several years ago before she discovered her HIV-positive status. She said, "I knew it would never work for me. I wasn't really serious about therapy. I either came late to sessions or didn't show up at all. The therapist would call me, leaving messages that I wouldn't return."

* * *

Beth is a 39-year-old Irish-American. Milton, her husband, is a 45-year-old Russian-Jew; they have been lovers for 18 years. Beth was diagnosed HIV-positive two years ago; Milton, three years ago. Milton has HIV-related dementia complex (HDC), suffering considerable cognitive impairment. Beth is HIV-symptomatic, with lymphadenopathy. Beth has five children: Roger, the oldest, is 23, and Billy is 22; both were born of an unmarried relationship with the same biological father. Kevin, 20, was placed in a foster home at infancy, biologically fathered from a different unmarried relationship. Sissy, 16, and Michael, 12, are both children of the only marriage. Currently, Michael, Sissy, and Roger live in their mother's former apartment in the same neighborhood.

In addition to her serostatus, Beth has a past history of several somatic disabilities, including hypertension and obesity. Additionally, she is an alcoholic in remission who recovered through the program of Alcoholics Anonymous (having attended meetings for a couple of years, but has since discontinued going). Alcoholism is prevalent, active and inactive, cross-generationally in her family, as well as within significant relationships. For instance, both of her parents were alcoholic; her husband, her unmarried relationships, each son, and her teenage daughter have all begun to exhibit symptoms.

*   *   *

Gladys is a 28-year-old Latina who is two months pregnant. Her partner has not tested for HIV. She has three children in foster care. Her mother died the previous year at age 48 in an HIV-disease nursing home. It was at that time that Gladys made the decision to be tested for HIV. Gladys has no history of substance use.

*   *   *

Jill is a 31-year-old Italian-American female with two children. She and her husband are each HIV-seropositive. Her husband's medical condition is more advanced. Her two children, neither of whom know of her HIV status, have questioned their parents about their frequent medical visits and have noticed the medications they take. Both Jill and her husband are in NA and have been in recovery for over three years. They met when they were adolescents and have been married for 15 years.

"I never thought we'd be together for so many years. I remember my wedding day–I didn't take it seriously. We were both using drugs at the time, and I barely made it down the aisle I was so strung out. Since recovery, I realize that we don't know each other and have very little in common. I often feel confused, and he tells me constantly that I'm crazy, that I don't know what I'm talking about. We do very little together, and I can't remember the last time we had a social evening together; I think it was a couple of months ago. We never discuss HIV. It's almost as if it doesn't exist, but I feel that it's like a time bomb. I'm not sure how I'd feel if I had to take care of him, because I know that he'll get sick before me. At least that's what I think."

Jill's parents were separated when she was about six, and she knows little of her father. Family legend is that he took a loaded gun one night and pointed it at the children when he and Jill's mother were having one of their violent quarrels.

* * *

Diann has been out of a substance-use rehabilitation residence for about two months and is in a treatment aftercare program. She was tested for HIV when at the rehab. She was shocked by the result, though she had been sharing needles for years (and many of her needle-sharing partners died). Her partner, Darren, was HIV-tested the month before she entered a drug rehabilitation program. She received a brief letter from Darren, letting her know he was HIV-positive. She said, "Damn. I was committed to the program for 18 months. I got this news the first month. I wanted to split. Wanted it real bad. I don't know what kept me there. I guess I was tired of self-destructing myself. They offered to do the test, but I said, 'No. I think I need more time.' I know I made the right decision. Coming back positive would have blown me away. Then I got word that Darren was sick. I got real scared. He was in the hospital with meningitis. I heard that he wasn't doin' too well. God. We had gotten through so much together. We lived on the streets and then in this crummy welfare hotel. But, I knew in my gut we wouldn't get through this one together. I was afraid I might never see him again."

She comes from a very deprived, dysfunctional, alcoholic, poverty-stricken background, with sexual and verbal abuse. She was also a battered wife. She said, "My life has been shit." During a late session, she revealed two important pieces of information. She had been hospitalized at Pilgrim State Hospital for almost a year when she was 17. This information had not been given during months of treatment, because she felt a sense of shame and fear of mental illness that prevented her from relating this pertinent information. She felt that she was hospitalized because her family was incapable of taking appropriate care of her, and this constituted a traumatic period of her life. The second piece of information was that she had been sexually abused by an uncle for several years. Her mother denied the incidents, and this forced Diann into secrecy.

*   *   *

Charise is a 36-year-old African-American who has been in therapy several times within an outpatient department (OPD) of psychiatry in a community hospital. She has been in treatment previously at the OPD for a duration of several months with the presenting problems of agoraphobia and panic attacks. During a session, she categorized her prior treatment at the OPD as ineffective; after terminating treatment at the OPD, she sought treatment at another hospital clinic, where the treatment modality included behavior modification therapy and hypnosis.

Socially, Charise has several neighborhood friends, maintains peripheral contact with members of AA, is a regular church-goer, and works as a volunteer to the homeless through her parish. She was, until recently, part-time employed, serving lunches in a parochial school cafeteria.

Of familial relations, she has limited contact with members of her extended family, except a tenuous relationship with her sister and with a brother-in-law from her divorced marriage. Her nuclear family appears to know little of Charise's social life except that she attends AA.

Predominant themes emerged about repetitive patterns in family functioning and the implications of cross-generational alcoholism. Charise's family relationships were characterized as distant, conflicted, and violent. Thomas, her son, employed as a messenger, is described by his mother as socially isolated and friendless, an active alcoholic and sociophobic (he retreats into his room during visits from family friends or relatives). His dyslexia, complicated by emotional difficulties, prevented him from getting a high school education. Charise describes him as always having been a problem.

"Even when he was a child, if he didn't get his way he would throw tantrums. As he got older, it didn't stop, it just got different. I think he likes to see me get upset. I get nervous and he laughs at me. I guess he knows how nervous I get, and he likes to taunt me. I just want to get rid of him. I hate him. I don't know why he won't leave me alone."

As a child, Thomas Jr. suffered from scarlet fever and was hospitalized for several months. When he returned, his maternal grandmother assumed active responsibility for him and became a principal in his childrearing. Charise expresses feelings that he had been spoiled by his grandmother. She has fears about his dependency upon her. Her descriptions of him resonate sexually and are repetitive of her relations with men. She says the basis of her fears are culturally reflective observations of African-American men and their mothers.

"Ya know. Seeing a mother and son walking down the street arm-in-arm, it gets me very upset. When he touches me, I get upset. I just want to get away from him. He thinks he's so cute. The thought of seeing a mother and son together sickens me."

Besides the presenting problem, Charise began to describe behavioral difficulties with her three other children (except for the youngest child). For instance, her oldest son, Steven, is a felon, arrested for possession of a weapon and assault. Around the same time, he attempted suicide and was hospitalized briefly. He refused therapeutic treatment, although he attended several sessions with a clinician. He is an alcoholic in remission and attends AA meetings.

Reframing shifted the focus of the immediacy of her problem with Thomas by expanding the meaning of the presenting symptom into a broader framework thus she was more able to understand her difficulties. Caution had to be exercised so Charise was not endangered and her self-interest was protected during this examination of the historical context of her problem.

One of her parenting role concerns in terms of Thomas was his inability to function socially and economically and that he would remain with her "forever." She noted, "When I see a mother and son walking down the street arm-in-arm, it makes me sick." If the clinician examines her anxiety solely from an intrapsychic perspective, he/she might consider the comment as a by-product of an unresolved Oedipal situation. However, within African-American culture, it is not uncommon for mothers to live with adult children who have not left home. On the other hand, there may be underlying sexual issues between Thomas and his mother; however, with the comprehension of ethnic influences, the puzzle has more pieces, is more intricate, and helps the clinician to be more sensitive to conflicts and biases.

Children of alcoholics (COAs) come from unmanageable back-grounds, and in Charise's case, both parents were afflicted by the disease of alcoholism. Several of her difficulties appear symptomat-ic of COAs, such as (1) having to guess at what normal behavior is; (2) having difficulty with relationships; (3) lacking the ability to gauge the effect of changes within the family; and (4) low self-es-teem manifested by constantly seeking a steady emotional state.

*   *   *

Group formation requires that group members understand and accept what membership in the group will mean, at both cognitive and emotional levels. However, acceptance of membership cannot be achieved before the group members come together. Until the group meets, members will not know at what emotional level mem-bership will mean for them. This testing takes place in the early face-to-face processes by which group norms are negotiated.

GROUP SESSIONS

It was a half-hour before the group session, and several members were socializing in the clinic reception area. Donna was introducing a woman to some of the members. Initially, I recognized her, but I couldn't identify from where I had known her. It provoked an exasperating sensation of déjà vu–my memory disappointing self-expectation. Preoccupied with the woman's face, I prepared the conference room for the group session, moving tables against walls, opening the space for a circle of chairs, convinced that I knew her. Then, at once, the memory came to mind and a chill ran through my body. It was Harriet, the sister of Cassandra, a former client who had died two years ago. I sat for a few moments utterly lost in reminiscence.

I had known Cassandra for several months before her death. Most PWAs express shame about being publicly exposed, and Cas-sandra a 32-year-old African-American woman with two children, ages 6 and 11, was no exception. She kept the diagnosis to herself, and those who knew felt confidanted with a sacred trust. The word "AIDS" was never spoken.

It was past visiting hours, about 9 p.m., and I was returning to the AIDS unit after dinner. My premonitions were not infallible, but I felt Cassandra would live until morning. At night, with the patients asleep, the unit was deceptively serene, an incongruency. Yet, the mixture of moaning and the vibration of machines create a disquieting unmusical contrapuntal rhythm that resonates through the corridors. The peculiar power of these sounds diminish, become remote after time, almost ordinary, so the listener is self-protected from the incalculable struggle for existence.

I entered Cassandra's hospital room to discover her mother sitting bedside, with one hand grasping her daughter's, balancing the Bible in another, reading a passage aloud. She chanted rapturously, powerless to oppose her daughter's delirium, but unable to restrain her spiritual enthusiasm and the demand for justification. Her daughter passed away despite all her petitions.

I was the only caucasian at the funeral service, sitting alone as the preacher spoke of Cassandra's struggle on this planet. The singer, a modest woman reminiscent of Bessie Smith, wore a housecoat as if seizing anything hanging on a clothing hook to visit a neighbor for a cup of coffee and chat.

> We'll meet again. Oh yes Lord. We'll meet again.
> I don't know when. I don't know how. Oh Lord.
> We'll meet again. Oh yeah.

She transformed the 1930s pop standard about unrequited love into an evangelistic promise of resurrection–a spiritual with gospel phrasing and inflection accompanied only by a saxophonist. The two, world-weary, walked deliberately down a side aisle, then leaned against the chapel wall.

A note was passed to me. I looked over my shoulder at a woman, several rows behind, who nodded at me as I opened the note. It read: "Cassandra's sister Harriet has a drug problem. Please help her." The note was unsigned.

*   *   *

Harriet: "Donna's my sponsor in NA. I've got 40 days' clean time, and when she mentioned the group to me I knew that I had to come. Then, she told me about the facilitator; I knew who it was. It wasn't easy to get her.

"I guess the whole time my sister was ill with AIDS, I denied that it had anything to do with me, that I was at any risk. I never did drugs IV. So I was okay. But when me and my man broke up, I was going to get even with him, and I went back to Daryl. I thought we could rekindle our thing. I should have known better. I don't think that Daryl knew he was HIV.

"I began to get symptoms. Swollen lymph nodes. I was tired all the time. I went to a doctor but he didn't suggest the test. I lied to him when he asked me questions about HIV. He sent me to an eye, ear, and throat clinic. They wanted to do a CAT scan. The doctor asked me about HIV again, but I didn't want to think about it. I didn't do the tests. They took some tubes of blood, but I didn't go back for the results. I guess I knew."

Laura: "I know what you mean. I went to this spiritualist in Bedford-Stuyvesant that I had been to once before with a boyfriend about five years ago. I remember that she had told me that I better watch my health, that something was wrong. I was lucky to have found her again because she's unlisted. I had to walk around the neighborhood to find the building and had gone up into a couple of buildings by mistake until I found the right one. Nothing's marked; no name on the bell or on the front door. When you enter her apartment, her assistant gives you a number, and you sit in a semi-dark living room with no furniture, except folding metal chairs. No one spoke, except occasionally, and always in whispers. I waited for about three hours until my number was called.

"I was terrified to see her again. The room had candles every-where along the floor, some in colored glass, others just stuck in cup saucers and plates. The walls were covered with pictures of the saints, all dark-skinned. She remembered me. I felt relieved, though she told me it was serious.

"She said that she healed people like me. Then I thought, 'Who the fuck does she think I am?' I felt guilty for thinking so negative. She was trying to comfort me. I couldn't wait to get out. I felt oppressed by the heat of the room, the candles, the tenement walls. It took such effort to understand her Jamaican dialect, and I began to tune her out. Although I heard her say something in Spanish, '*No hay santo sin ewe.*' She said it meant, 'There is no saint without herbs.' She recommended coming back the following week, lighting certain colored candles, reading certain Biblical passages. I kept saying yes, but I knew I wouldn't follow her suggestions. She confirmed my fears, that something was wrong."

Donna: "I was bottoming out on drugs. Doing things, seeing things, becoming something that I never wanted: an addict. I knew that it was almost over. But what?"

Laura: "The night after I saw the spiritualist, I did a colon cleansing. I stayed in bed for two days. A friend found me in my apartment. That night I went to NA. I don't know how I got the strength. Donna told me not to test. It was too soon in my sobriety, but I knew that I wouldn't stay clean unless I knew for sure."

Carmen: "When I found out, it was like my life was changed forever. I would never be the same person anymore."

Donna: "Yeah, I remember when I found out. Well, actually, I'd taken the test months before I was ready to go back to get the results. Ya know what I mean? I knew. I knew I was positive, but to actually see it down on paper. . . . That counselor had shown me the form where I get the results. I used to imagine the boxes checked. I could actually see it. I wasn't ready to face it. My feelings were gettin' so fucked up that I hadda go back. I guess it took the time it takes."

Tonya: "I took the test two weeks after my husband died. He died of AIDS. I never knew it. If he were alive, I'd kill him. I didn't know what was wrong. He just closed up. I felt there was something wrong with me. What did he think? Couldn't he trust me? I wouldn't have deserted him. There I was, volunteering my time in the AIDS ward at a hospital, and my husband was dying. He went so fast. He was in the hospital for a couple weeks; [he] never said a word about AIDS."

Beth: "I tested when I found out that some guy I had sex with a couple of times was ill, had pneumonia. When I tested positive, I hadda take it one day at a time. Do what I gotta do. I'm not ill. Don't have any symptoms. I think about nine years of marriage. I felt so shut out. I felt abandoned."

Gladys: "I found out when I had my baby. They tested the baby and it was positive. The baby's with my mother in the hospital. He's got pneumonia. I see my body changing. Every day I notice something. I'm pregnant now. Six weeks. I don't know what to do. The other day, I was ready to take an abortion. I was already at a clinic. I was in a robe when they tell me that my Medicaid ain't good. I took it as a sign. I'm not sure what to do. Maybe I need to test again."

*   *   *

Beth: "I need to talk about somethin'. I just moved into my new apartment. I hadda tell Thomas that he wasn't movin' in with us. I left him in the old apartment. I feel that I'm in physical danger–that he would actually do somethin'. I says to myself, 'What does he want from me?' He keeps callin' me up, makin' threats that if he catches me on the street, he'll bash my head in. I've been plannin' this move for about two years."

There had been no discussion with her children about plans to reorganize familial living arrangements or the imminent move to a new apartment. She is incredulous that her son is upset about being left in the old apartment. He has made threatening attempts to pursue her into the new apartment. She feels victimized by her son, but is unable to self-examine in order to see her participation in the current difficulty. From early childhood, her son has been unreasonable and problematic and is currently alcoholic.

Beth: "I went over there the other day, and I don't know how they can live like that. There was garbage piled in the kitchen since when I moved out. It was disgustin'. I know that they want me to clean up after them, but I won't do it. There were cans of beer everywhere. The other one is at least sober. He went to a rehab and goes to AA. But this one. . . . He won't admit that he's an alcoholic."

After many threats, her son moved into her new apartment, and revealed to me that they had made a prior agreement for a time-limited stay to appease him. Currently, he has expressed that he won't leave and will stay as long as he chooses. Beth's current situation is a repetition of others, particularly those involving her father and former husband.

Beth: "When I was a child, my father would come home drunk. He'd shake me until I woke. It was horrible. He would stand over my bed and begin to question me. 'Where's ya mother. I told ya not to let her out. How'd she get outa here?' I never knew what he'd do when he got home. Then he'd demand that I make dinner for him. He'd be drunk, and, at times, he'd pass out while I was cookin' his meal.

"So I don't wait up for Thomas, but he comes through the apartment, making noise, and it wakes me up. That feeling of being awakened from sleep terrifies me. Reminds me of my father. There have been several relationships that I had to end. My husband [was one]. I just wanted him to leave. It took a while, but I finally got him out. Just before my husband left, he chased me through the apartment, and I fell, breaking my leg. I had to get a court order against him. But I got him out."

After several Tough Love meetings, Beth made a decision to remove her son forcibly. She collected his belongings and took them to her old apartment, instructing the doorman not to allow her son to come up to the apartment.

Beth: "He's still outa the house. He hasn't been callin'. He hasn't called or anything. A new tactic I think. About two weeks ago, Steven called me and said Thomas hadn't been home for three nights. So I said. . . . Well, I said, 'He's 21. I'm sure he's all right.' Steven said, 'Well. . . . yeah. It just seemed funny doin' it.' So I was thinkin' about it all that day. It did seem funny. He showed up. I don't know where he was or anything. But I hadn't seen him or anything since he left.

"It was hard to get him out. It wasn't easy. Let me tell you. It was terrible. I wouldn't wish it on anybody. Every day, I'd say to myself, 'I wish the time would go.' It was like . . . wake up . . . think about it . . . go back to sleep. I wouldn't take him back. The hardest part to . . . get him outa the house. I don't know. I just think, with me, it had to get to the point where I couldn't tolerate it anymore. And that's what happened. He more or less did it to himself. He pushed me to it when he said, 'I'll stay two or three more years if I feel like it.' I felt backed to the wall. It wasn't two or three months.

"I was readin' this AA book, and it describes a pine cone fallin' from a tree. And it stays there for decades until a forest fire comes. The heat forces the seal open. The seeds fall out. And things grow and flourish. [Hearty laugh.] That's me. I was readin' that two weeks ago and connected to it."

* * *

Carmen: "I hadda a friend call dentists to see if they'd treat someone HIV-positive. I couldn't handle it alone. Some of them hung up on him. Some said they didn't have the equipment. I finally found a clinic that would do my teeth. They took X rays and told me that I needed a root canal and two extractions. Then I found out that Medicaid wouldn't cover the work I needed. They wouldn't do the root canal. They wanted me to have all my bottom teeth pulled."

Donna: "I goes to sign up for Medicaid. I said I had the virus. And the worker just looks at me, then she disappears. I never see her again. A supervisor appears. She was actually quite nice to me.

Then I hadda get my T cells done. I waits two weeks for the result. Then they lost the blood. How did they lose the blood? I gots to go in again. They're 249. How could they be so low?

When I was druggin', it was a scam. I had three welfare cards. I didn't care. Now I'm tellin' the truth and it doesn't work. The caseworker said she didn't have time for me and hung up. I felt like a piece of shit. All these feelins' kicked up. I felt inadequate."

Rhonda: "Inadequate?"

Donna: "For me, it's the stigma. You know whatta I mean? I hate this fuckin' virus. It's not the medical that's so hard to deal with. It's the way people treat you out there. Don't get me wrong. I have a lotta friends who understand. I know that I can call Laura anytime. Here I am clean for three years, and I think that they just look at me as Donna the Junkie. That's how I feel."

Steven: "You've described this feeling before in group. What do you think it's about?"

Donna: "The damn social services."

Steven: "Who in your life treats you that way?"

Donna: "The system's a bitch."

Steven: "Who did that to you?"

Donna: "My mother treats me that way. Nothin' I do is right. She's always sayin', 'Donna, get on with it.' It makes me feel like Donna the Complainer. Donna the Junkie."

Donna: Out there, the nine-to-fivers on the conveyer belt, off to work. They're gettin' on with their lives. My mother works no matter what–102° fever, [she's] off to work. Every week it's somethin' else. Stu was bleedin' from his ass and won't go to the doctor. I had a vaginal infection. My kid's actin' out.

* * *

Harriet: "There was this friend over the other day, and he's talkin' to Herbie about women, that they're different now. I just thinkin' about my doin' the laundry after a D and C and carryin' it up five flights of stairs. And moppin' the floor. And givin' Herbie his AZT, and goin' to the clinic for me. Ya know what I mean? And this prick is talkin' about women. What am I supposed to be: super-mom and superwife? Give me a break. I hadda leave the house. And do you know what? He don't want me to come here. To come to group. We fight about it."

Beth: "Yeah. Mike's hangin' out the window waitin' for me to come home."

Steven: "What do you think that's about?"

Beth: "The women here know what it's about. Control!"

Donna: "I gotta negotiate to get here. I stopped callin' after the meetin' was over. I used to call to say I was on my way home. What for? So I get home and the place looks like a tornado hit. I need this for me."

Rhonda: "My husband doesn't tell me not to come. He gets this look. All sad and helpless. A guilt trip gets laid on me."

Harriet: "I just want ta shut down with this. I didn't want to come here. I had to force myself. I walked to the bus, then turned back. Then walked back. I take it all home. It's a lot to handle. You supposed to be a rock. My God, my mother died a coupla months ago. I went to a fuckin' NA meeting and this woman came up to me and said, 'You gotta accept it.' I wanted to punch her. She said she was positive. She played it off and was in control. She was comin' off to me. I felt I had no right to these feelin's. I've seen a lot of shit with my partner. I used to take him everywhere. I knew where to go for everything. Now it's me. When is it goin' to stop?"

Rhonda: "I done hit him with somethin' when he puts his face in mine. He don't seem to take it serious. He want everything to be the same . . . like it's nothin'. He done prayed for forgiveness. That's it. Very simple. He says, 'What you got to complain. I'm the one's sick.' But I got the virus, too. We sleeps together at night. At times, I turns over and his face is there. I thinks, why don't you dumps your load somewhere out in the yard. I's got to be there for him. He don't have anyone else. But I don'ts want him to touch me.

When were in bed, I feel him move, and I can't sleep because he might want sex.

"The other day, he says, 'Honey, let's do it.' And he gets this condo and puts it on. Then he goes into the bathroom. I said, 'What's you doin'?' God. I thinks he's cuttin' the condo. After we finish, I feels his meat, and the condo breaked. I panicked. I thinks he cut it."

Laura: "I don't think I could be that kind. To forgive him would be a process for me. It would take time. I'd be so angry."

Rhonda: "I don't know what I feel. I'm not angry."

Laura: "I think you are. That's why you keep reminding him to turn his head when he coughs. And you wear rubber gloves."

Rhonda: "Theys told me to do that."

Laura: "It's one way you keep remindin' him."

Rhonda: "My husband can't read. Doesn't do nothin'. Is you gonna bring me the water?"

Beth: "I've been through that. All they have to do is breathe and shit. I waited on him hand and foot."

Harriet: "With sex, I set the stage. He just played with it. I went through with it. Faked it.

"He was god of all gods on a throne. I created my own misery. I came out of it slowly. I closed the book. Fuck it. I used to make all the appointments and I spoke to the doctors. He was so passive. Didn't even get up to go to the bathroom. I mopped the floor. Then he's in my face: 'Baby. Oh baby.'"

Billie: "You can't turn back the clock. You never know. You never know. I'm the relationship, preserving and protecting. The universe is falling apart. My relationship was sex-centered. I do everything. Running around buying condoms. Extra-large. I was in the hospital last week, running 105°. He went to a conference. I told him to go. Then when I was home, I discovered a hotel receipt for Pittsburgh. He flew to Pittsburgh. I feel so deceived. I don't have the time to rebuild the trust. I don't know about the foundation. I said to him, 'This is God's test for you.'

"He says no one appreciates what he does. What did he do? I was in the hospital for a month, and he took care of things. What about the future? God forbid. What if I'm in the hospital for a couple of months? I've been goin' 24 × 7 [24 hours a day, 7 days a week,] for someone else. One month. He did it for a month.

"I keep everything together. It's all filed from A to Z. When I'm gone it can all be thrown in the garbage."

Steven: "Are you going to be filed in the garbage?"

Billie: "That's how it feels. I went through changes. The sex was cut off. It's been a fuckin' year without sex. This shit kicks up. He don't feel it."

Harriet: "When I play through the role. I feel like shit after."

Rhonda: "I be praying he don't go through with it."

* * *

Donna: "I feel really lost since leaving the group. I feel like a ship at sea. It's a real loss for me."

Steven: "It seems that this is a realization for you–something that you were unprepared for feeling."

Donna: "I had no idea how much the group meant to me. When Thursday comes, I think to get ready for group. But then, I remember that I'm not a member of the group anymore."

Harriet: "I'm thinking that I'm sliding back without group. You know, I've gained over ten pounds in the past two weeks since I left group. I feel that I'm getting depressed. I need to be out. I can get very isolated, and group gave me some place to go."

Steven: "Your decision to leave group is part of a process, and I think that you have learned something about being a member of group that you might want to share with other members."

Harriet: "That's very hard for me to do. I don't like to show that side of me."

Tonya: "How do you think of that side."

Harriet: "People look at me and they don't know how I feel inside. I look like the life of the party, and I'm always giving to other people. But inside . . . there's sadness. People don't realize that I have diabetes. They say to me, 'You can't have diabetes. You look so good.'"

Carmen: "When you think about your anger, can you tell me what makes you mad?"

Harriet: "People think that I'm very strong. But inside, it's something else."

Steven: "That seems to be a consistent theme since we've had our sessions together. That people don't know how you feel."

Harriet: "Yes."

Steven: "But it's very difficult for you to express your feelings. You can express anger, but when you're hurt, that's another matter."

Donna: "I think that's why I felt that I couldn't stay in the group."

Steven: "You felt hurt by your friend Vera's comment about the way you dress?"

Donna: "You bet I did. I was very angry. Who's she to tell me how to dress?"

Harriet: "Do you think that there would have been a way that you could have expressed that hurt to her?"

Donna: "No. I was so angry at her."

Steven: "Perhaps we could think of another response that could have been made. We could think of it as an exercise."

Donna: "I got so angry at her. I felt attacked."

Carmen: "Do you think you could have told her that you felt attacked?"

Donna: "No."

Steven: "Perhaps you could have said to her, 'Vera, how I dress is very important to me. It's a part of me. It reflects a lot of care, and it hurts me when someone says something negative about my appearance. I try to take care of myself.'"

Donna: "I don't know if I could say something like that to her."

Tonya: "What feelings does it bring up for you."

Donna: "I think that it would show her something about myself."

Gladys: "Would it be showing her something about what's going on inside?"

Donna: "Yes."

Rhonda: "What do you think will happen if you show sadness?"

Donna: "It's a sign of weakness. I think that if I show my sadness, people will take advantage of me."

Steven: "When you were a child, were you allowed to express sadness?"

Donna: "Oh no. My father would hit me, and he would tell me not to cry. If I cried, he would threaten me even more. So I . . . .

"You know, I was thinking the other day, since we had spoken about me singing at church, that he forbade me to sing. I used to love to sing. I think I wanted to have a career as a singer, but he told me that I'd become a whore. That people would take advantage of me, so I was not allowed to continue. I had a beautiful voice. I don't know what my voice is like now, because I rarely use it."

Lynne: "You look very sad right now. How are you feeling?"

Donna: "I was thinking of the Bette Midler song "Wind Beneath My Wings" and that if I heard it right now, I'd begin to cry."

* * *

Carmen: "But you know, I forgive my father. He did the best he could."

Steven: "Can you describe how you came to forgive your father?"

Carmen: "I guess that I realized things about my mother. She was having an affair with his best friend. I told her to have an abortion. That the child would be a monster."

Steven: "How old were you when you mother became pregnant?"

Carmen: "I was about 12. My mother used to discuss a lot of sexual feelings with me. That she wasn't satisfied with my father. She used to confide in me. I suppose that was okay."

Rhonda: "Do you think it was okay?"

Carmen: "I don't know. I was always asked to do things as a child."

Steven: "Can you give me an example?"

Carmen: "I can even remember a teacher who wanted to have sex with me. I told him no. He said he had taken hormones and wanted to have sex with me.

"I haven't had sex with anyone since 1974. I'm not interested in sex anymore. I'm not interested in Mike.

"I feel that I need to be controlling my anger. I've told you before. I feel this rage. And I have to control it."

Steven: "Yes. You've told me a lot about violence. Your family was very violent. There was also a lot about sex in your family."

Carmen: "Yes. Even my sister. She's got three children. One from her husband. One from her husband's brother. And one from her husband's best friend.

"Yeah. And violence. I once hit Mike with a flower pot. Cracked his head open. I have to sit on my violence–keep it under control."

GROUP PROCESS

Intervention within a group session is directed toward problem-solving, education, and crisis intervention, but it also focuses on encouraging fundamental personality and behavioral changes. During the group sessions, members may express intense emotion. Through the release of emotional affect, a member presents underlying thoughts, values, beliefs, and attitudes that suggest a history of difficulty. The examination of member's belief systems is derived from cognitive-oriented psychotherapy. The cognition or thought of a group member–especially when she has conscious knowledge of an idea, image, or meaning–is a symbolic representation of her interpersonal behavior. Cognitivists maintain that behavioral change occurs when there is a modification of goal-defeating emotions and actions. Self-disturbing beliefs and assumptions are identified, with the focus on the individual group member. The dictum "feelings are not fact" accepts the reality of a feeling but suggests that the feeling may derive from an irrational belief. Irrational beliefs consist of distortions of reality, exaggerated evaluations, and must-statements–all of which promote erroneous expectations or anticipations.

Group Matrix

- Cohesiveness, a sense of belonging and acceptance
- Capacity of the group to control, reward, and punish behavior
- Confirm the authenticity of the individual's experience by peers
- Induce and release powerful feelings
- Provide a contrast for social comparison and feedback
- Encourage risk-taking behavior
- Increase self-esteem through disclosure and self-revelation
- Experience of common crisis
- Intimacy and support

The therapist and group members offer direct feedback to the focal client to get her to adopt more realistic perspectives on self, other people, and the world in general. Clients are helped to modify dysphoric moods and maladaptive behaviors so they may learn to help themselves.

Group Therapeutic Experience

- Installation of hope
- Universality (universalization)
- Imparting of information (intellectualization)
- Altruism
- The corrective recapitulation of the primary family group development through socializing techniques
- Imitative behavior (spectator therapy)
- Interpersonal learning (reality testing)
- Interaction
- Group cohesiveness
- Catharsis (ventilation)
- Existential factors

Most of the group members have a history of substance use, with low frustration tolerance (LFT). Substance users, particularly in early recovery (the first several years of abstinence), present an inability or unwillingness to withstand discomfort, inconvenience, or frustration. The consequence of LFT is a set of beliefs, often unconscious, that promote procrastination, withdrawal, and avoidance.

Most schools of group psychotherapy would argue that an individual's interpersonal behavior in the group is analogous in many ways to the individual's social behavior in the real world, and that personal problems occurring in the group also occur outside the group. However, the degree to which the group context is used to address, analyze, and modify these problems is limited. Although interpersonal relations among members and group dynamics are stressed, the foci of the group has been presenting problems of individual members rather than dealing with the so-called treatment of the group. The self-help modality is intrinsic to the power of the group, so networking and formation of relationships outside the group session is encouraged.

However, this also presents difficult therapeutic concerns, because members may attempt to work through group reactions outside of session. According to Getzel, four prototypical solutions occur through the group process of sharing and mutual aid.

Once a group member's problem has been delineated, the problem is explored. Whether or not its cause is construed as occurring in the past or present, the goal is to increase the member's understanding of the problem and its cause through further interpretation, such as destructive patterns within relationships. Conversely, there are problems that are addressed in the *here and now*, with rejection of the belief that interpretation and understanding will produce positive change (for example, procrastination regarding seeking medical treatment).

When an individual or family applies to the group to resolve a presenting problem, the problem itself is symptomatic of a systemic malfunction. Generally, the problem itself suggests more pervasive underlying issues that have created an inexpiable situation or condition. Therefore, a primary goal for the clinician is the gathering of as much information as possible during the assessment process to determine family history and methods of interaction and reaction as well as coping mechanisms: "Missing information about important family members or events and discrepancies in the information offered frequently reflect charged emotional issues in the family."[3]

During a group session, deeper awareness surfaces by graphically revealing repetitive symptoms, untimely life-cycle transitions, and the assignment of parent-child roles. Clinically, it involves reframing the presenting problem by enlarging its significance into a familial context (which is a primary goal of therapeutic intervention with the client).

Each woman has expressed the burden of the stigmatization of HIV disease. All are struggling with issues of disclosure and some have been unable to discuss HIV with their partners. HIV is a "family disease," meaning that all members of a patient's support network are influenced dramatically by an individual's diagnosis. Therefore, the category of identified patient must be defined systemically, so the identified patient is a unit–the entire support system–that requires social work treatment. Often, patients have experienced HIV disease in their social network, with spouses, children, and friends who have HIV or have died of the disease. It is rare that a patient has not been affected by HIV disease or known families with multidiagnosed members. Individuals, therefore, may have experienced the loss of a spouse of child. The population affected by HIV disease may be three-generational. For example, an individual has HIV herself, lost her spouse, and her sexually active 14-year-old teenage daughter is pregnant. Her daughter's HIV serostatus is unknown, but she and her unborn child may be considered "at risk" and require intervention. These problems are exacerbated by the "outcast" status assigned to persons with AIDS (PWAs). This status is primarily due to the general population's misunderstandings regarding the nature of HIV transmission and with the identification of HIV with groups outside the social mainstream (predominantly, gay men and intravenous drug users).

REFERENCE NOTES

1. Nicholas Freudenberg, DrPH, *Preventing AIDS: A Guide to Effective Education for the Prevention of HIV Infection* (Washington, DC: American Public Health Association, 1989), p. 169.

2. Gloria Steinem, *Revolution from Within* (Boston: Little, Brown & Company, 1992), p. 33.

3. Monica McGoldrick and Randy Gerson, *Genograms in Family Assessment* (New York: W. W. Norton & Company, 1985), p. 38.

Chapter 8

Frankie

There are those who no matter how perfect your attire
Will find you queer
Who don't realize that what you do
Is quite natural
These people don't know you
And don't want to
Therefore it makes no sense trying to explain.

–Roy Gonsalves, "Que Sera Sera"

THE SOCIAL WORK ROLE

When, in the 1980s, as the first social worker with an exclusive, inpatient, HIV-disease practice in a Brooklyn hospital, I felt disfavored as an activist by other health-care providers who were challenged by the escalation of HIV disease patients from the community. Shernoff pointed out that HIV disease will touch the practice of most social workers in health-care settings. They are often the first to see the illness present in a community.[1] Some of the serious barriers to the provision of quality medical care for individuals with HIV disease that existed in the 1980s persist into the 1990s. These include underdiagnosis, resistance by certain medical providers to perform essential diagnostic testing, continuity of medical care from inpatient hospitalization to a clinic or community health setting, and insurance restrictions for certain excessively high-priced medical treatments. Prejudicial attitudes and unfounded anxiety toward individuals with HIV disease continue, so, for instance, when food trays are left outside the rooms of nonambulatory patients, they go without meals. Hospitalization itself has profound psychosocial implications, with the patient in a helpless and dependent role unlike how they function in the community. The impact of any hospitalization precipitates a crisis for a patient and puts them into a vulnerable state marked by disequilibrium and disorganization.[2]

Staff at most hospitals are struggling with fear of HIV transmission and their prejudice toward the patients. Surgeons frequently refuse to perform diagnostic procedures, such as a bronchoscopy (a lung tissue biopsy essential to the definitive diagnosis of *Pneumocystis carinii* pneumonia [PCP]). When a discharge results without diagnosis, the patient is uniformed of aftercare, such as antiretroviral therapy and prophylaxis treatment, safer sex to prevent viral transmission, and awareness of disease progression necessary to monitor symptomatology.

Social workers render indispensable services within host medical settings. They must reconcile the primary emphasis on discharge planning with the pressures of the diagnostic-related group (DRG) system to expedite discharges.

The earliest roots of clinical social work in the health field began in 1905, and the practice and theory base has been evolving continually. Social work pioneer Harriet Bartlett defined medical social work as a process of treatment that emphasizes psychological support, interwoven with the illness and medical care, and the collaboration with the physician and other professionals.[3] The practice of social work, however, has become more complex with the rising incidence of substance abuse during the 1980s and the paucity of treatment facilities available. Financial cutbacks have affected aftercare in community-based mental-health facilities, creating a mentally ill homeless population.

Social workers walk a tightrope, balancing clinical and therapeutic responsibilities with administrative directives. My sessions with Frankie took place in his hospital room once a week during his six-month hospitalization. There is minimal control of the therapeutic spatial environment in a hospital setting, and so there are many interruptions. Most medical personnel are insensitive to the primacy of psychological support for ill patients. They must suppress their feelings to provide care, which takes its toll emotionally. The sessions with Frankie also had limited privacy–within the hospital, medical interventions are most important.

SESSIONS WITH FRANKIE

The hospital visitor's room was monochromatic, a study in institutional drabness: grey walls, gun-metal folding chairs, and slate-hued tile floor. Even the patient's gowns were ashen. It was a week before Christmas, but the room wasn't portentous of the holiday; there were no wreaths, cards, or mistletoe. The hospital corridors were decorated with construction paper stars hung randomly from ceilings. The nurse's stations had diminutive metallic Christmas trees, blinking colored lights.

The patient's HIV-disease support group used the visitor's room for an hour-long inpatient meeting. This hospital didn't have a dedicated HIV disease unit; instead, it was a scatter-bed system, with patients on different floors (some doubled in rooms together). Each week, the patients were escorted to the fifth-floor meeting, falling into place outside their rooms and at elevator banks.

A procession of HIV-disease patients advanced through hallways. Some dragged their intravenous poles, careful not to tangle tubing in the wheels. Other patients helped less-ambulatory patients, confined to wheelchairs, to the support group. The parade route attracted fascinated sideline attention–many staff had expressions of disbelief. It was anomalous within this hospital to see patients together, rather than insulated within their rooms. The patients were aware of their spectacle, that they were known to have HIV disease, but they proudly made their way to the meeting room.

Frankie stalked the room during the support-group meeting. It was disruptive to other patients, who were distracted and threatened by him. He was mumbling under his breath, but loud enough for other members to hear: "This is all bullshit. I ain't afraid to die. It's all bullshit." I asked him to sit. He refused, threateningly pointing at me with a cigarette dangling from the corner of his mouth, ashes falling onto his hospital robe.

Frankie had been hospitalized since his diagnosis in September. He had Kaposi's sarcoma, with lesions on his feet, legs, arms, wrist, and neck. They were so dense that they appeared as patches, not as isolated lesions. They covered the heels and soles of his feet, swollen balloon-like, causing edema (an excessive accumulation of fluid in body tissues), which affected blood circulation. He had wasting syndrome: he was an emaciated 116 pounds on a 6'2" frame. He was toothless. Actually, he had slivers of teeth that lined his mouth. Teeth are a class privilege.

Sessions with Frankie began two months ago in his hospital room. Frankie, a seasoned manipulator, began testing me during our first session. "I'm sorry," I told him. "In all conscience, I can't buy you cigarettes. It's against my principles." "A who? Principles?" he said mockingly. My God, the man smoked with tuberculosis. Now, in recovery, he smoked more. He chain-smoked, using the radiator as an ashtray. He threw butts out the window, aiming at people. He hit a doctor, passing under his window, with a lit butt.

Frankie's main prop, a cigarette, was familiar to me. He used it to punctuate sentences, to emphasize and underscore every point that he needed to make. His cigarette was a weapon. "No," I said to myself, "I won't do it." I remembered smoking four packs a day. I was never without a cigarette, sometimes smoking two at a time, moving through my office, forgetting the one already lit. It's been three years, and I can still taste them; I still missed the burning sensation, the aftertaste. I remembered the disdain of nonsmokers. I always felt self-judgmental about smoking, which I defined as destructive acting out and lack of discipline. I turned from Frankie and sprayed my mouth with spearmint-flavored Binaca, a carryover.

*   *   *

During this session with Frankie, he was on autopilot and began a self-narrative in a bizarre, breathless, staccato-like rhythm, that was ostensibly effortless. The recitative, the story of his life, was not responsive to any question I had asked. He delivered a speech by rote, as if from a street-corner soap box. The monologue was directionless, not toward me; it was for an imaginary audience, probably the cosmos. The delivery was obsessional, with repetitious content about victimization. Oliver Sacks recognized such behavior:

> We have, each of us, a lifestory, an inner narrative–whose continuity, whose sense, is our lives. It might be said that each

of us constructs and lives, a *narrative*, and that this narrative is us, our identities.[4]

I recognized Frankie's life story as self-creation, an amalgam of fiction and fact from which he couldn't differentiate. But the characterization was self-preservative, a defense mechanism that served his ego.

Frankie defied the upwardly mobile, educated (he hadn't completed grammar school), artistic stereotypes about gay men. He laid no claim to any consciousness of a gay sensibility. Frankie had always been poverty-stricken, a life of abandonment, institutionalization, violence, disruption, and illiteracy. His was a marginal existence. He could spell his name, and he read the newspaper's picture captions and comics. His life may have been marginal, but it was a life nonetheless. He was going to claim it no matter what the price, no matter how.

He felt enraged and expressed it randomly, particularly toward those he identified as authority figures. Rage was his métier. I anticipated his rage toward me, recognizing that devaluation and contempt toward a therapist is common with the borderline personality disorder.[5]

"My mother deserted me on a subway platform when I was five," Frankie told me. "She called my father from a street-corner pay phone and said, 'Come and get the brat. He's on the BMT station, Delancey Street stop. You can have him.' She hadn't seen my father in years. She left him because of his drinking. He used to beat on her. I waited for her on the platform bench for hours until my father got there. He took me to my grandmother's house. He didn't want me. My mother disappeared. I never saw her again.

"Some doctor told my father that my sex organs were tied in a knot. That I'll grow up queer. My father had me put away in Manhattan State Hospital. I was there until a teenager."

As an adult, he was hospitalized at Creedmore and Pilgrim State. Deserted. Untaught. Unwanted. The rich have places to go and are not subjected to the institutions of poverty.

* * *

We had a session the day after Thanksgiving. His room was changed on the holiday, when he felt particularly vulnerable. Long-term hospitalized patients are traumatized by any radical environmental change. Frankie was moved to an alternate level of care (ALC) floor used for homeless people, nursing-home placements, and people not receiving acute care. ALC patients do not require hospitalization but are not discharged to the community because they are unable to perform the activities of daily life.

Frankie cried himself to sleep; his eyes were red from weeping. He was depressed about his confinement in the hospital, and it triggered past unresolved feelings about protracted institutionalizations. Cynically, he attempted self-humor, saying, "No partying here. I went to sleep early. In the good ole days I'd wear black leather. I had these pants especially made. The fact is, I was some figure. Chains too. No one would go near me. Sometimes, I'd wear black velvet, a jump suit, and platform shoes. [Laughing.] No one would go near me."

Frankie was homeless. For the last several years, he lived in and out of New York's gay bathhouses: the Everard and Beacon, Y's, McBurney, and 63rd Street. A vision of him came to mind during a session as a Damon Runyan-type, a time-warp from another era, socializing at bathhouse coffee shops, sitting for endless hours, drinking cup after cup of coffee, smoking cigarettes endlessly, and philosophizing. That was home. Check in for the evening, check out around 6 a.m. Day after day. His belongings, all his worldly possessions, fit into a gym bag and wetpack; with everything he could settle into any two-by-four foot space.

Frankie faced me, away from the window out of which he had been staring, flicking ashes into the window-sill ventilator as if it were a wall-to-wall ashtray. He mockingly said, "Do you want to be my hubby wubby? My other half? Yes? I want to be buried in a wedding gown like Mae West." He laughed.

* * *

The following week, he called my office six, seven, eight times a day. He had an insatiable need, and any ear would do. I always kept my answering machine on. He got used to leaving long messages. The answering machine became an acceptable substitute: "Cough. Cough. Cough. Cough. Cough. Cough. Sorry, wrong number." He even used disguised voices. I felt invaded.

He was homeless, but not friendless. There was one person, Clarabel, whom he called his niece. Then, he added: "Well not my niece. I call her my niece. I want you to call her, meet with her." Clarabel was Frankie's former neighbor from Manhattan's Lower East Side; she was married, with one child. I agreed to meet her, and on the afternoon of the appointment I saw her walking through the hospital corridor at a distance. She appeared childlike, diminutive, 4'10" or so, worn and tired, anemic, and looked ill herself. She brought her friend, Theresa, for our meeting. Theresa lost her husband, an IV drug user, from HIV disease a few months ago.

Clarabel told me, "Ya gotta understand. I'm not his niece, justa friend. Not a relative. Frankie stayed with me for a couple of months afta he was kicked outa his apartment. I hadda throw him out. It was impossible. Then I didn't see him for a coupla years. Maybe two. Then he shows up drunk on my doorstep. I feel sorry for the guy, but I can't do much. He calls me day and night. I got a kid to take care of. I can't take him on. The guy wants to move in. I can't. Is that why you wanted to meet me?"

I responded that Frankie wanted us to meet as a connection to his world. I said, "He can be demanding." She replied, "No kiddin'." Clarabel was resolute about not being part of a solution for Frankie. She had no problem expressing her need for distance. It was clear Clarabel felt manipulated by Frankie and couldn't always find a way to back out. She wasn't a relative; the niece title was a manipulation on Frankie's part.

* * *

After my meeting with Clarabel, I felt helpless to resolve Frankie's multiple problems. Feeling that I needed to solve them made me uncomfortable. In some way, I wanted to provide an answer. I had a sleepless night. Countertransferential material emerged about my father, which needed to be examined. A dream. Frankie looked familiar. Like who? Could Frankie have been the return of my manic-depressive father, Morris? When I awoke, I mentally composed a letter in the spirit of Morris.

When Morris was under lock and key at Pilgrim State Hospital, I visited once. I needed to be self-protective, since I was an adolescent at the time. I resented him, so visiting was painful. I was unable to feel compassion for him. Ten years after his discharge, he was murdered in his apartment by a band of teenage thrillseekers. My countertransferential epiphany that Frankie reminded me of my father further challenged an already complex treatment.

At the end of November, all hell broke loose. Clarabel hadn't visited for a month. Each time, she had a different reason. She began to distance herself further as Frankie's medical condition deteriorated. He felt victimized, and he obsessed about all of life's injustices. Every session and rambling phone message was about Clarabel: "Damn her. I'm gonna get her. Because of this and that . . . . The fact that . . . . On account of the fact . . . . Get the message?" He felt deserted, and his life's difficulties were displaced onto Clarabel. He felt she had an obligation to him. Frankie was aware that he was friendless, so he tempered reality by emotionally blackmailing people, drawing them in, exacting commitments with one-sided interpretations.

*   *   *

During a session, Frankie reminisced about the Village before the epidemic, a memory triggered by feelings of desertion and abandonment that were integral to his grieving process: "All my friends are dead. Hundreds of them. I'll take you to this Mexican restaurant in the Village. Well. Uh. Not there. I can't go back there. You know what, we'll take a trip to New Hope. Right, hubby wubby. You'd like that. We'll go to this bar . . . The Red Velvet. No. Not there. Can't go there." Many of Frankie's bar stories ended with arrests, fights, and/or bannings. A vague expression appeared on his face, and he was unable to remember all the details of the story–no doubt one told numerously. He may have had organic memory loss due to HIV dementia complex (HDC), and I suggested a neurological consult (to no avail).

*   *   *

During the first week of December, a plan to take Frankie out for the day was discussed with hospital staff by David, a Gay Men's Health Crisis (GMHC) buddy, Clarabel, and Theresa. It was unheard of–acute-care hospitals don't give day passes. However, they received the cooperation of Frankie's doctor, a rare supportive physician. They were going to a restaurant at South Street Seaport, signing him out against medical advice (AMA) for the day.

Frankie was dressed, sitting in a wheelchair, waiting impatiently. No, the attending nurse said she knew nothing about it. It's completely against hospital regulations. She threatened to call administration. No, she said she won't give them the AMA form. No, she doesn't know who the intern is for the day. No, she won't help with this plan for a day's outing, an adventure, for a patient who hasn't been outside the hospital for two months. No. No. No.

An administrator arrived. Frankie ridiculed him, shouting, "Hospital rule number 135B243C11-2D. Blah. Blah. Blah. Can't be done. Just watch us." They wheeled Frankie to the elevators, with the administrator trailing them, holding out an AMA form in his hand for Frankie's signature. The elevator doors closed in the administrator's face, but when they reached the lobby, he was there with the form. He ordered a nurse to "Strip the bed. Clear the room. The patient's discharged. Strip the room." Frankie shouted, "I'm going to get that faggot."

I imagined a five-hour wait in the emergency room when he returned. What if they won't readmit him? What if they try to farm him out to a city hospital? Frankie knew the basement passages well: he received radiation treatment in the bowels of the hospital. He returned through a back-door ambulance entrance that was kept open. The four of them moved past a suspicious security guard, who didn't stop them. When you have a clear purpose, it has its own authority.

They went back to the fifth floor and found his room bare. There weren't sheets on the bed. His belongings were thrown into a plastic Hefty bag. Frankie stripped nude. I watched David get a clean set of sheets from the hallway supply cabinet. He made the bed, and he lifted Frankie up and tossed him into it.

Frankie yawned. "Let them try to evict me," he said. "Just let them."

"You okay?" I asked.

"Yup," he replied. "This will be the talk of the hospital. There's a crowd outside my door. Boy, I'm tired."

All eyes of the support group members were on Frankie as he settled into a chair. I asked, "Frankie, are you upset? Do you want to tell us what's happening?" He said, "I'm leaving this joint. They're gonna send me someplace else."

* * *

Frankie's physical condition had not improved during his four-month hospitalization, so he couldn't be discharged back to the community. He was essentially homeless. He couldn't live as he had before, at YMCAs and bathhouses (most of the latter had been closed during the early years of the epidemic by the New York City Board of Health). He could not survive independently. There are few facilities for a person with HIV disease; in New York, only one nursing home accepts patients. Even the Bailey House in Greenwich Village isn't an option for Frankie, since he requires a health aide to perform the basic tasks of daily living.

He was transferred to Weller Hospital, which is located on a small island in the East River and has an HIV disease unit. Frankie acutely felt the threat of institutionalization, since he had a long prior history. It was as if Weller was the last stop on his journey. He said: "I'll never leave there. I'm goin' to die there. I know that. Why can't I stay here? I don't want to go. They can't make me. I'll sue them."

Within a week he left, packing his belongings and anything he could carry into red plastic bags. He had collected cans of Ensure, a liquid dietary supplement, over the months, preparing for the return to his previous transient lifestyle. He packed an egg-crate mattress, a thermometer, chuck pads, several pieces of plastic-wrapped cake from previous days' meals, and an assortment of crumpled papers in stained envelopes. On the day of the transfer, he argued with various staff, making verbal threats, but he managed to smile when saying goodbye to the staff as he was wheeled off the floor. He turned toward me while waiting for an elevator. "See ya," he said. The transfer occurred quickly, without time for us to think about the termination of our therapeutic relationship.

* * *

About a month passed, with no word from Frankie. I had spoken to his new social worker and knew that he was attempting to adjust to Weller. I returned to my office one afternoon to find a message on my answering machine: "I want to see you. When can you come? Get here. Oh. Listen, doll, this is your other half, the real half, the real thing. It's Frankie. When you come, bring me the Sunday *Daily News*; an olive loaf sandwich on white with mayo; a sour pickle, very sour; a danish, no raisins; coffee with Sweet 'n' Low; three plants; some underwear; a TV Guide; nail clippers; emery boards; clear nail polish; and a plastic bag. Ha! Ha! Ha! By the way, I fired David, my Gay Men's Health Club [sic] buddy." Click.

The deserted road to Weller had no sidewalks, with both sides of the road overgrown with back-lot flora. At one turn, there is a pseudo-Greco ruin, a concrete staircase leading nowhere, 20 or 30 steps with no edifice. I reached the nondescript building, but I couldn't distinguish the front from the back with no directional signs and all the doors locked. There was no one on the grounds. Then, a nurse headed up the deserted road and directed me to a side-door entrance.

Weller's interior was unimaginable, although it bore a resemblance to the main waiting room at Grand Central Station (but it smelled of hospital cooking). There were scores of homeless people, paraplegics, amputees, the poor, the mad, the forgotten. "Our Lady of the Door" asked for spare change; she was a version of Bette Davis as Baby Jane Hudson. The Man on the Transom left alone in a corridor motioned in thin air.

Frankie's room was unlike any other at Weller: he had a Louis Quartorze white telephone ($29.95 from a discount store). It took a month to get it installed. When the telephone company realized it was being installed in a room occupied by an HIV disease patient, they said the union allowed them to refuse. It was the inventiveness of the social worker, who moved all three patients from the room for a day, that allowed the phone to be installed.

Plants lined the window: one bought by a nurse, Persian violets from David, and a philodendron that Frankie picked out at Kmart. There was a ten-inch color TV with a stand, purchased with money Frankie had saved during his hospitalization. The room was transformed into a home. Here was Frankie's creativity–his will, his design.

When I arrived, he had begun packing for a picnic on the grounds on the East River, facing Manhattan's Upper East Side. Sailboats passed by as we sat on a hospital blanket. He yawned, stretching his arms to the azure sky, saying, "Maybe your next husband will get you that. Would you like that yacht?" I questioned, "My next husband?"

Frankie had nothing to do all day but think and review all the past, present, and future injustices he felt or would feel. I suggested some comic books. "Nah." Some magazines? "Nah." Some music? A healing tape? "A who?" Maybe a tape recorder to dictate your life story? "Nah."

He said, "Ya see that blackbird on the building ledge? It's chirpin, 'Fuck you. Fuck you. Fuck you.' I don't have much time left. Something's happening. I feel it. I don't know what it is, but it's beginning. I signed a living will. You know, I spoke to Father O'Malley about why I fight with everyone. I just don't understand it. I'm not used to someone trying to help me. It's never happened. Except once, when I was 13 at Manhattan State, with my first lover. He was in his thirties. He left. Went to Chicago. I remember he died in a plane crash, and I read his name in a newspaper list of passengers. Maybe it was a dream. Father said we all have moods. Ya know, sometimes after I fight, I just cry. I just cry after we fight. Are you having a nice day?" I nodded yes.

"Listen," he said, "you brought the wrong nail polish."

"What?" I said.

"I don't know what this stuff is. Hardener? Get it. The fact of the matter is, you brought the wrong stuff. $4.99 down the tubes. . . ."

When we returned to his room, he said, "I've lost my freedom. This is the last stop. I'm never going to leave this place." There were two other patients in Frankie's room; one didn't move, just stared wide-eyed at the ceiling and wouldn't speak at all. The other was clearly dying, curled into fetal position, moaning. Frankie said to him, "If you're going to croak, *croak*. I can't take your noise anymore. Don't come to me to borrow cigarettes or money or to watch TV."

He was in a rage. "Who put me here? You put me here. Who put me here? Tell Clarabel to get the fuck outa my life. You're fired. David's fired. Out! Out! If you don't get outa this room, I'm calling the security guard. Get it?" I replied, "I get it."

The next day, there were messages from Clarabel, David, the lawyer, the social worker, the physician's assistant, the crisis intervention worker, my ex-lover, and Frankie. I had had a summer cold. I missed two days of work and just wanted to sleep. I was running a slight fever.

Back to setting limits.

"I'm not interested in ducking your anger. I won't be afraid of you. You can't fire me. I haven't been hired." I was talking to myself, walking down Madison Avenue, stopping to look at the windows of Givenchy. I wondered if anyone noticed me. I remembered an axiom: Whenever we are disturbed, no matter what the cause, there is something wrong with us. Unbeknownst to me, Frankie named me executor of his will. Several weeks after the Weller visit, I received a telephone call from a funeral home. He was cremated, and they wanted me to come in to pick up the ashes. I hadn't even been informed of his death. A GMHC volunteer and myself picked up the container of ashes. We followed the instructions in Frankie's will by taking the container to a remote cemetery where his grandmother was buried. We found her gravesite, removed the ashes from the container and buried him with a garden trowel.

BIOPSYCHOSOCIAL DIAGNOSIS

The biopsychosocial diagnosis includes the history of the present illness, the mental status of the individual, past psychiatric and substance use history, relations with support system and family, and ecosystemic resources (such as community and religious affiliations).

Frankie's Biomedical Diagnosis

Neuropsychiatric difficulties are prominent in HIV-infected individuals, so HIV dementia complex (HDC), cryptococcal meningitis, cranial lymphoma, and toxoplasmosis affect all levels of the central and peripheral nervous systems as complications of HIV-induced immunosuppression. The potential for neurologic manifestations are contingent on the progression of HIV disease. There are complex diagnostic difficulties due to the effect of HIV on cerebrospinal fluid parameters. For instance, the management of neurosyphilis is a complication in an HIV-infected individual. The principal objective of neurodiagnosis is to determine the treatable components of neuropsychiatric dysfunction.[6]

Studies indicate 30% to 40% of individuals with symptomatic HIV disease develop some neurological dysfunction. A survey of 180 patients at San Francisco General Hospital determined that 50% of patients followed over a three-year period developed cognitive dysfunction (including forgetfulness), poor concentration, lack of interest, and difficulty with complex tasks. Neurologic complications further impair an individual's adaptation to the stressors of HIV disease.[7]

Mental Status Examination

- Appearance
- Psychomotor state
- Relation to interviewer
- Speech
- Thought content
- Thought processes
- Mood
- Cognitive functioning
  orientation
  attention and concentration
  memory
  immediate recall
  five-minute recall
  recent memory
  remote memory
  fund of knowledge
  calculations
  ability to abstract
  sensorimotor tasks
  insight and judgment

HIV infection causes subcortical neuropathology, while dementia is rarely the initial presentation. Also occurring are organic cognitive and psychological alterations resembling functional disorders. The organicity of HDC present mood disorders that can be differentiated from functional depression. The two classifications manifest differently according to Perry, so symptomatology such as "apathy, withdrawal, mental slowing, and avoidance of complex tasks associated with early HIV-induced organic mental disorders are clinically distinct from low self-esteem, irrational guilt, and other psychological features of depression."[8]

It is difficult to distinguish depression from HIV-induced mental disorders, such as those caused by HIV-related dementia or toxoplasmosis. One marker when making a differential diagnosis is these patients do not subjectively feel depressed or exhibit suicidal ideation. However, depression, along with social withdrawal, is a frequent symptom of early HIV-related dementia. Studies document elevated proportions of current and lifetime mood disorders in individuals at risk from HIV infection. A clinician will often make and treat a dually diagnosed individual.[9] There have been some detailed reports of psychiatric consultation with individuals with HIV disease who present depressed mood, major depression, dementia, delirium, and panic disorder.[10] When HDC does not exist, psychological and psychiatric problems are remarkably characteristic over the course of HIV illness. Identification of premorbid psychiatric conditions is integral to initial counseling and screening, because these individuals are at risk for decompensation during the progression of illness.

Differentiating Between Delirium and Dementia

DELIRIUM
- increased psychomotor activity
- fluctuating level of consciousness
- disordered thinking
- perceptual disturbances
- disorientation
- memory impairment

DEMENTIA
- patients are alert, but can be hostile or violent
- suspicious
- irritable personalities intensified

Anxiety and minor depression frequently present in individuals without prior psychiatric histories:

> Anxiety is almost ubiquitous in HIV-infected populations, peaking early, at the time of notification of HIV seropositivity, and late, as complications of disease progress and death is anticipated. Depression is increasingly common and may mimic some of the nonspecific organic complaints caused by HIV infection. Insomnia may also be a prominent complaint.[11]

The treatment of anxiety and depression for these individuals must consider their history of substance use. There is a correlation between idiosyncratic side effects of many classes of drugs in HIV-infected individuals.

As a result of impaired thinking and perceptual disturbances, violence in organic mental disorders and syndromes may be the result of the patients' decreased control over aggression and other impulses, poor social judgment, and paranoid thoughts (or even delusions). In short, they feel threatened by their cognitive impairment:

> In delirium, there may be increased psychomotor activity with violence accompanied by disordered thinking, fluctuating level of consciousness, perceptual disturbances, disorientation, and memory impairment. In dementia, patients are more alert but can be irritable, hostile, and violent as a result of their frustration with impaired memory and higher cortical function. In addition, suspicious, irritable personalities may be intensified with dementia.[12]

Psychological

The process of making a differential diagnosis first requires an examination of the symptoms manifested in the individual. Further, the assignment of a diagnostic category assumes that these symptoms appear as part of a behavioral cluster, a style of interpersonal interaction, a patterned collection of symptoms defined as a syndrome. The accuracy of diagnosis is critical to the formulation of a treatment plan and requires considerable clinical skill. The *Diag-*

nostic and Statistical Manual of Mental Disorders (DSM-III-R) is the evaluative tool utilized by mental-health professionals to make "diagnostic judgments," and it is organized into categories of psychopathology according to symptoms.

Controversy surrounds the process of clinical diagnosis itself. No responsible clinician denies that troubled people manifest disturbing behaviors that endanger their well-being, as well as those in society, and that they have a right to receive professional help to cope with such disturbances. However, categorizations have been questioned by entire classes of people not only because issues of social class, race, ethnicity, sexism, or sexual orientation have not been taken into account but because those very differences have formed the basis for theoretical, so-called scientific biases. For instance, when surveying psychoanalytic theory that relates to narcissistic personality disorder, there is a *blame-the-mother* ideology that scrutinizes her ability to provide adequate, phase-appropriate, and unimpaired love during critical stages of infant development. The DSM-III-R's definition of borderline personality disorder (BPD) includes "a pervasive pattern of instability of mood, interpersonal relationships, and self-image, beginning by early adulthood and present in a variety of contexts."[13] BPD presents particular resistance characterized by mood instability with abrupt affectual transitions and intensely emotional expression, shifting short- and long-term goals, and conflict about the therapist. The borderline client esteems and denigrates the therapist simultaneously. For example, Frankie said, with praise and hostility in a paradoxical assertion, "You've helped me so much. I love you to death." He then described a dream in which he took a pen I often hold during session and repeatedly stabbed my tongue with it. The dream conveyed the twofold symbolization of silencing me and feelings of sexual aggression. Frankie's verbal assaults were ubiquitous when he considered interventions to be unsupportive or he felt misunderstood.

Affinity with BPD clients is difficult to establish, so the therapist must maintain empathic behavior while isolating pathology that requires examination. Ever-changing feelings, judgments, and goals affect the client-therapist alliance, and the client's inconsistency will have a negative influence. BPD clients have the inclination to shift discussion from one subject to another and require support to pursue a theme, a holding environment. Clients fluctuate from enthusiasm to devaluation.[14] The essence of borderline pathology is the developmental failure to acquire holding and soothing introjects. Their intention is not subversion of what exists or what is malformed but to actualize what was not a component of their life experience. Healing proceeds less from interpretation than from the therapist's stable, consistent care. The therapist is nonpunitive, surviving the client's rage and destructive impulses while promoting holding and soothing functions the client cannot.[15]

Criteria for Borderline Personality Disorder[16]

- Recurrent suicidal threats, gestures, or behavior.
- Self-mutilating behavior.
- Labile affect and affective instability, shifting from baseline mood to depression, irritability, or anxiety, that lasts a few hours and only rarely more than a few days.
- Impulsivity (e.g,, spending, sex, substance use, and binge eating).
- Temper tantrums and lack of control of anger.
- Intense and unstable relations characterized by alternating extremes of overidealization and devaluation.
- Disturbed identity with uncertainty about self-image, sexual orientation, long-term goals, type of friends, and preferred values.
- Chronic feelings of emptiness or boredom.
- Frantic efforts to avoid real or imagined abandonment.

According to Segal, the interpersonal phenomena in borderline pathology requires a multidimensional approach, including the quality of manifest interpersonal behaviors, patterns of core interpersonal conflicts, capacity for processing complex emotions, patterns of defensive operations, and the capacity for differentiating mental images of others from perceptions of the self.[17]

Frankie's polarity of self-aggrandizement, grandiosity, and superiority fused with a sense of vulnerability, helplessness, and weakness suggested a narcissistic personality type. He exhibited hostility, aggressiveness, a compulsion to lie, and manipulative behavior that also implied a diagnosis of narcissism. He was isolated from functional object relations. He felt victimized by people. And, although he denied substance use as a problem, the abuse of alcohol was integral to his life story.

Frankie's situation was complicated by a tripartite convergence of substance use, chronic mental illness, and HIV disease. Unlike mental-health professionals in private practice, agency, institutional, or hospital practice does not allow for choosing appropriate and easily engaged or successfully treatable patients. Microsocial issues (those that are interpersonal and intrapsychic) and macrosocial issues (those that are societal) are complex. They must be addressed by the social worker through a comprehensive biopsychosocial assessment. This diagnostic assessment considers both the response of the patient to the hospital setting and their ability to cope with illness.

THE COUNTERTRANSFERENTIAL MATRIX

The impact of AIDS on both the therapist and client introduces significant issues that can be emotionally distressing for both. The therapist often has unconscious feelings and attitudes toward the client throughout the psychotherapeutic encounter, composing a countertransferential matrix. The therapist may have intense emotional reactions to the client that indicate a countertransference position rooted in the therapist's own past. Borderline clients make exceptional demands on the emotionality of the therapist. As Searles indicates, the borderline client's ego functioning is at a symbiotic, preindividuation level. The therapist's awareness, by accessing unconscious experiences, can formulate and verbalize the client's still-unconscious conflicts. The conflicts are recognized through identification with the therapist "into whom they have been able to flow, as it were, through the liquidly symbiotic transference."

Both Stephen Levine and Ram Dass have written excellent books on the helping professions and have conducted workshops on burnout. (See also Figure 13.)

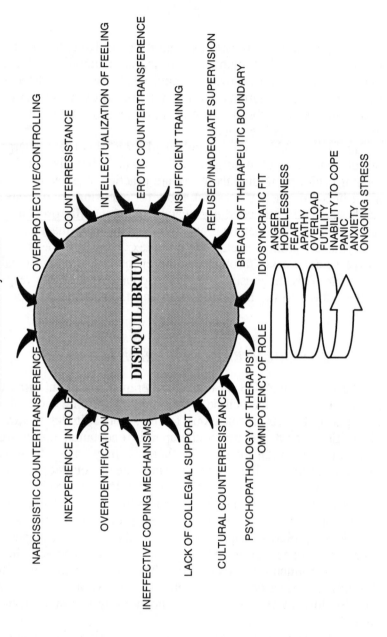

FIGURE 13. Burnout Syndrome

Burn-out occurs when we give from the little self, the small mind. We give from who we think we are. We become 'helpers.' Because the little mind, the little personality, doesn't have much room, we don't have space enough for the suffering of others. We feel isolated and struggle to keep from being submerged in our separate suffering.[18]

Ram Dass warns the following:

Frequently, our reactiveness to suffering takes the form of having instantly to do something, do anything. It's the "we gotta" syndrome. "We gotta" fix this up right away. "We gotta" call this person for advice. It's tricky, because this impulse may arise from genuine empathy, but the form of action is compulsive. Often what's happening is that "we gotta" rid someone's pain because it's hurting us too much.[19]

The profound distress of HIV-related psychotherapy requires continual self-examination. In the following, providers describe how dreamlife is affected.

Dreams[20]

- "I recently dreamed that I was infected due to a needlestick. I received the diagnosis with horror."
- "I dreamed that while going through my patient's HIV-positive results, there was a report with my name on it marked "POSITIVE" in bold letters."
- "The majority of time, I have dreams about patients who are special to me or with whom I've had difficulty making discharge plans or someone I feel emotional involvement. Sometimes, I also have dreams related to what would happen if I'm HIV-positive."
- "I dream of finding a cure for AIDS. I have a son with HIV, and it's very hard for me, my family, and friends."
- "I have nightmares of being attacked by someone with an infected needle."
- "No dreams. I hope for a vaccine."

With clients in the early, asymptomatic, stage of HIV disease, the ability by the therapist to form a therapeutic alliance is considerably less impeded than with the occurrence of symptomatology, particularly neuropsychiatric aspects or when the client is homebound or hospitalized. Individuals with advanced HIV disease experience difficulty engaging in psychotherapy that is interpretive or analytic; instead, they require a supportive bond. For the therapist, the apprehension that a client will deteriorate medically is omnipresent, and often, at times unconsciously, the therapist prepares for this eventuality. During the course of treatment, certain boundaries fluctuate, such as when a client is hospitalized when physical contact between therapist and client may occur, resulting in a changed therapeutic frame. The shift is more acute when a patient may be dying.

One of the singular features of psychotherapy is that the therapist expends much of his or her professional time forbidding or restricting self-expression (See Figure 14): "Much more than any other professional, the psychotherapist, whilst on the job, needs to be less than normally self-assertive; if not an enigma, at least not a completely known quantity. His own personality is never fully expressed, but always orientated toward the needs of the other."[21] Inevitably, inadvertently, or impulsively, a therapist may disclose countertherapeutic reactions to a client. Whether these are based on the client's behavior or are caused by something within the worker, they may be expressed in a way that is not in the client's interests.[22]

When a therapist has unresolved problems related to his or her own aggression, for instance, they may placate or be ingratiating to the individual: "The client, therefore, cannot improve because it is not safe to express aggression toward the therapist, and she may have to act out unverbalized hatred by quitting treatment."[23] Schwartz forewarns that homophobia deteriorates the value of psychotherapy and can transpire even with therapists who are self-homophobic:

> Mutual "blind spots" can lead to a collusion to avoid conflicted areas shared by the client and therapist. The anticipated blanket acceptance by the therapist expected by the client may act as a resistance to exploring the intrapsychic conflict that brought him to therapy.[24]

FIGURE 14. Limit-Setting

THE CONSCIOUS USE OF SELF
The counselor must be present if there is helping, rather than inattentive, absent-minded, abstracted, or day-dreaming. A counselor's detachment or preoccupation induces boredom and makes helping impossible. Counselor stress is routine in the helping role. The counselor needs to value his/her feeling as well as the client's. The counselor may need to have his/her own needs met, i.e., to identify, be loved, react, or exercise power. The professional self requires examination and reflection.

METHOD–THE WORKING ALLIANCE
The counselor engages the client. The counselor encourages trust, encouraging the client to accept guidance. The counselor must present him/herself as authentic while maintaining a professional role with the client. Self-disclosure by the counselor may not facilitate the working alliance. Instead, self-disclosure can be experienced by the client as the counselor's self-involvement and inability to actively listen. The counselor needs to recognize the client as an individual human being.

STRUCTURE–EMOTIONAL REACTION TO CLIENT
The structure of the session must be client-centered. However, the counselor must contend with the client's anxiety, feeling self-doubt about his/her ability to help. The counselor may cling to didactic model without engaging the client, becoming excessively directive or reciting at the client. In response to the client's stress, the counselor can develop rescue fantasies in a quest for omnipotence.

GOALS–CONTENT OF SESSION
Providing the client with the opportunity to share responsibility during the session helps mobilize participation promoting a higher level of adaptation to the outcome of the session. When self-defeating behaviors are identified, the client may be able to modify them without any injunctions from the counselor, thereby acquiring an opportunity for mastery and enhanced self-esteem.

The therapist's susceptibility to feelings of inadequacy are characteristic when treating clients with BPD. This is not an indicator that the therapy is retrogressive. For the client to acknowledge progress, it necessitates recognition of the significance of the therapeutic relationship and the therapist's capacity to generate corrective change. The therapeutic relationship may induce unbearable vulnerability and envy in the client and the terror of loss and abandonment.[25]

Over the course of treatment, borderline clients may develop a transference psychosis that induces feelings of guilt and responsibility in the therapist. With BPD individuals, the therapist experiences well-meaning interventions and being subjected to renunciation and rejection in exchange. This is the inspiring and challenging ingredient of the work. Therapists nearly masochistically submit to their client's aggression, feel disproportionate questionings of ability, and fear criticisms by third parties.[26]

> [W]e must recognize that the analyst's blind spots are always a hazard. However, the hazard is greater when there is a stake in denying them. Not only is the patient needlessly confused by this, but, possibly even more important, denial aids the analyst in repressing his own possibility of insight. A frank discussion with the patient, encouraging him to tell all that he has observed or thinks he has observed may actually increase the analyst's insight into himself to the benefit of both.[27]

On the other hand, Winnicott recommends against the therapist's guarded professional stance that results from defenses, inhibitions, and obsessional orderliness: "The professional attitude is rather like symbolism, in that it assumes a *distance between analyst and patient*. The symbol is a gap between the subjective object and the object that is perceived objectively."[28] If the therapist is struggling because of the structure of his or her ego defenses, this lessens the ability to meet the client's needs. The therapist must endure vulnerability counterpoised against the professional role. Personal evolution is promoted so the therapist is genuinely congruent with the client. Rogers defines congruence as therapist feelings that are experienced, consciously available, and tolerable and as the talent to communicate them when appropriate. Rogers writes, "No one fully achieves this condition, yet the more the therapist is able to listen acceptantly to what is going on within himself, and the more he is able to be the complexity of his feelings, without fear, the higher the degree of his congruence."[29]

REFERENCE NOTES

1. Michael Shernoff, "Why Every Social Worker Should Be Challenged By AIDS," *Social Work*, January 1990, Volume 35, Number 1.

2. Naomi Golan, "Crisis Theory," in *Social Work Treatment*, edited by Francis J. Turner (New York: The Free Press, 1986), p. 297.

3. Harriet M. Bartlett, *Social Work Practice In The Health Field* (Washington, DC: National Association of Social Workers, 1961), p. 189.

4. Oliver Sacks, *The Man Who Mistook His Wife For A Hat* (New York: Summit Books, 1985), p. 105.

5. Otto F. Kernberg, "Further Contributions to the Treatment of Narcissistic Personalities," in *Essential Papers On Narcissism*, edited by Andrew P. Morrison, MD (New York: New York University Press, 1986), p. 255.

6. Harry Hollander, MD, "Neurologic and Psychiatric Manifestations of HIV Disease," *Journal of General Medicine*, Volume 6, January/February Supplement, 1991, p. 525.

7. James Dilley, MD, "Psychosocial Impact of AIDS: Overview," in *The AIDS Knowledge Base*, pp. 2–5, 13.1.

8. Samuel W. Perry, MD, *American Journal of Psychiatry*, 1990, 147: 702.

9. Perry, p. 702.

10. Michael E. Faulstich, MD, "Psychiatric Aspects of AIDS," *American Journal of Psychiatry*, 144:5, May 1987.

11. Ibid.

12. Kenneth Tardiff, MD, MPH, *Assessment and Management of Violent Patients* (Washington, DC: American Psychiatric Press, 1989), p. 49.

13. *Diagnostic Criteria from DSM-III-R* (Washington, DC: The American Psychiatric Association, 1987).

14. Ekkehard Othmer, MD, PhD, and Sieglinde C. Othmer, PhD, *The Clinical Interview Using DSM-II-R* (Washington, DC: American Psychiatric Press, 1989), p. 397.

15. Robert J. Waldinger, MD, and John G. Gunderson, MD, *Effective Psychotherapy with Borderline Patients* (Washington, DC: American Psychiatric Press, 1987), p. 13.

16. Adapted from the *Diagnostic Criteria from DSM-III-R*, op. cit.

17. Barry M. Segal, MB, BCh, "Interpersonal Factors in Borderline Pathology," in *Family Environment and Borderline Personality Disorder*, edited by Paul S. Links, MD, MSc, FRCP (Washington, DC: American Psychiatric Press: 1990), p. 59.

18. Stephen Levine, *Who Dies?* (New York: Anchor Books, 1982), p. 170.

19. Ram Dass, *How Can I Help?* (New York: Alfred A. Knopf, 1985), p. 63.

20. From a questionnaire designed by Zachary Rosen, MD, and distributed to providers at the conference, "The Second Decade: HIV in Primary Care Practice," Bronx, New York, February 6, 1992.

21. Anthony Storr, *The Art of Psychotherapy* (New York: Methuen, 1980), p. 171.

22. Florence Hollis and Mary E. Woods, *Casework: A Psychosocial Therapy* (New York: Random House, 1981), p. 293.

23. Herbert S. Stream, "Psychoanalytic Theory," in *Social Work Treatment*, edited by Francis J. Turner (New York: The Free Press, 1986), p. 37.

24. Robert D. Schwartz, MD, "When the Therapist is Gay: Personal and Clinical Reflections," *Journal of Gay & Lesbian Psychotherapy*, Vol 1(1), 1989.

25. Lawrence Epstein, "The Problem of The Bad-Analyst Feeling," paper presented at the National Association for the Advancement of Psychoanalysis Conference, New York, May 2, 1987.

26. Otto Kernberg, *Borderline Conditions and Pathological Narcissism* (Northvale, NJ: Jason Aronson, Inc., 1987), p. 61.

27. Clara Thompson, "The Role of the Analyst's Personality in Therapy," in *Essential Papers on Countertransference*, edited by Benjamin Wolstein (New York: New York University Press, 1988), p. 122.

28. D. W. Winnicott, "Counter-Transference," in *Essential Papers on Countertransference*, pp. 264-265.

29. Carl Rogers, *On Becoming a Person* (Boston: Houghton Mifflin, 1961), p. 61.

Chapter 9

Jose

Charles Villaborg and Gilbert Rodriguez came to this country ten years ago from Costa Rica. According to *The New York Times,* in a two-paragraph news story of the joint suicide, they tied themselves together with a bed-sheet and jumped to their deaths from their 35th-floor apartment on 3rd Avenue and 91st Street.

–Contents of a letter from a friend

FEAR AND TREMBLING

Recently discharged from a hospital after a 21-day treatment for *pneumocystis carinii* pneumonia (PCP), Jose, a 29-year-old Latino, returned to life as usual. He was a well-respected costume designer who worked throughout the country in the regional theater circuit. His long-awaited break came a year before his diagnosis, when a Broadway producer optioned a play during a new play festival in Louisville, Kentucky. The play moved to Broadway for a brief run with the entire creative team. Jose was a Tony Award nominee.

His concept of theater design attempted to evoke a psychological scenario that defied the boundaries of the proscenium, of convention itself. The fabric of costumes absorbed him sensually as he sat in a wing chair for hours stroking a velvet square between his fingers before deciding. He lived on New York's Upper West Side, in a large apartment with the floor of his large work room ankle deep in fabric scraps.

A well-known, but out-of-work, Hollywood director signed him for a project scheduled for filming in New York. The director was also well known for his difficult temper, which was probably exacerbated by substance use, particularly cocaine and alcohol. Jose, used to the theatrical collaborative medium, was ill-prepared for the dictatorial style of film. Work on the film was exhausting in every conceivable way–emotionally, physically, and creatively. Since he believed it was an accident of fate, it became difficult to enjoy the special success. Jose became preoccupied with self-doubt about future projects. He worked on the film with intemperate speed and daring, balancing creative and business temperaments with the increasing fear for his health.

Jose envisioned himself having a Byronic temperament–a neurotically fragile nineteenth-century Romanticist, vacillating between flippant defiance and honest, heart-of-sleeve expression, with many subtle variations between moods.

He designed most of his own clothing, combining improbable patterns in the Japanese style, always wearing boots to augment his height and masculinize his gait. He wore his long jet-black hair pomaded and pulled into a ponytail and tied with a black-velvet ribbon. Despite the idiosyncratic fashion, he was inconspicuous–the effect was style, not ostentation.

He described himself as physically limited and hypochondriacal; he always carried a black-leather case filled with over-the-counter and prescription medications. After reading that aspirin prevented heart disease, he took one every day. The case contained several bottles of various antibiotics for sexually transmitted diseases (STDs), which he saved after treatment for syphilis or gonorrhea; Naprosyn for lower-back spasms, to which he was prone; antihistamines for allergies; an inhaler for asthma; Seconal for sleep; Prozac for depression; and low-dosage multivitamins for balance. He smoked three packs of cigarettes a day with a tortoise holder to decrease nicotine.

For years, he took for granted he was HIV-positive, internally adjusting to the monumental supposition, unable to constrain his unconscious, and often awakening from nightmares in dread. Jose relegated HIV to the sphere of dreams, scrupulously avoiding those he knew who were HIV-positive, turning from any mention of the disease. He knew nothing of the disease except a conviction he would die from it.

He most feared disfigurement after seeing an actor acquaintance who developed Kaposi's sarcoma (KS). The actor, a soap-opera idol, had lesions all over his face, which he covered with makeup. No makeup camouflaged the swelling that remodeled his facial structure, broadening his nose and puffing the tissue around his eyes so they appeared half-open. Jose reflexively turned from the friend, sensing the contraction of his body, the aspect of a death mask. Pity deflected into self-pity, and Jose felt humiliated by fear—the fear that death would infect him.

He endured fatigue, fever, shortness of breath, and chest pains because he was energized by the film project. Despite the exhaustion, the interfering apprehension of illness complicated sleep. Roberto, his lover, was in Puerto Rico visiting relatives. Jose skipped dinner, favoring a hot rosemary oilbath to sedate his anxiety. He smoked marijuana to Peter Gabriel's macabre soundtrack for the film *The Last Temptation of Christ*, which he played through the night with the tape deck set for auto-reverse. He consoled himself by thinking it was paranoiac to worry. He fell asleep ruminating about the difference between the artistic processes of film versus theater.

The answering-machine message counter blinked silently. It was almost noon when Jose awakened, undisturbed by two alarm clocks placed on opposite sides of the bedroom. He boasted that his biological timekeeper preferred nighttime, so he set two blasting alarms for 7 a.m., neither clock within reach from the bed. His pajamas soaked through a dressing gown to a feverishly, aching body.

He telephoned his assistant, who was already on the set, saying he would be there in an hour. He was barely able to walk to the bathroom to splash cold water on his face. An hour later, Roy, his assistant, held his finger on the downstairs doorbell, and when no one answered, he arrived with the superintendent, who had a spare set of keys to the apartment. They entered the apartment and found Jose on the bathroom floor, his face covered with blood.

The ambulance arrived at the emergency room of a world-famous municipal hospital, where Jose remained on a gurney for 18 hours before admission. The 10th floor was not an officially designated HIV ward, but most patients had an HIV-related infection. In the adjacent room, a Rikers Island prisoner contorted against the chains wrapped around his bed; Jose heard the rhythmic clanging of the sweat-soaked links in his room. It bewildered him witnessing a dying man chained to a hospital bed with an armed floor-police patrol.

Jose recalled a story about another patient. "I know the man in 10W," he said sheepishly.

"Oh," I asked.

"About ten years ago. An East Side bar. What's the name? *Conoces*? *Digame*! Ay. The Parrot? Well, he was the bartender. I had such a crush on him. His waist was smaller than Vivian Leigh playing Scarlet. What a doll. I would sit at the bar all night, flirting with him. He was unapproachable, although friendly. We called him the Contessa. I would wait until the bar closed. I was so drunk, it was a technical feat to get off the bar stool without falling. Oh, we used to snort cocaine right at the bar. What a divine combination—rum and coke and coke.

"I'd need someone to help me, lend me an arm. Then that someone, whoever, would escort me home. Escort? It sounds so pretentious. He'd stay the night. Someone would be there in the morning, a total stranger. God knows what I promised them the night before. They wouldn't even get a cup of coffee the next morning. Up and out.

"Why did they always look like a Japanese C horror film? Godzillas. Ah, but the Contessa, the stuff of sweet dreams, and right next door. Roberto called GMHC [Gay Men's Health Crisis] for a buddy who brought me these cookies: 'I'll eat every one for you, Contessa.' "

Jose began to laugh and laugh, then cough and cough, then choke. He turned purple, amusing himself. Until chills overtook him; then Roberto threw himself on top of him. He had piled blanket upon blanket, attempting to keep him warm. The chills had become uncontrollable. Nothing stopped the fevers. No medication lowered his temperature. Not even medications to counter medications. Or drugs with side-effects prescribed for drugs with side-effects. He was having an allergic response to a pharmacological combination. Paging a nurse got no response, so Roberto went to the nurses' station. Overwhelmed with other patients, the nurses ignored the poorly phrased, nonmedical appeal until he shouted at them: "Jose Borges, room 11B. High fever, more than 106. Tylenol isn't bringing it down. Severe chills. Uncontrollable. Please help!"

* * *

Carmen was Jose's sister, and she had been feeling rage toward him because she felt that he was unresponsive to her efforts to be supportive. "I ain't goin' call him anymore. He doesn't return my phone calls. He's changed. We used to be so close. When I found out he had HIV, I didn't abandon him. I thought it was disgusting, but he's my brother. When I asked him questions, he just turned to me and slapped me with some pamphlet. I pleaded with him, 'Talk to me. I don't want to read something.' He turned to me with disgust and said, 'Go educate yourself.' Well, I did. I went to a counselor, and tried to understand why I was so angry at him. You see, I'm eight years older than he, and my role was to protect him. I protected him all his life, but I couldn't save him from this damn virus. I feel so guilty. Like I failed.

"But, I found a way to be there for him. This last hospitalization was the worst. They said he attempted suicide by drinking several glasses of Clorox. I remember the night I called. I tried his phone several times. I thought where could he be? I waited ten minutes . . . still, no answer. I panicked and called the nurses station. I'm certain the bleach was left on his nightstand for him to drink. He just wouldn't have done it, not my brother. Jose's throat was badly burned; he couldn't eat, even talking was difficult. They posted a policeman outside his door to keep 24-hour vigilance. He seemed a prisoner. After all, suicide is a crime."

Carmen had moved into Jose and Roberto's apartment to help them–neither had been capable enough to cope with the devastating emotional or physical effects of AIDS for awhile. I had the impression that Carmen needed to be there as much as they needed her.

Jose's apartment interior showed no trace of being inside a tenement: the walls and ceiling had been replaced, so they met at perfect right angles with no cracks, bumps, or buckles. Several walls had been shifted to make the standard railroad arrangement appear larger. The walls covered with ticking were hung with photographs: on the beach, in Paris, as children, the poodles as puppies, the parents. Fabric was everywhere. Yards and yards of it draped over everything. Art books were piled on the floor, and on table tops. It was a romantic apartment.

Roberto is indifferent to me. No, skeptical. He's always been there. Their relationship had endured all the tests—conscious and unconscious, those ideological, and those for thrill and intoxication. Roberto also has AIDS. It had been less than a year since he had PCP. He's a Vietnam Vet, silent and protective of his lover.

Jose denied having lesions for months. He hoped they would go away, that they were something else. When his strength began to weaken, he feared what was happening. It was becoming undeniable. He was running a fever, Roberto was in Puerto Rico on business, and he unplugged the phone, locking himself into the apartment for over a week until he was found by Carmen, dehydrated and delirious.

*   *   *

Jose said: "I'm writing a children's story, which I think could be animated, like *The Little Mermaid*. I'd like to read it to you."

In former times, enthralled spirits ceaselessly wandered Earth, encircling the planet. They levitated serpentine through the heavens, adventurously gliding above the planet euphoric. They were inspired by self-transcendence, witnessing life as eternal transformation—the unfolding of formlessness into substance. They were obligated to creativity, the interdependence of chromaticity and patterns, and the mathematics of vibration and cadence. They witnessed processes hidden within atomic synapses, experiencing neutrons struggling to transform through change toward perfection. They were moved by this passion and agony, beholding life as the implication of unknown. For Spirits, holy intention was revelry and their charismatic aura illuminated the skies. It came to pass that a group of men forbade the passage to see the face of ancestors, banishing themselves from the community. So for millennia, humans have had to die a little to evoke mystery and suffer the face behind the mask. Many legends attempted to explain the phenomena. Some thought these men were an aberration, a mutation, a challenge. The spirits were powerless to prevent their renunciation of change and could only accept the inevitable. Some believed it was the depravity of power. Power existed before the Men of Denial left the community, but it was creative and life-sustaining. The Men of Denial challenged the Great Mother, attempting to prevail over Her singular genius to procreate. They lusted after nature.

The Men of Denial lived in a hidden valley called Abyss, between two mountain ranges. They organized a society through rituals and trials of dominion, administered by the Elite, patriarchs who designated a Master. It was celebration to sacrifice the Master through torture every decade and to glory in his wretched submission to destiny. The Elite also imposed classifications corrupted by power dominance, so they bonded from fear. The Men of Denial assaulted other communities, enslaving many peoples, particularly women and children. They lived in clusters each with one, or several, women and many children.

It was universal law in Abyss that every infant after birth be confirmed before a tribunal of Elite during an Examination of Infants. The Examination was a trial, a prosecution, to mandate an infant's fate. The abandonment of infants was common practice when considered irredeemable. When sentencing an infant, the Tribunal applied many doctrines that were codified in a large Encyclopedia of human characteristics, such as skin tone, hair texture, physique size. As the infant grew into childhood, it was summoned before the Tribunal for miscellaneous ideosyncracies of behavior (quirks, mannerisms, oddities, disabilities) or for gender defilement (womanlike or mannish deportment).

A child named Noble was born within a cluster. His parents, Mercy and Jack, received a Tribunal notice to present the infant. The Chief of the Tribunal, Malleus, presented the verdict. He said, "This child, Noble, of three months, is short by three millimeters and is underweight by seven grams. Therefore, the infant is of delicate and frail physique and will develop a sensitive nature and an effeminate character. This is unacceptable to the men of Abyss. The infant is sentenced to abandonment in a designated cave in the mountain range."

His parents begged for mercy; Noble was their only child. Malleus responded to their helpless supplication, feeling a surge of eroticism toward Mercy. He said, "You must commit yourselves to maintain the Golden Rules of Pedagogy in all affairs of this infant's childraising. Jack, you must become a member of the Elite and report for duty, working long hours away from your wife and child. You will observe them as a bystander to monitor compliance with the Golden Rules. Mercy, you will become a communicant and periodically appear before me in my private chambers, confessing when you transgress from the Golden Rules, and I will extricate you from conflict and relieve your anxiety. If you both obey these commandments, I will suspend the sentence." And so they both agreed, and the infant was spared the fate of abandonment.

Years went by, and Noble fulfilled Malleus' ominous prophesy and became a child of sympathetic nature, captivated by sensation and inspired by consciousness. He concealed emotions, feeling that no other in Abyss was kindred. He was brokenhearted and survived through imagination and phantasmagoric seclusion, tendering a secret life.

One night, in honor of the full moon, Noble lay under the night sky, falling asleep. He was startled awake by moonlight, as clouds passed, and he heard the bidding of a warm, fierce current: "Here I am, unto you. First, grieve the Men of Denial. You must journey alone for the way. I warn you not to misunderstand this loss for intolerable agony. Second, be life-sustaining through creation. You must search alone for the way. I warn you not to misunderstand this reward for intolerable suffering. Third, return to Abyss and confide to all who listen. You must find the course homeward. I warn you, do not abuse power by misunderstanding what you have heard. You will not break if you follow my guidance."

The Spirit disappeared, as the moon was obscured once again by clouds, and the night sky was dimmed into star brightness.

* * *

Jose said to me, "Roberto left. I know that he's never coming back. He's HIV-positive. He's been in such deep denial about it. I knew the first time he got symptoms, he wouldn't be able to handle it. He said he was going to visit family in Puerto Rico, but I know that I'll never seen him again."

* * *

Jose never emotionally recovered from Roberto's disappearance. We had several sessions in his apartment. He spoke of his impending death: "The house is on fire. No one knows how to put it out. Every one is running haywire."

* * *

Jose maintained a stash of Seconals that no one knew about. When his sister arrived on Easter morning, she found her brother lying in bed with his stereo headphones on. He had been listening to an environmental tape of the ocean when he died.

THE SICKNESS UNTO DEATH

Suicidal thoughts are prevalent for infected individuals during the course of HIV disease. This is particularly the circumstance with individuals who have a history of depression. In 1985, 12 suicides were studied among individuals with an AIDS diagnosis:

> All committed suicide within nine months of receiving the diagnosis of AIDS, most within six months of diagnosis. On autopsy none of the victims appeared to have been wasted, suggesting all were at relative early stages of the illness.[1]

Clinicians should distinguish endogenous depression from advanced debility or dementia and, when appropriate, have consultation services available for both the client and the therapist. (See Figure 15.)

According to Dilley, depression commonly accompanies either

FIGURE 15. HIV/AIDS-Related Illness and Depression

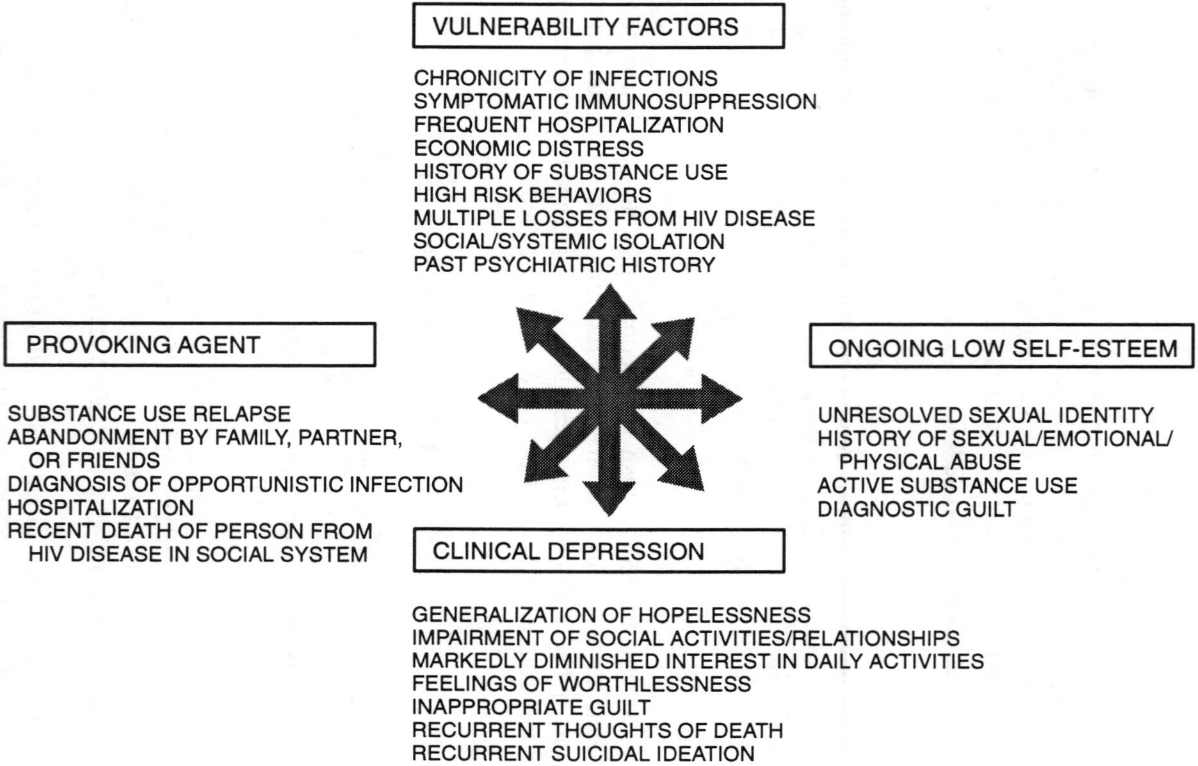

VULNERABILITY FACTORS

CHRONICITY OF INFECTIONS
SYMPTOMATIC IMMUNOSUPPRESSION
FREQUENT HOSPITALIZATION
ECONOMIC DISTRESS
HISTORY OF SUBSTANCE USE
HIGH RISK BEHAVIORS
MULTIPLE LOSSES FROM HIV DISEASE
SOCIAL/SYSTEMIC ISOLATION
PAST PSYCHIATRIC HISTORY

ONGOING LOW SELF-ESTEEM

UNRESOLVED SEXUAL IDENTITY
HISTORY OF SEXUAL/EMOTIONAL/
PHYSICAL ABUSE
ACTIVE SUBSTANCE USE
DIAGNOSTIC GUILT

PROVOKING AGENT

SUBSTANCE USE RELAPSE
ABANDONMENT BY FAMILY, PARTNER,
OR FRIENDS
DIAGNOSIS OF OPPORTUNISTIC INFECTION
HOSPITALIZATION
RECENT DEATH OF PERSON FROM
HIV DISEASE IN SOCIAL SYSTEM

CLINICAL DEPRESSION

GENERALIZATION OF HOPELESSNESS
IMPAIRMENT OF SOCIAL ACTIVITIES/RELATIONSHIPS
MARKEDLY DIMINISHED INTEREST IN DAILY ACTIVITIES
FEELINGS OF WORTHLESSNESS
INAPPROPRIATE GUILT
RECURRENT THOUGHTS OF DEATH
RECURRENT SUICIDAL IDEATION

progressive debilitation or dementia. Depression also presents with the diagnosis of specific opportunistic infections, such as toxoplasmosis or cryptococcosis meningitis.[2]

Signs And Symptoms of Major Depression

* Low mood
* Difficulty concentrating
* Lowered self-esteem
* Guilt and/or shame
* Anger
* Hopelessness
* Suicidal ideation

HIV-infected individuals, predominantly during progressive disease conditions, sustain a profound biological loss of control of their bodies. They may experience a combination of some of the following: bowel control loss, disabling neuropathy, vision impairment, suppressed appetite with accompanying taste deprivation, memory limitations, and neurologic damage with involuntary movements. There are visible, prominent, vital body alterations, such as wasting syndrome, routine dermatological conditions, and disfiguring lesions generated by Kaposi's sarcoma.

Individuals with advanced HIV disease may be dependent on intravenous therapies, such as total peripheral nutrition (TPN) and other life-sustaining medications that require body-altering surgical insertion of catheters for infusion therapies. Individuals must construct their daily activities to comply with extended therapy cycles, which customarily last for several hours. Beyond doubt, these complex treatments require skillful, well-functioning individuals or the supervision of members of the support system and health-care professionals.

Many people with HIV disease live in poverty, within chaotic environments, in inadequate housing (such as single-room-occupancy (SRO) units or as the "shadow homeless"), in family systems already burdened by multiple members with HIV disease, or are totally isolated from supports. All of these factors inhibit life-enhancing therapeutic interventions.

Emotionally, previous dispositions become restimulated as a

consequence of disease progression. The virus is experienced as quasi-anthropomorphic countenance signified through the duality between morality and corruption. The individual faces the conflict of maintaining self-esteem in the face of social prohibitions against identity and prior behavior. Becker distinguishes this tension by contrasting the allegedly modern neurotic with the classical sinner:

> Traditional religion turned the consciousness of sin into a condition for salvation; but the tortured sense of nothingness of the neurotic qualifies him now only for miserable extinction, for merciful release in lonely death.[3]

He observes the experience of human insufficiency undermining the contemporary individual from transforming limitations into heroism. Gertrude and Rubin Blanck write that once a therapist commits to treat the individual, there must be availability at all times, at all hours:

> Availability is more than physical availability or a good telephone answering service. It is an attitude. At the outset of treatment, of course, it is difficult to convey it all at once. It has to be done repeatedly and consistently.[4]

The case example of Jose is active, unassisted euthanasia. Jose never disclosed his intent or that he had concealed lethal pills. Therapists who experience a case of suicide have meaningful self-doubts. When a therapist finds him or herself in this situation, they must seek consultation services.

Gay men are often disunited from their spiritual aspect because of disaffection from organized religions that assign their identity to a sinful state. The suicidal ideation must be seen as serious and not an attention-getting threat. When there is ideation, the individual has thoughts and can verbalize intention, such as "I want to kill myself." When there is the threat of suicide, the individual can disclose suicidal action, such as "I'm going to run in front of a car." With a mild attempt, there is an actual self-destructive action, such as the ingestion of a bottle of aspirin. The serious attempt is a self-destructive action that is life-threatening and requires medical intervention. Suicide ideation, and suicide itself, may be the corrupted aspiration of appropriating control. Levine comments that suicide often emanates from the passion for life:

> The being who commits suicide as a means of escaping life is a manifestation of the pain of us all. Suicide is not the answer. But neither is a life of coping and holding to a hope that things will be different or that survival must be maintained at any cost.[5]

Suicide can be the manifestation of the frustrated will to live.

REFERENCE NOTES

1. Peter M. Murzuk, MD et al., "Increased Risk of Suicide in Persons with AIDS," *Journal of the American Medical Association (JAMA)*, March 4, 1968, Volume 259, Number 9, p. 1335.

2. James Dilley, MD, Jay Baer, MD, Alicia Boccellari, PhD, and Herbert Ochitill, MD, "Altered Mental States: Clinical Syndromes and Diagnosis" in *The AIDS Knowledge Base*, edited by P.T. Cohen, MD, PhD, Merle Sande, MD and Paul A. Volberding, MD. p. 4, 5.13.2.

3. Ernest Becker, *The Denial of Death* (New York: The Free Press, 1973), p. 197.

4. Gertrude and Rubin Blanck, *Ego Psychology: Theory and Practice* (New York: Columbia University Press, 1974), p. 267.

5. Stephen Levine, *Who Dies?* (New York: Anchor Books, 1982), p. 219.

Chapter 10

The Substance of Dandelions

We reach for destinies beyond
what we have come to know.

–Alice Walker, *We Become New*

THE INQUISITOR'S PRICK

In each of the preceding chapters of this book, there is an attempt to examine historical and social realities that influence the response to the HIV epidemic. HIV conjures images of the Other, whether the difference is of gender, sexual identity and conduct, or certain behaviors, such as substance use. HIV can be observed as the confluence of several central issues facing this planet in the twenty-first century, including the economic concerns of poverty, healthcare, and homelessness. However, the superstructure that provides the underpinning for economic disenfranchisement is the institutionalization of each male and white supremacy. Almost all empirical knowledge, scientific theory, and intrapsychic reality is filtered through a perceptual system guided by the domination of one person over another.

Freud's influence on contemporary twentieth-century life is incalculable from the theories regarding intrapsychic structure to dream interpretation: even the vocabulary of psychoanalysis is everyday, such as the oft-cited Freudian slip-of-the-tongue or the notion of unconscious motivation. For several decades, Freudian theory has been scrutinized for its male supremacist view of women–for instance, the deceptive theory of female sexuality.

(Freud's Eurocentric bias has been examined as well.) In particular, Alice Miller broke with the practice of psychoanalysis because of its denial of childhood sexual abuse as a major etiologic factor underlying several pathological conditions. Current research indicates that childhood traumata from sexual abuse is frequently discovered in substance abuse and borderline personality disorders. Many HIV-positive individuals, especially women, suffered childhood sexual abuse often masked through substance use. (An argument can be made for the emotional and sexual abuse of all gay men whose central identity was forced into submission in our dominant heterosexual culture.)

Dora was one of the most famous of Freud's patients, and his case study of her analysis influenced the entire practice of psychoanalysis with women. Many HIV-positive clients come to psychotherapy initially due to a medical diagnosis, but when there is a remission of symptomatology, especially in early HIV disease, individuals seek to resolve the identical life issues that introduce anyone to treatment. The predominance of sexual abuse in patriarchical cultures requires psychotherapists to assess all clients from this perspective. Many women are powerless to implement safer sex guidelines because they do not have control over their bodies. The case of Amy Fisher captured attention because of the convergence of sexuality, drugs, and violence: sexuality, because there is a quasi-Oedipal triangle between Amy, Joey, and MaryJo, and the suspicion of sexual abuse of Amy by her father and Joey; drugs, because substance use seems to provide the fuel for much of the criminal behavior; and violence, because our male-dominated society is obsessed with it. For myself, Amy is a prototype of many women who also become HIV-infected. She is a contemporary rendering of Dora.

In 1896, Freud published *Etiology of Hysteria*, an initial study on hysteria based on research into the sexual abuse of children. Freud's paper presented astonishing evidence of such abuse after clinical findings. Prior to writing his work on hysteria, Masson surmises, with abundant evidence, that Freud was exposed to demonstrations of child sexual abuse in the Paris morgue.[1] Freud concluded that "at the bottom of every case of hysteria there are one or more occurrences of premature sexual experience, occurrences which belong to the earliest years of childhood."[2]

The paper was very poorly received, with a response from the medical and scientific community constituting unmitigated ostracism. Freud disavowed his former theoretical position on the etiology of hysteria as originating from childhood sexual abuse and incest. Instead, to gain acceptance, he postulated that the experiences of puberty were harmful because they repeated, or stirred up, unconscious memories of early traumatic events. The adolescent experiences were unconsciously repressed (or even consciously suppressed) because they were reminiscent of earlier, far more painful ones. He submitted that early childhood traumas were a consequence of fantasies, rather than authentic events. Freud promulgated a theory that the locus of psychiatric illness originates within the fantasy life and desires of childhood, rather than real-life incidents and the adult inclination to commit incest. For instance, without the Oepidus complex, the foundation of psychoanalytic theory would be questionable, as Masson cites in a letter he received from Anna Freud:

> Keeping up the seduction theory would mean to abandon the Oedipus complex, and with it the whole importance of phantasy life, conscious or unconscious phantasy. In fact, I think there would have been no psychoanalysis afterwards.[3]

As a result, any adolescent may be seen to be neurotic whenever they do not acknowledge their own sexual desires or repel the seductive attacks by adults.

After discarding the seduction theory, Freud wrote one additional major clinical study of hysteria–the Dora case. No history of an early seduction was described in the case report. From childhood on, however, the teenage patient was deeply enmeshed in her parents' marital conflicts and in the liaisons of her seductive, syphilitic father, his mistress, Frau K, and the latter's husband, Herr K. A definition of sexual abuse incorporates several constituents, including an age difference between partners, the presence of force of coercion, and the developmental appropriateness of the behavior itself. With abuse between children, an age difference of five years of more would be an indicator. It is clear in the case illustration that

Dora was a victim of such abuse. Freud's psychoanalysis of Dora, presented in "Analysis of a Case of Hysteria," constituted one of the essential building blocks on which the foundation of psychoanalytic theory and treatment was built.

Dora is a classic case study within psychoanalytic literature of a hysterical personality disorder, a diagnosis that is no longer categorized in the *Diagnostic and Statistical Manual III-R* (DSM-III-R). However, histrionic personality disorder is contained in the DSM-III-R with many identical characteristics to designate the disorder. The case of Dora was decisive for two reasons. First, it gave Freud an opportunity to utilize his theory of dream interpretation, and second, Freud was able to present an organic etiology for mental illness that further supported a scientific view of psychology that was a new discipline during the early part of this century (when this paper was published).

Dora was brought to Freud for treatment by her father. She presented several somatic complaints. Dora suffered from a vaginal discharge and enuresis that recurred after she had achieved several years of nocturnal continence.

> Vaginal discharge as well as regression in bladder control have frequently been described in modern reports on sexually abused children. Freud, on the other hand, ascribed these problems to masturbation ending at about 8, when Dora's first hysterical symptoms appeared.[4]

Dora was 18 when she entered treatment. Her father was an affluent, upper-middle-class manufacturer. When the young woman was about 12 years old, she was suffering from migraine headaches and an ailment defined in Freud's paper as "attacks of nervous coughing." Various treatment methods were used with Dora to relieve her symptomatology, including hydrotherapy and local applications of electricity. Her conditions became chronic, and none of the treatments proved to be effective. Dora became reluctant when her father demanded that she continue to seek specialized medical treatment. However, in spite of her unwillingness to seek treatment, she didn't object to consultations with her family physician. When Dora was 16, she first met Freud; he suggested that she begin psychological treatment with him, but the family decided against it.

Dora was intelligent and attractive, but she was neither satisfied with herself or her family. She was sociophobic, particularly toward men, and avoided any social contact. Dora was described by her father as depressed, with numerous somatic complaints. She wasn't suicidal, but she had expressed a desire to "take leave" of her parents because "she could no longer endure her life" with them. Dora wrote a note in which she expressed dissatisfaction with her life situation, and when her father discovered the note, he angrily confronted her. An argument ensued, during which her father reported that she had an attack that he described as a "loss of consciousness."

As for her parents, Dora's father suffered numerous physical and mental difficulties: His vision was permanently impaired due to an improperly treated detached retina. He had become immobilized with symptoms of paralysis that was not related to any physical condition. He suffered a "confusional attack" and was diagnosed as having "slight mental disturbances." Dora's mother was incapable of dealing with familial issues: Her primary concern had been expressed as compulsive homemaking, and she appeared to have "no understanding of her children's more active interests." She and Dora had difficult relations and were antagonistic to one another.

Due to Dora's father's illnesses, a married couple, the Ks, became caretakers in their household. Mrs. K nursed Dora's father through an extensive convalescence, and he expressed a sense of deep indebtedness and loyalty to her. When Dora was 14, Mr. K had become very attentive to her, giving her small presents. He sought her company on many occasions, joining her on lakeside walks on her parent's property. His interest in Dora didn't arouse anyone's suspicion, until he made a violent and overtly sexual advance toward Dora. He forced himself on her, and he began to kiss her. Dora fought against him, tearing herself free.

Dora immediately told her mother of the incident, and her parents confronted Mr. K. Mr. K, however, emphatically denied having attacked Dora. His counterclaim consisted of an accusation against Dora. He stated that she made it a habit to read sexual literature and, having been aroused by it, conjured up the scene. To Dora's dismay, Mr. K's version was believed by her father, and he expressed to her his conclusion that the event was a fantasy.

Dora felt betrayed, and she pleaded with her parents to break off their relationship with the Ks. Her father reiterated his devotion to the Ks for having helped him through his recovery. Dora then discovered that her father's relationship with Mrs. K was sexual. She believed that was the primary explanation for her father's betrayal of her. She felt lost and victimized and that none of her feelings were taken into account. Further, Dora felt that her father had conspired with the Ks against her and that she was part of a trade-off in a negotiation. She believed she had been bartered to Mr. K so her father could continue his affair with Mrs. K.

Freud diagnosed Dora as having been already "entirely and completely hysterical" at the time of Mr. K's attack upon her. Freud suggested that any person "in whom an occasion for sexual excitement elicited feelings that were preponderantly or exclusively unpleasurable" was, without question, hysterical.

Freud suggested that Dora's somatization was a displacement of sensations: "Instead of the genital sensation which would certainly have been felt by a healthy girl," she was overcome with unpleasurable feelings. Further, Dora's symptoms that related to the oral cavity, her persistent coughing, were reminiscent of her habit of thumb-sucking and its later repression as a form of erotic pleasure.

Freud also theorized about Dora's attacks of illness during Mr. K's absence: "Could it be that the presence or absence of the man she loved had an influence upon the appearance and disappearance of the symptoms of her illness." When it was discovered there wasn't a correlation, he hypothesized it had become necessary for Dora to "obscure the coincidence between her attacks of illness and the absence of the man she secretly loved."

Dora consistently felt that her father's affair with Mrs. K should be addressed, although she also complained that "we children have no right to criticize this behaviour of father's." Freud felt that Dora was suffering from an exaggerated and pathological train of thought, and that it "must owe its reinforcement to the unconscious." According to Freud, Dora's continual questioning of her father was pathological in nature because it masked feelings of jealousy toward Mrs. K, as well as an infantile attachment to her father vis-à-vis an unresolved Oedipus complex. Freud further felt that concealed in Dora's jealousy were feelings "which could only be based on an affection on Dora's part for one of her sex." Freud felt that Dora exhibited a strong homosexual predisposition and that her pathological concern with her father's relations masked her love for Mr. K.

Contemporary critics uncovered ethical issues regarding the case and a misalliance between Freud and the interests of his patient. Apparently, Freud had a professional relationship with Dora's father and had also known Mr. K. Both factors might have called into question whether Freud could have established an unbiased therapeutic relationship with Dora. Dora insisted there was more than friendship between Mrs. K and her father. Indeed, when she was brought to treatment, her father handed her over to Freud, stating, "[T]ry to bring her to reason." Therefore, subduing Dora's accusations became the primary motivation of Dora's father, and it overshadowed any wish that she be relieved of her somatic symptomatology.

Freud's original theories regarding psychopathology advanced sexual seduction in childhood by an adult or older child as the basis for neurosis. He considered the etiology of neurosis to be sexual seduction as "red-hot." In a letter to Wilhelm Fliess in 1897, he wrote this enigmatic paragraph:

> Once more, the inquisitors prick with needles to discover the devil's stigmata, and in a similar situation the victims think of the same old cruel story in fictionalized form (helped perhaps by disguises of the seducers). Thus, not only the victims but also the executioners recalled in this their earliest youth.[5]

The references of the passage are peculiarly metaphorical, although references to the Inquisition appear elsewhere in his writings:

> I dream, therefore, of a primeval devil religion with rites that are carried on secretly, and understand the harsh therapy of the witches's judges. Connecting links abound.[6]

Freud relegated the pathogenic event or trauma of childhood sexual seduction described by patients to the phantasmagoric, though the patients knew the events were authentic. Freud rejected the seduction theory principally for reasons of professional self-interest within the scientific community.

It is equally important to regard the historical context of this momentous decision. Millet characterizes Freud as the most vigorous reactionary force in the ideology of sexual politics during the first phase of the feminist movement, from 1830 through 1930. She defines the sexual politics of this era as the quintessential challenge to the patriarchal structure most represented by male domination of the family unit:

> Although generally accepted as a prototype of the liberal urge toward sexual freedom, and a single contributor toward softening traditional inhibitions upon sexuality, the effect of Freud's work, that of his followers, and still more that of his popularizers, was to rationalize the invidious relationship between the sexes, to ratify traditional roles, and to validate temperamental differences.[7]

Essentially, Freud is a modern Moses, transposing the Judeo-Christian God–the Father myths–into scientific theory. Each Western religion and Freudian theory promotes an externalized image of power that is symbolized through domination. The resolution of the Oedipal predicament guarantees the authority of the father.[8]

THE SECRET UNMASKED

On an early spring afternoon at my office, while I was retrieving messages off the answering machine, there were a few mystifying, sequentially recorded hang-up calls. An imperceptible presence was distinguishable on the tape–not the resonance of breathing, but more like an idiosyncratic heart-beating vibration. Then, my receptionist announced that a woman was waiting to see me. It was too early for the next scheduled appointment, so I questioned who it was. The patient said only: "Tell him that Shirley is here."

Shirley was a diminutive African-American woman in her mid-thirties. She was sitting in a far corner of the waiting room with her young son. Both were reading: she, a Bible, and he, a large picture book. They impressed me as solitary. They were huddled protectively, with their bodies positioned as if to shoulder weight, each tilted slightly toward the other. In a slurred, almost imperceptible voice, Shirley said, "I tried calling you a couple of times, but I kept getting your machine. So I thought I'd just come in person. Doctor, I need to speak with you. It's very important. A friend told me that you could help me. I need to speak to you. Could you spare a few minutes?" Her plea conveyed urgency. I invited her into my office so we could speak privately for a few moments. Her narrative impressed me as a rehearsed speech.

"I had open-heart surgery about five years ago," she began. "I had many transfusions. They gave me bad blood. I'm unclean now. I know that I got HIV. I don't want to give it to anyone. People look at me different since the open-heart surgery. They know. I be riding the subway and people move away from me. They change their seat, and they be staring at me. I try not to notice them looking. I be reading my Bible. But they know. I know, too. And my family knows. They see that I'm different. I be getting small. I visited my mother in North Carolina, and she says, 'Why you getting so small?'"

The HIV-antibody tests were developed and in use by 1985. Their initial purpose was to screen the blood supply, since transfusion recipients had faced the risk of receiving HIV-infected blood. Shirley's surgery had been in 1984. I assessed from our initial session that there were underlying issues that were distinct from the presenting problem of her presumed HIV serostatus.

* * *

The following week, Shirley arrived about 45 minutes early again, with her seven-year-old son, Antoine. They sat together as they had the previous week–shrunken together in a far corner of the waiting room. When I approached her, she lifted herself from the reception-room chair with an audible sigh, then followed me quietly to my office.

She was living with her younger sister, Ruth, in a one-bedroom apartment in northwest Bronx, having moved there after she and her husband, Carl, separated a year ago. Her sister slept in the living room, while she and Antoine slept in a small bedroom. Shirley spoke of a marriage distinguished by alienation and exploitation. Her husband was inattentive to her emotional, physical, and financial needs. He was verbally abusive to her, sexually unfaithful, and he drank heavily. After she decided to proceed with open-heart surgery, the relationship deteriorated further.

She said, "When I first got sick, before the open-heart surgery, my husband wasn't worried about me. I couldn't even sleep at night. I would toss and turn until it be 5:00 in the morning. I be coughing, then I be throwing up. I couldn't keep food down. Everything I ate would back up. I be losing weight. During the summer, I got really weak, and my brother was up here and went to the doctor with me.

"One weekend, I got real sick, and my husband knew I was sick. He wanted to go to his niece's wedding. That was more important than me. The wedding was down South, in Bucksport. That night, I went to the window, and was looking out, and my body started shaking. I thought that I couldn't sit back down on the bed. My breathing was kind of short. He didn't say, 'Well, I'll cancel my trip. I stay home with you and take you to the doctor.' He just asked me if I be okay, and I said, 'I guess I'll be okay.' Then, he went.

"I thought he would cancel the trip, but he didn't cancel the trip. He went on with his trip. I said to myself, 'If your trip is that important, then go. I'm not goin' to make a fool out of myself.' My sister brought me to the hospital while he was away.

"The doctor at the hospital made me sign this paper. I kept putting off the operation because I was 'fraid. Then he would say that I was crazy not to have the operation. I said that 'I don't know what choice I have.' So, I remembered what another doctor told me, my heart specialist. He said I didn't need to have an operation if I took my medicine, that I'd be fine. So I did that. And I put it off again until I couldn't anymore.

"I knew that I had a leaky heart valve ever since I leaved high school. I had rheumatic fever down there in the South. I didn't think that I would get sicker and lose weight. You know, one of my co-workers told me she had this friend. . . . And this friend went and had heart surgery and died on the operating table. I be scared. Before I had the heart surgery, I would read up on all that I could learn about heart surgery.

"I got a temperature one evening, and I took aspirin that doesn't work with the blood thinner. I went to the hospital, and I thought they'd admit me there. We stayed until 4:30 a.m. They took a lot of

X rays, and told me I had a really bad infection. They said to take these pills, and I took the pills. I thought that I should be admitted.

"A friend told me, 'What you have to do is fall out on the floor. Then they'll admit you to the hospital.' But, I thought that wouldn't really make them look into it. They'd think I was crazy. Or he would just think that I needed a drink of water, or something. But my co-worker said, 'You gotta do somethin' so they can find out what's the matter with you.' So, I signed the papers and got ready to go to the hospital.

"Carl and my mother had a fallout when I came back after the surgery. My mother told my husband over the phone that it was his duty to take me back and forth to the doctor. So my husband blew off, and he told my mother off. He told her to mind her own business, that she was putting him through changes. But I be thinking that my sister shouldn't have to do it for me. It's not my sister's job. But he didn't want to do it for me, you know. He didn't want to do it.

"I knew something else was goin' on, because once he claimed his hours was changed. He used to drive me to work. I discussed it with a cousin, and I told her that he claimed he had to leave home before 7:00 a.m. And my cousin says, 'He doesn't start work until maybe about 9:00 a.m. or something.' 'Well,' I said, 'he acted like he had to get out of here in a hurry.'

"I didn't argue with him. My cousin says: 'He be sleeping with someone. You be crazy not to know that.' I knew that because I knew who it was. It be this woman in the neighborhood. One morning, when I was takin' Antoine to school, I seen Carl leave her building. He didn't see me. But Antoine and me seen him. Then I looks up and she be in the window. And we looked at each other. We just stood in the street looking up, and she stood there in her slip. In those few minutes, we recognized each other, and we both knows what it be all about.

"I didn't felt angry at my husband. He should have been here for me, but he wasn't. Like what I told you, doctor, about the time he got back from his niece's wedding, he said, 'I didn't thought that you'd get sick. But then, we was having arguments before the surgery. Because I had to go through a lot of problems with him money-wise. Always fussing about who's goin' to pay what. Because he figured I had more money than him I should pay for everything.

"I am very close to my family, and he resented it. He said I be doin' things in his face. That if I did something for my sister, how come I don't make a big deal of it, like I do with him. He says, 'I make a big deal about what he do.' And I'd say, 'I don't make a big deal out of it. What do you want out of my life?'

"He would get into his car and go with his friends. And I would be mad sometimes, for a day-and-a-half. We didn't really speak. I would say, 'Good morning.' I don't remember if I would even say, 'Good morning.' Antoine and me would eat without him because he wasn't usually home at dinner, and he would fix his own food. Or heat it up. We were silent. Only the kids would talk. Oh, I didn't tell you that his son from his other wife lived with us. His name's Donny. He's 15. But I didn't really used to have to say anything to Carl. What did I need to for? Finally, I be the one to give in all the time.

"I would leave it alone. The money that is. I never mention the other woman. If I be bringing up the money again, say after a couple of months, we would go into a frenzy over it. Get all crazy. He got to the point where he didn't want to give my money in my hand. He tell my son. He would have it in a little paper that comes from the bank. He would say, 'Give this to your mother. This is for the rent.' Antoine, he would bring it to me.

"I would say, 'Why can't you give it to me yourself? Why do you have to give it to him? You know I'm coming into the room; you can give it to me then.' He would leave it on the dresser sometimes, and he would say, 'There go the rent money, or there go the food money.' He would give what he wanted. I didn't know what he made. Sometimes, I would send money to my mother, but I didn't tell him. If he know, he would say, 'Give that money to me.' If I did something for my family, he wanted to know everything that I did. I didn't know everything *he* did.

"After my surgery, I be very sick and I had a stroke a month later. My husband acted like he didn't know how to use the washing machine. I had to do everything. I would say, 'What's so difficult. You ought to learn how to use the washing machine. You press a button and the water comes in by itself. And it goes off by itself. He couldn't use the washing machine to do the laundry. My husband acted like he was some kind of king or something.

"I could barely walk or get around. My husband would be lying on the chair when I tried to cook. My sister got so mad, she would curse him because she would say, 'Why do Shirley have to scrub and cook, and you lying down on the chair?' She had to bite her tongue, and she let it go at that. He began to feel guilty, so he do some of his own ironing. My sister would come over and said: 'I ain't doing your ironing, you big enough to do your own.

"My sister and me had this really close bond, you see. My husband was kinda jealous because I confide in my sister and my sister confide in me. I said, 'Why should I has to tell you everything? If she wants to tell you something, she will. What's discussed between me and her is discussed between me and her.' He would go into a rage about things. He said, 'I wish I could be close to my family like you are to yours.' They weren't like that.

"He just tole me they should be close. It used to upset him that when summertime came, he wanted to send his son down South, and his brother then would charge him to take his son to his mother. We would scream and argue. I hit him just one time. I said something to him. I don't remember what. I hit him in the face, and he knocked my glasses off. That was that. He tole me that I better never hit him again. So, I never raised my hand again. I just leave it alone. Most of the time, I couldn't win a point of view with him anyway. He had to be right all the time. I had to be wrong. That how it was with him.

"I didn't feel he was responsible for my having the stroke after the surgery. But I don't know. Maybe it was me. I missed my medication. Maybe I did too much too soon. So, I can't say. After I had the stroke, I went through a few different phases, and I asked him certain things. I just leave it alone.

"I had this silver bracelet, and it be missing. I asked him about it, but he didn't answer me. He just look at me. When we were at dinner, I would see him staring at me. Then he notice that I'm looking, he would go out of the room or something. He goes out.

"After the stroke, I was seeing double. They gave me CAT scans and brain scans. And this and that. I didn't look to go through all those things. I don't know what happened. I doubt that he gave it to someone else.

"I don't know what happened when I got sick the second time. I woke up in the intensive care. I didn't know anyone. When I woke up,

I saw all those sick people, and I said, 'What am I doing down here?' Then I hesitate. That was it. I stayed there for a week. My husband came to visit me, and he didn't want to kiss me. 'Do you think I have germs or something?' I asked. He didn't want to come close to me. I don't know. Even my family–they wouldn't stay in the room.

"Because I didn't know what happened to my life at that point. I really didn't know. That's when I asked them how I got to the hospital. My husband didn't exactly tell me that I had a stroke. I asked my doctor. He said, 'Didn't your husband tell you? You had a stroke.' Then, I wondered why he didn't tell me at first.

"I was already in a room with another patient when I found out. My sister told me, but my husband didn't tell me. I didn't expect it to happen. After the heart surgery, my doctor said I was in good health. I went home. I don't know if I caused it. The stroke. We had bought the boys a new bed, and I was saying, 'Twist it that way. Twist it this way. Turn it.' I don't know if I got myself fatigued. Tired. A few days later, I went outside and was walking along a fence. I felt it in the pit of my stomach; suddenly, it was dark. 'Oh God. What's the matter with me?' A friend got me back up, and all I did was sleep.

"I used to ask him, 'Is there something that I'm doing wrong that make you unhappy, then you should tell me. If you want to leave, leave. I can raise my son on my own.' I don't think that he wanted to do nuttin' because I was doing more than my share. I did *more* than my share.

"I told my sister and brother that one of these days, I'm goin' to have enough, and I'm goin' to walk straight out the door. He started laughing. He thought I was kidding. The next day after I seen him [Carl] leave that women's apartment, that Saturday morning at the end of March, he asks me what will I buy for dinner. I said, 'I don't know if I'm going to be here when you come back.' He just laughed. My sister said, 'If you have to move, move now.' Because she was having to go somewhere for a week. Or something. For two years, I had been going through a lot of ups and downs. I had had it.

"I left him. I packed my things and Antoine['s], leaving everything I couldn't carry. My sister took me in. He calls me on the telephone and asks how I be doing, and I said I was doing fine."

During the year-long separation, Carl has not visited with Antoine, and his contacts with Shirley have been minimal. Shirley describes her son as resistant to speaking with his father, and she says that she doesn't enforce any notion that he should be in touch with his father. Shirley is very bitter toward her husband, and she frequently repeats similar anecdotes during sessions–that he didn't provide for the family financially; that he didn't appreciate that Shirley helped rear his son from another marriage; that he didn't seem to care for her after a major surgery.

*   *   *

During another visit, Shirley told me more about her new life. "Since I've been living with my sister, I keep getting hang-up calls. The person wouldn't answer. I don't know. I don't know if it's him or someone else or what. I don't let it bother me. At first, I used to let it bother me. It used to get on my nerves, you know. But I didn't care after a while, and my sister would answer the phone. Or my son would answer the phone. It would be off and on. It had stopped already, and then my sister went away to Panama.

"Then, the night before, I got a call. Then uh, today, I got another call. My son said, 'Mommy don't worry. And we went ahead and played our game. I don't really know how to play backgammon, so we played another game, matching baseball cards. Like that. You know. Or it's reading whatever. I tries to spend more time with him because his teacher said his reading isn't so good.

"This person would call two times a week. If it wasn't in the morning, it would be at night. About 2:00 a.m. at night. My sister said we could accuse nobody because, when she lived alone, she would get calls late at night and early morning. She used to tell me about it. I told her to report it to the telephone company. The telephone company got no get-go behind it. So that was the end of that.

"She said she couldn't figure nobody. I just leave it alone. I thought it probably was my husband, but my sister said, 'No, you can't say it's him because you don't have proof that it's him. You have to leave well enough alone. Don't worry about it.'

"It doesn't upset me. I mean, he doesn't really call my son that often anyway. Neither my stepson does. But he always tells my son to call, and my son gets to the point where he doesn't want to call. He remembers what happened with my husband and his grandmother. And he figures with all the changes that I went through, I didn't want to call his father anyway. My sister said, 'If he doesn't want to call his father, don't make him.' So I don't do it."

"My brother calls my sister because I got sicker over the weekend, and he says, 'Shirley' He calls me Shirley because that's my name. 'She need to go to the hospital to see what really the matter.'"

* * *

"You said that when you had awakened in the ICU that you didn't know what had happened to your life. What does that expression mean to you?" I asked.

"I didn't thought I'd get upset," Shirley said. "When I think about that period of my life . . . what happened along the way . . . what I couldn't do . . . I don't know how I became so sick in a short space of time and what caused it. I mean, it's not like I didn't used to take my medication. Not like when I was menstruating and didn't take the blood thinner. It's like what I my doctor who wants to take my stomach tests. To see why I have the jerking motion. He wants me on intravenous so when I'm off the pills, the same thing doesn't happen. He could tell me if the pills caused the stroke. It's not that I was worried. I didn't overdo it. I don't know what really caused [it]. I didn't expect it to happen.

"Doctor, I see this white stuff. I be trying to get this white stuff off me. I be riding the train, and I see it on my coat and I be trying to get it off. Sometimes, I see it the air and it be landing on me. I try to brush it off. I'm not sure if anyone else sees it. My sister tells me not to worry about the white stuff. But I keeps thinking about it. I don't want it on me. People on the train see me and they be movin' away. I just be reading my Bible, and I try not to pay attention to them. They know.

"They know that I be different now. That I be chosen. I think that, sometimes, they can see the scar. You can see it. Here. If I wears a dress or sweater with a V-neck, you can see it. It's the mark. That I be chosen. Different. The white stuff–it be in the air. My sister says it be all in my head. She says I be under a lot of pressure, with the surgery and Carl. But I knows that the white stuff is there. I'll bring a piece of the white stuff to show you.

"When I returned to my job . . . they could tell. It be very hard there because I needed to take a lot of time off. My co-workers be annoyed with me. That I be treated special. But, I had all these doctors appointments. I worked there for 15 years. I worked very hard.

"One day at work, I smelled something. It smelled like perfume, and I asked my friend about it. And she don't smell it. I looked everywhere for it. I don't know where it be comin' from. I looked inside my desk. But I couldn't find where the smell be coming from. I got very upset. No one could calm me down. I be smelling it everywhere, all around me. I had to leave the office. My co-workers be lookin' at me like I was crazy or something. I couldn't go back to work for a week, and when I returned . . . well, the smell was gone, so I was okay.

* * *

"My father used to hit me when he be drinking," Shirley continued. "I used to think, what did I do? I used to hate him. But there were times when he would hold me in his lap, and I could hear his heart beating. It would feel so good. Safe. There were times when I be home from school when I be sick, and he would play the radio while I was in bed. I liked that. He would leave for work and the radio be playing.

"But when he be drinking, they'd fight. I be very scared when they'd fight. Sometimes, it be in the middle of the night. My mother would come and get us kids and take us out to her sister's house. I be half asleep and we be walkin' along the road in [the] dark to my aunt's house. When the moon be out, it wouldn't be so bad, but when it be all dark and cold, I be scared. She would tell me to hush up and she'd drag me along the road. We'd stay at my aunt's house for a couple of days, then go back.

"It would start all over again. I be in school, fallin' asleep at my desk. The teacher would get angry at me. It seemed like I was always tired. Even now, I wake up in the middle of the night. Sometimes, I be checkin' the door to make sure it's locked, and I be lookin' in the closets to make sure there be no one there. Once, my father broke down the door. He came through the door with a knife. I think that happened, but I'm not sure. It may be a dream I had. I remember a dream with blood all over the walls. I guess it didn't happen.

"There were times when I hated them both, but they did the best they could, and my sister says, 'Get on with your life. Forget it. It's the past.' There was one day–my mother called him for dinner. She made a roast beef. He came to the table, looked at the roast beef, and spit on it. It was disgusting because his phlegm be a big glob.

"And one time, he shit on the living-room floor, and my mother made me clean it up. I didn't know why she made me do it. It weren't my fault. I started to cry and she threatened me with a beating if I didn't stop. She used to keep this strap hung from the bedroom door, and, once, my brother said he was goin' to steal it away from her when she weren't home. But he be afraid to do it. It just hung there.

"Finally, she kicked my father out. I guess he was ready to go because she had threatened him many time, but he's never leave. She had this boyfriend after she kicked him out. People said that this man's wife had killed herself–jumped out of a window and died. She and this man, his name was Williams, they used to fight, too. I used to be afraid of him. One time, when I be home sick, he came into the house. He showed me pictures. They were dirty pictures. I was about 12. He didn't touch me. At least, I don't remember. He made me promise not to tell my mother. It would be our secret."

*   *   *

"This has been one of the most terrible weeks of my life." Shirley said at another session, "I got this call from a doctor at a hospital in New Jersey. He told me that my husband has AIDS. He came to the hospital with a very high fever. In a couple of days, he was on a respirator with a pneumonia. He's not conscious anymore. He's in an ICU. He may die."

*   *   *

Shirley decided to have an HIV antibody test. When she entered my office, I knew instantly the test result was HIV-seropositive. The faces of many came to mind when I used to do HIV testing. At times, people with seronegative results would weep uncontrollably from relief. They'd promise to change behavior, educate others, or contribute to AIDS organizations. At times, I would hear from them. One woman became a volunteer, showing HIV-related video tapes at a women's health clinic. Memories of those individuals with seropositive results are indelible. Tears showered from Shirley's eyes as her past became the present.

I left my office for lunch and for several city blocks, the air was adrift with dandelion pappose seeds blown by a late autumnal whirlwind. White stuff.

THE OFFENSES OF SEXUAL AGGRESSION

The definition of incest is inconsistent, for our purposes, with its medical definition: "Sexual intercourse or other sexual activity between persons so closely related that marriage between them is legally or culturally prohibited."[9] The extensiveness of sexual abuse can have a cross-generational component that is misperceived as a taboo. In family therapy, cross-generational alliances that contribute to adversity for the members of the family system may be the result of incest.[10]

Children cope with sexual abuse by blocking the memory or forgetting the abuse, although some survivors remember the event. Many adults completely forget the traumata. Davis maintains that remembering is an ongoing process of discovery, and she provides the following list of defenses that need to be worked through during healing.

List of Defenses to Memory[11]

If I remember the abuse,   *I'll die.*
If I remember the abuse,   *my Dad will come and get me.*
If I remember the abuse,   *I'll end up in the hospital.*
If I remember the abuse,   *I'll kill myself.*
If I remember the abuse,   *I'll lose my family.*
If I remember the abuse,   *it will mean my Mom was bad.*

The unholy silence that shrouds the interfamily sexual abuse of children and prevents a realistic appraisal of its true incidence and meanings is rooted in the same patriarchal philosophy of sexual private property that shaped and determined historic male attitudes toward rape. If a woman was man's original corporal property, then children were, and are, a wholly owned subsidiary.[12]

Many psychological disorders, including borderline personality, originate from a traumatic experience during early childhood with prolonged childhood physical and sexual abuse.[13]

Long-Term Effects of Childhood Sexual Abuse[14]

* Depression, low self-esteem
* Psychiatric hospitalization
* Substance abuse
* Self-abuse
* Somatization disorder
* Erotization
* Learning difficulties
* Post-traumatic stress disorder, anxiety
* Dissociative disorders
* Conversion reactions
* Running away, prostitution
* Revictimization
* Impaired interpersonal relationships
* Poor parenting

Russell acknowledges the centrality of incest in female development because "every little girl may be affected by the incestuous urges–overt, covert, or repressed–that the males in their families often feel toward them."[15] She recognizes that incestuous feelings are frequently projected onto children. The accusations by fathers and other male relatives of a girl's seductive behavior serves as a rationalization for acting upon sexual feelings:

> Even the widespread use of the word *seduce* in this context is an offensive misnomer. It assumes a mutuality–if not initially, then once the child has submitted. But the notion that a father *could* seduce, rather than violate, his daughter is itself a myth. And the notion that some daughters seduce their fathers is a double myth.[16]

The inference that the incest survivors accept or seduce is false:

> Whether or not the daughter overtly resists the sexual relationship with her father, the resulting emotional and behavioral

problems demonstrate her emotional resistance and her awareness that this kind of relationship is not socially acceptable. As for the victim's so-called "seductivity," her passive and submissive character at home suggests that she would lack the assertiveness necessary to "seduce" her father, as well as the emotional strengths to resist his advances.[17]

Sexual offenses are predominantly committed by males–of four million known offenders, only 5% are women. Males are the most dominant part of the sexual addiction population. When incest is present, in a family other patterns of violence and conflict are prevalent; incest is not an isolated phenomenon. Bradshaw says "instant numbing" through dissociation, a defense mechanism against victimization, accounts for the incested disconnection from conscious memories of the transgression:

> Incest clearly focuses on the major problem of abandonment. This problem can be expressed as the disconnection between the act of victimization and the response to being victimized. Because the violation is so profound, the defense is equally profound.[18]

A CHECKLIST FOR PRETEST COUNSELING[19]

- Ask the patient about any history of HIV counseling and testing.
- Explain the difference between anonymous and confidential testing.
- If the patient has tested negative, and has an ongoing identified risk, proceed with counseling to repeat HIV testing. If the test was with within the past six months, and there is no identified risk since testing, offer the patient the option of counseling and retesting if the patient wishes.
- If the patient has tested HIV-positive, determine whether the patient is receiving appropriate medical care and support services. If the patient is not receiving care, offer to provide it, or refer him or her to medical and support services.
- If the patient was tested previously, whether negative or positive, explain that it is important to have the test result in order to provide medical and other care. Ask the patient for permission to contact the care provider for verification of the test result.

- Provide basic information of transmission and prevention.
- Discuss the nature of the antibody testing procedure and its use as a diagnostic tool. Also discuss what an antibody is, the risks and benefits of being tested, false positives, false negatives, and inconclusive results.
- Inform the patient that anxiety about the HIV test result is a common feeling. Assure the patient that you will assist with identifying psychological and emotional support services if needed.
- Have patient read and sign an informed consent form.
- Encourage patient to discuss HIV transmission, risk reduction, and the availability of counseling and testing with partner(s).

A CHECKLIST FOR POSTTEST COUNSELING[20]

If Seronegative

- The patient should receive the posttest result in person. Begin by providing the test result and showing patient the lab slip.
- Give patient time to react to the test result, and address the patient's immediate concerns.
- Interpret test results. Explain that a negative result does not mean that the patient is immune to infection. Help the patient to understand the negative test result in relation to personal risk.
- Help patient to develop risk-reduction strategy.

If Seropositive

- Provide the test result and show the patient the lab slip result.
- Give the patient time to react to the test result and encourage the patient to express feelings and concerns.
- Address the patient's immediate concerns.

Helping the Patient Cope with the Test Result

- Set a supportive and encouraging tone.
- Be prepared to deal with the patient's emotions, which may include disbelief, anxiety, anger, guilt, depression, apathy, and fear of death. If the patient becomes distressed:

- Stay with the patient and respond to the situation; listen to the patient's concerns;
- Help sort out the issues
- Help identify coping mechanisms used in other crisis situations
- If necessary, call for assistance from a mental-health professional
- Provide telephone numbers for 24-hour crisis hotlines
- Offer to assist the patient in contacting crisis support services, and provide place for the patient to use the telephone.

• Discuss the patient's feelings about the test result and how the patient anticipates handling this information during the next 48 hours (and over time).
• Remind the patient about supports identified in the pretest session. Ask who the patient can talk to about the test result, such as a family member, friend, mental-health professional, or a member of the clergy. If the patient identifies someone, discuss how the patient might tell that person and what the reaction might be.
• Provide the patient with referrals for emotional support.

Meaning of Positive Test Result

The test shows that the antibody to HIV was present.

• A positive HIV test result means:

- The patient is infected with HIV, and antibodies to the virus were produced.
- The patient has active virus and can infect others.

• A positive test result does not mean the patient has AIDS.

Medical Follow-Up

• Explain the importance of getting into medical care as soon as possible.

- Laboratory tests can tell how the immune system is functioning and show if HIV-related infections or cancers are present.
- Treatments are available that may slow the progression of HIV disease and prevent some infections.

• Explain that a medical evaluation includes:

– Medical and personal history
– Physical examination
– Tests of immune system functioning
– Tests for other infections, such as sexually transmitted diseases and tuberculosis.

• Emphasize the importance of following good health-care practices.
• Stress that it is important to stay in a medical treatment program to get regular medical checkups and information about new medical treatments.
• Explain that a positive test result may mean that partners and children could be infected with HIV.
• If this is the patient's first HIV test, the patient should be encouraged to refer partners and children (born since 1976) for HIV-antibody testing and medical evaluations. Provide the patient with medical and counseling referrals for partners and children.
• If the patient is pregnant or has recently delivered, inform her that:

– All babies are born with their mother's antibodies; therefore, if the mother has antibodies to HIV, her baby will test HIV-antibody-positive at birth.
– The mother's infection does not necessarily mean that the baby is infected with HIV; research studies suggest that approximately 30% to 50% of babies born to infected women are infected themselves.
– If the baby is not infected, the baby should test negative by 18 to 24 months of age.
– If the baby is infected, it is possible that the baby will test positive at birth, test negative for a period of time, and then test positive again (after the production of the baby's own antibodies).
– It is important for the baby to receive regular medical care from a physician who is knowledgeable about HIV, and that the physician providing care to the baby be aware of the mother's infection so that the health status of the infant can be closely monitored.
– Women who are breastfeeding, or planning to breastfeed, should discuss the risk of possible HIV transmission with a physician

who is knowledgeable about HIV. The Centers for Disease Control (CDC) have recommended that HIV-infected women should be advised against breastfeeding to avoid post-natal transmission of HIV.

Transmission Reduction

Emphasize that although the patient may not have any signs or symptoms of HIV infection, the patient can transmit infection by:

- Having sex without a condom, or incorrectly using a condom.
- Sharing intravenous needles, works, and other drug paraphernalia.
- Passing it to the baby during pregnancy, birth, and breastfeeding.

Stress that HIV is not spread through casual, household transmission. Discuss risk-reduction strategies, based on a review of the patient's sexual and/or drug-use behaviors. Offer to explain risk-reduction strategies to both the patient and the partner.

REFERENCE NOTES

1. Jeffrey Moussaieff Masson, *The Assault on Truth: Freud's Suppression of the Seduction Theory* (New York: Farrar, Straus and Giroux, 1984), p. 53.

2. Sigmund Freud, "The Etiology of Hysteria," in *The Standard Edition of Complete Psychological Works of Sigmund Freud*, edited and translated by Strachey J. London (New York: Hogarth, 1962). p. 203.

3. Masson, *The Assault on Truth*, p. 113.

4. Richard J. Lowenstein, MD, "Somatoform Disorders in Victims of Incest and Child Abuse," in *Incest-Related Syndromes of Adult Psychopathology*, edited by Richard P. Kluft, MD (Washington, DC: American Psychiatric Press, 1990), p. 81.

5. Jeffrey Moussaieff Masson, translator and editor, *The Complete Letters of Sigmund Freud to Wilhelm Fliess* (Cambridge, MA: Harvard University Press, 1985), p. 225.

6. Masson, *The Complete Letters*, p. 227.

7. Kate Millet, *Sexual Politics* (New York: Equinox, 1970), p. 178.

8. Steven F. Dansky, "God, Freud, Daddy, and Us Faggots" in *Faggotry* (New York: Templar Press, 1972), p. 12.

9. *Dorland's Illustrated Medical Dictionary*, 27th edition (Baltimore: W. N. Saunders, 1988).

10. Jay Haley, "Toward a Theory of Pathological Systems," in *Family Therapy and Disturbed Families*, edited by G. H. Zuk and I. Boszormenyi-Nagy (Palo Alto, CA: Science and Behavior Books, 1969), p. 40.

11. Laura Davis, *The Courage to Heal* (New York: Perennial Library, 1990), p. 214.

12. Susan Brownmiller, *Against Our Will: Men, Women, and Rape* (New York: Simon and Schuster, 1975), p. 281.

13. Paul S. Links, MD, MSc, FRCP, and Heather Munroe Blum, PhD, "Family Environment and Borderline Personality Disorder: Development of Etiologic Models" in *Family Environment and Borderline Personality Disorder*, edited by Paul S. Links, MD, MSc, FRCP (Washington, DC: American Psychiatric Press, 1990), p. 16.

14. Diane H. Schetky, MD, "A Review of the Literature on the Long-Term Effects of Child Sexual Abuse," in *Incest-Related Syndromes of Adult Psychopathology* (Washington, DC: American Psychiatric Press, 1990), p. 41.

15. Diana E. H. Russell, *The Secret Trauma: Incest in the Lives of Girls and Women* (New York: Basic Books, 1986), p. 392.

16. Ibid., p. 393.

17. Francis J. Turner, editor, *Differential Diagnosis and Treatment in Social Work* (New York: The Free Press, 1976), p. 783.

18. John Bradshaw, *Bradshaw On: The Family* (Deerfield Beach, FL: Health Communications, 1988), p. 115.

19. *A Guide to HIV Counseling and Testing*, New York State Department of Health, February 1991.

20. Ibid.

Suggested Readings

Allport, Gordon W., *The Nature of Prejudice*, Reading, MA: Addison-Wesley Publishing Company, 1987.

Altman, Dennis, *AIDS: In The Mind of America*, New York: Anchor Press, 1987.

Andolsen, Barbara Hilkert, Christine E. Gudorf, and Mary D. Pellauer, *Women's Consciousness, Women's Conscience*, New York: A Seabury Book, 1985.

Baldwin, James, *The Evidences of Things Not Seen*, New York: Holt, Rinehart & Winston, 1985.

Bartlett, Harriett M., *Social Work Practice In The Health Field*, Washington, DC: National Association of Social Workers, 1961.

Bataille, Georges, *Death and Sensuality*, New York: Walker and Company, 1962.

Bayer, Ronald, *Homosexuality and American Psychiatry*, New York: Basic Books, 1981.

Beck, Ernest, *The Denial of Death*, New York: The Free Press, 1973.

Benjamin, Jessica, *The Bonds of Love*, New York: Pantheon Books, 1988.

Blanck, Gertrude and Rueben, *Ego Psychology: Theory and Practice*, New York: Columbia University Press, 1974.

Bowlby, John, *Attachment and Loss, Volumes I, II, and III*, New York: Basic Books, 1980.

Bradshaw, John, *Bradshaw On: The Family*, Deerfield Beach, FL: Health Communications, 1988.

Briffault, Robert, *The Mothers: The Matriarchal Theory of Social Origins*, New York: Grosset & Dunlap, 1963.

Brill, A. A., *The Basic Writings of Sigmund Freud*, New York: The Modern Library, 1966.

Brown, Norman O., *Life Against Death*, Middleton, CT: Wesleyan University Press, 1969.

Brownmiller, Susan, *Against Our Will: Men, Women, and Rape*, New York: Simon and Schuster, 1975.

Campbell, Joseph, *The Masks of God: Primitive Mythology*, New York: The Viking Press, 1973.

Carnes, Patrick, *The Sexual Addiction*, Minneapolis: CompCare Publications, 1983.

Chesler, Phyllis, *Women & Madness*, New York: Avon, 1972.

Chodorow, Nancy J., *Feminism and Psychoanalytic Theory*, New Haven, CT: Yale University Press, 1989.

Chodorow, Nancy J., *The Reproduction of Mothering: Psychoanalysis and the Sociology of Gender*, Berkeley: University of California Press, 1978.

Chopra, Deepak, *Quantum Healing: Exploring the Frontiers of Mind/Body Medicine*, New York: Bantam Books, 1990.

Cohen, P. T., *The AIDS Knowledge Base*, Waltham, MA: The Medical Publishing Group, 1990.

Collier, Helen V., *Counseling Women: A Guide for Therapists*, New York: The Free Press, 1982.

Cousins, Norman, *Anatomy Of An Illness*, New York: Bantam Books, 1980.

Daly, Mary, *Beyond God The Father*, Boston: Beacon Press, 1973.

Daly, Mary, *Gynecology: The Metaethics of Radical Feminism*, Boston: Beacon Press, 1978.

Dass, Ram, *How Can I Help?*, New York: Alfred A. Knopf, 1985.

Davis, Elizabeth Gould, *The First Sex*, New York: G. P. Putnam's Sons, 1971.

Davis, Laura, *The Courage to Heal*, New York: Perennial Library, 1990.

de Beauvoir, Simone, *The Second Sex*, New York: Vintage Books, 1975.

Diagnostic Criteria from DSM-III-R, Washington, DC: The American Psychiatric Association, 1987.

Downing, Christine, *Myths and Mysteries of Same-Sex Love*, New York: Continuum, 1991.

Dworkin, Andrea, *Our Blood*, New York: Harper & Row, 1976.

Dworkin, Andrea, *Intercourse*, New York: The Free Press, 1987.

Erikson, Erik H., *Childhood and Society*, New York: W. W. Norton, 1963.

Erikson, Erik H., *Identity and the Life Cycle*, New York: W. W. Norton, 1980.

Fanon, Frantz, *Black Skin, White Masks*, New York: Grove Press, 1967.

Fee, Elizabeth, and Daniel M. Fox, *AIDS: The Burdens of History*, Berkeley: University of California Press, 1988.

Feldman, Douglas A., *Culture and AIDS*, New York: Praeger, 1990.

Foucault, Michel, *The Birth of the Clinic*, New York: Vintage, 1973.

Foucault, Michel, *The History of Sexuality: An Introduction, Volume 1*, New York: Vintage, 1990.

Frankl, Viktor E., *The Doctor & The Soul*, New York: Vintage, 1973.

Frazer, James, *The Golden Bough*, New York: Macmillan, 1941.

French, Marilyn, *Beyond Power: On Women, Men, And Morals*, New York: Summit, 1985.

Freud, Sigmund, *Leonardo da Vinci and a Memory of His Childhood*, New York: W. W. Norton, 1964.

Freud, Sigmund, *Totem and Taboo*, New York: W. W. Norton, 1963.

Freudenberg, Nicholas, *Preventing AIDS: A Guide to Effective Education for the Prevention of HIV Infection*, Washington, DC: American Public Health Association, 1989.

Friedman, Richard C., *Male Homosexuality: A Contemporary Psychoanalytic Perspective*, New Haven, CT: Yale University Press, 1988.

Fromm-Reichmann, Frieda, *Principles of Intensive Psychotherapy*, Chicago: The University of Chicago Press, 1960.

Gilman, Sander L., *Difference and Pathology: Stereotypes of Sexuality, Race, and Madness*, Ithaca, NY: Cornell University Press, 1985.

Goffman, Erving, *Stigma: Notes on the Management of Spoiled Identity*, New York: A Touchstone Book, 1986.

Gomez, Jose, *Demystifying Homosexuality: A Teaching Guide About Lesbians and Gay Men*, New York: Irvington Publishers, 1984.

Graves, Robert, *The White Goddess*, New York: Farrar, Straus and Giroux, 1972.

Graves, Robert, and Raphael Patai, *Hebrew Myths: The Book of Genesis*, New York: McGraw-Hill, 1964.

Green, Richard, *The "Sissy Boy Syndrome" and the Development of Homosexuality*, New Haven, CT: Yale University Press, 1987.

Hay, Louise L., *The AIDS Book: Creating a Positive Approach*, Santa Monica, CA: Hay House, 1988.

Hays, H. R., *The Dangerous Sex*, New York: G. P. Putnam's Sons, 1964.

Hildalgo, Hilda, Travis L. Peterson, and Natalie Jane Woodman, *Lesbian and Gay Issues: A Resource Manual for Social Workers*, Silver Spring, MD: National Association of Social Workers, 1985.

Hoffman, Lynn, *The Foundations of Family Therapy*, New York: Basic Books, 1981.

Hollis, Florence, and Mary E. Woods, *Casework: A Psychosocial Therapy*, New York: Random House, 1981.

Horney, Karen, *Feminine Psychology*, New York: W. W. Norton, 1967.

Hughes, Pennethorne, *Witchcraft*, New York: A Pelican Book, 1965.

Illich, Ivan, *Medical Nemesis*, New York: Pantheon, 1976.

Illich, Ivan, *Gender*, New York: Pantheon, 1982.

James, William, *The Varieties of Religious Experience*, New York: Penguin Books, 1982.

Janssen-Jurreit, Marielouise, *Sexism: The Male Monopoly on History and Thought*, New York: Farrar, Straus and Giroux, 1982.

Katz, Jonathan, *Gay American History*, New York: Thomas Y. Crowell Company, 1976.

Kluft, Richard P., *Incest-Related Syndromes of Adult Psychopathology*, Washington, DC: American Psychiatric Press, 1990.

Kovel, Joel, *White Racism: A Psychohistory*, New York: Columbia University Press, 1984.

Kramer, Larry, *Reports from the Holocaust: The Making of an AIDS Activist*, New York: St. Martin's Press, 1989.

Laing, R. D., *The Politics of Experience*, New York: Ballantine Books, 1967.

Laing, R. D., *The Politics of the Family*, New York: Vintage, 1972.

Laing, R. D., *Self and Others*, New York: Penguin Books, 1987.

Levine, Stephen, *Who Dies?*, New York: Anchor Books, 1982.

Lewes, Kenneth, *The Psychoanalytic Theory of Male Homosexuality*, New York: Simon & Schuster, 1988.

Licata, Salvatore J., and Robert P. Peterson, *The Gay Past*, New York: Harrington Park Press, 1985.

Links, Paul S., *Family Environment and Borderline Personality Disorder*, Washington, DC: American Psychiatric Press, 1990.

Locke, Steven, *The Healer Within*, New York: E. P. Dutton, 1986.

Masson, Jeffrey Moussaieff, *The Assault on Truth: Freud's Suppression of the Seduction Theory*, New York: Farrar, Straus and Giroux, 1984.

Masson, Jeffrey Moussaieff, *The Complete Letters of Sigmund Freud to Wilhelm Fliess, 1887-1904*, Cambridge, MA: Harvard University Press, 1985.

McGoldrick, Monica, and John K. Pearce, *Ethnicity and Family Therapy*, New York: Guilford Press, 1984.

Memmi, Albert, *The Colonizer and the Colonized*, Boston: Beacon Press, 1972.

Meyers, Jeffrey, *Disease and the Novel: 1890-1969*, New York: St. Martin's Press, 1985.

Miller, Jean Baker, *Toward a New Psychology of Women*, Boston: Beacon Press, 1986.

Millet, Kate, *Sexual Politics*, New York: Equinox, 1970.

Minuchin, Salvatore, *Families and Family Therapy*, Cambridge, MA: Harvard University Press, 1974.

Morgan, Robin, *Sisterhood is Global*, New York: Anchor/Doubleday, 1984.

Morgan, Robin, *The Demon Lover*, New York: W. W. Norton, 1989.

Neumann, Erich, *The Origins and History of Consciousness*, Princeton, NJ: Princeton University Press, 1973.

The New English Bible, New York: Cambridge University Press, 1971.

Othmer, Ekkhard and Sieglind, *The Clinical Interview Using DSM-III-R*, Washington, DC: American Psychiatric Press, 1989.

Paglia, Camille, *Sexual Personae*, New York: Vintage Books, 1991.

Parad, Howard, *Crisis Intervention: Selected Readings*, New York: Family Service Association of America, 1983.

Patton, Cindy, *Sex and Germs: The Politics of AIDS*, Boston: South End Press, 1985.

Pederson, Paul, *Handbook of Cross-Cultural Counseling and Therapy*, Westport, CT: Greenwood Press, 1985.

Plant, Richard, *The Pink Triangle: The Nazi War Against Homosexuals*, New York: A New Republic Book, 1986.

Rabinow, Paul, *The Foucault Reader*, New York: Pantheon Books, 1984.

Ranke-Heinemann, Uta, *Eunuchs for the Kingdom of Heaven*, New York: Doubleday, 1990.

Reinisch, June M., PhD, *The Kinsey Institute New Report on Sex*, New York: St. Martin's Press, 1990.

Rich, Adrienne, *Of Woman Born: Motherhood as Experience and Institution*, New York: W. W. Norton, 1976.

Rieder, Ines, and Patricia Ruppelt, *AIDS: The Women*, San Francisco: Cleis Press, 1988.

Russell, Diana E. H., *The Secret Trauma: Incest in the Lives of Girls and Women*, New York: Basic Books, 1986.

Sacks, Oliver, *The Man Who Mistook His Wife For A Hat*, New York: Summit Books, 1985.

Sedgwick, Eve Kosofsky, *Epistemology of the Closet*, Berkeley: University of California Press, 1990.

Shilts, Randy, *And The Band Played On*, New York: St. Martin's Press, 1987.

Siegel, Bernie S., *Love, Medicine & Miracles*, New York: Harper & Row, 1986.

Siegel, Larry, *AIDS And Substance Abuse*, New York: Harrington Park Press, 1988.

Sontag, Susan, *Illness as Metaphor*, New York: Vintage Books, 1977.

Sontag, Susan, *AIDS and Its Metaphors*, New York: Farrar, Straus and Giroux, 1989.

Starr, Paul, *The Social Transformation of American Medicine*, New York: Basic Books, 1982.

Steinem, Gloria, *Revolution from Within*, Boston: Little, Brown & Company, 1992.

Stroebe, Wolfgang and Margaret, *Bereavement and Health*, New York: Cambridge University Press, 1987.

Storr, Anthony, *The Art of Psychotherapy*, New York: Methuen, 1980.

Szasz, Thomas, *Ceremonial Chemistry*, New York: Anchor Press, 1974.

Turner, Francis J., *Differential Diagnosis and Treatment in Social Work*, New York: The Free Press, 1976.

Turner, Francis J., *Social Work Treatment*, New York: The Free Press, 1986.

Waldinger, Robert J., and John G. Gunderson, *Effective Psychotherapy with Borderline Patients*, Washington, DC: American Psychiatric Press, 1987.

Wolstein, Benjamin, *Essential Papers on Countertransference*, New York: New York University Press, 1988.

Yalom, Irvin D., *The Theory and Practice of Group Psychotherapy*, New York: Basic Books, 1975.

Yalom, Irvin D., *Love's Executioner: Tales of Psychotherapy*, New York: Basic Books, 1990.

Zuk, G. H., and I. Boszormenyi-Nagy, *Family Therapy and Disturbed Families*, Palo Alto, CA: Science and Behavior Books, 1969.

Appendix

MEDICAL PROXY

A Medical Proxy Assists Patients in Controlling Their Medical Treatment by:

- Ensuring that someone can decide about life-sustaining treatment if they are unable to decide for themselves.
- Choosing one family member to decide about treatment because they think that person would make the best decisions, or because they want to avoid conflict or confusion about who should decide.
- Choosing someone outside the family to decide about treatment because no one in the family is available or because they prefer that someone other than a family member decide about their health care.

A Medical Proxy Meets the Needs of Health-Care Professionals by:

- Clarifying who should decide for an incapable patient.
- Providing legal guidance and protection for health-care providers.
- Providing a vehicle for professionals and patients to plan for the patient's future incapacity.

LIVING WILL

To my family, friends, loved ones, physicians, and all those concerned with my care, I _____, presently residing at _____, and being capable of making decisions with respect to my health care, make this statement as a directive to be followed if I become unable to make or communicate my decisions regarding my medical care.

I am aware that I am presently infected with the Human Immunodeficiency Virus (HIV) and/or have been diagnosed as having Acquired Immunodeficiency Syndrome (AIDS). I have known about my conditions since _____. During that time I have had the following intermittent illnesses:

[Please fill in the following space if relevant]:

_____

_____

_____

I have been told that the infections and cancers associated with AIDS or HIV may be treatable, and that treatments are being developed for the virus itself. Still, I realized that my overall prognosis is poor.

Therefore, the following is my directive as to my future care:

In 1 - 5, for each section, choose the sentence (a) (b) or (c) that expresses your wishes; then check and initial it. In addition, read (d) in each section; if you decide to refuse food and fluids, check and initial (d). The treatments you might want to refuse are:

–diagnostic procedures
–cardiopulmonary resuscitation
–intubation
–antibiotics
–dialysis

–surgery
–blood transfusion
–other drugs not for comfort

IF YOU WANT TO REFUSE ALL THESE TREATMENTS, YOU SHOULD CHECK OPTION (c) FOR EACH SECTION.

1. If I should contract an illness from which my doctors expect me to recover to my present state of health:

_____ [   ] (a) I want my doctors to prolong my life and use all medically accepted treatments or interventions, or

_____ [   ] (b) I want to refuse only the following treatments or interventions :

_____

_____

_____

_____ [   ] (c) I want no medical treatments or interventions except those designed solely for my comfort.

_____ [   ] (d) I expressly refuse food and fluids administered by any artificial means or technology.

2. If I should contract an illness from which my doctors do not expect me to survive:

_____ [   ] (a) I want my doctors to prolong my life and use all medically accepted treatments or interventions, or

_____ [   ] (b) I want to refuse the following treatments or interventions :

_____

_____

_____

_____ [   ] (c) I want no medical treatments or interventions except those designed solely for my comfort.

_____ [   ] (d) I expressly refuse food and fluids administered by any artificial means or technology.

3. If I should contract an illness from which my doctors expect me to survive but likely at a significantly lesser level of well-being:

_____ [   ] (a) I want my doctors to prolong my life and use all medically accepted treatments or interventions, or

_____ [   ] (b) I want to refuse only the following treatments or interventions:

_____

_____

_____

_____ [   ] (c) I want no medical treatments or interventions except those designed solely for my comfort.

_____ [   ] (d) I expressly refuse food and fluids administered by any artificial means or technology.

4. If I am irreversibly demented and am unable to recognize or respond to family and friends:

_____ [   ] (a) I want my doctors to prolong my life and use all medically accepted treatments or interventions, or

_____ [   ] (b) I want to refuse only the following treatments or interventions:

_____

_____

_____

_____ [   ] (c) I want no medical treatments or interventions except those designed solely for my comfort.

_____ [   ] (d) I expressly refuse food and fluids administered by any artificial means or technology.

5. If I am irreversibly in a deep coma or persistent vegetative state:

_____ [   ] (a) I want my doctos to prolong my life and use all medically accepted treatments or interventions, or

_____ [   ] (b) I want to refuse only the following treatments or interventions:

_____

_____

_____

_____ [   ] (c) I want no medical treatments or interventions except those designed solely for my comfort.

_____ [   ] (d) I expressly refuse food and fluids administered by any artificial means or technology.

6. I would like to live out my last days in a hospice/palliative care program, at home if possible, and if not, in an environment guided by the principles of hospice care.

_____ YES   _____ NO

This statement is made after careful consideration. It is in accordance with my strong convictions and beliefs and based upon my legal right to consent or refuse care. I therefore expect my family, my loved ones, my doctors and all personnel concerned with my care to regard themselves as legally and morally bound to respect my directives.

I have read this directive, asked questions about it, understand it, and have had an opportunity to make any and all changes to it that I might wish to make. It accurately reflects my intentions and wishes and I am signing this document of my own free will. No one has pressured me to sign this document. I understand that I may cancel or change this Living Will at any time.

If I do not cancel or change it, this Living Will/Medical Directive shall be effective for the duration of my life.

IN WITNESS WHEREOF, I have hereunto set my hand and seal this _____ day of _____, 19_____.

_____
DECLARER SIGNATURE

The foregoing, consisting of _____ pages, including this one, was signed, sealed, and declared by the above named Declarer in our presence and hearing, and whereupon on request in the presence of each other, subscribed our names as witnesses thereto this _____ day of _____, 19, ____.

FIRST WITNESS: _____

ADDRESS: _____

_____

SECOND WITNESS: _____

ADDRESS: _____

_____

HEALTH-CARE PROXY

(1)   I, _____ hereby appoint

Name   _____

Home address   _____

Telephone number   _____

as my health-care agent to make any and all health-care decisions for me, except to the extent that I state otherwise. This
proxy shall take effect when and if I become unable to make
my own health-care decisions.

(2) Optional instructions: I direct my proxy to make health-care
decisions in accord with my wishes and limitations as stated
below, or as he or she otherwise knows. (Attach additional
pages if necessary.)

_____

_____

_____

(Unless your agent knows your wishes about artificial nutrition
and hydration [feeding tubes], your agent will not be allowed to
make decision about artificial nutrition and hydration.)

(3)   Name of substitute or fill-in proxy if the person I appoint is unable, unwilling, or unavailable to act as my heath-care agent.

Name   _____

Home address   _____

Telephone number   _____

(4) Unless I revoke it, this proxy shall remain in effect indefinite-
     ly, or until the date or conditions stated below. This proxy
     shall expire (specific date or conditions, if desired):

     _____

(5) Signature _____

     Address _____

I declare that the person who signed this document is personally
known to me and appears to be of sound mind and acting of his or
her own free will. He or she signed (or asked another to sign for him
or her) this document in my presence.

Witness 1 _____

Address _____

Witness 2 _____

Address _____

BILL OF RIGHTS
FOR
HIV ANTIBODY TESTING*

You, and only you, have the right to decide if you want to take the HIV antibody test, often called the "AIDS test." No one can test you without your written permission. You should know that these people are always tested with or without their knowledge or consent: Those applying to the military, Job Corps, Peace Corps, State Department, Foreign Service, Immigrants "Green Card," prisoners, donors or blood/body organs/body tissues/sperm. If you are one of these people you may or may not have the right to pre- and posttest counseling or know your test results.

Before you sign anything, please remember that you have the right:

■ To take the test without giving your name or any other information (anonymous testing). If someone tries to take your name (confidential testing), you have the right to ask where you can have the test without giving your name.

■ To take the test for free.

■ To refuse the test if someone tries to get you to take it. No one can deny you any other services (except, in some cases, insurance) if you decide not to take the test. And, by law, even if you decide to take the test, you can change your mind at any time.

■ To decide if you want to take the test before having a baby or having an abortion. Know the facts and your options.

■ By law, to have someone explain the test to you in private and answer all your questions with the facts in a language and way that you understand. The person who does this cannot try to persuade you one way or the other.

---

*Adapted from New Yorker's Bill of Rights for HIV Antibody Testing, sponsored by a coalition of community-based organizations, c/o Community Health Project, 208 West 13th Street, New York, New York 10011.

■ Not to tell others about taking the test or your test results. But sometimes, those who know your results may tell others.

■ To refuse to tell anyone about the people you've had sex with or shared needles with. If someone asks you for this information, you have the right to ask why they want it and how it will be used.

■ To know health-care and treatment options if you test HIV positive, and who will pay for it. It is important to know that not everyone has equal access to health care.

■ To file a complaint, in those localities that have laws governing HIV testing, if you are discriminated against because of taking an HIV antibody test or because of your results.

■ To be given referrals to HIV/AIDS service organizations in your community, state, or national hotlines.

Index